A Grower's Guide to
Water, Media, and Nutrition
for Greenhouse Crops

edited by David Wm. Reed

Ball Publishing

Batavia, Illinois USA

Ball Publishing
335 North River Street
Batavia, Illinois 60510 USA

Library of Congress Cataloging-in-Publication Data
Water, media, and nutrition for greenhouse crops / edited by David Wm. Reed
     p. cm.
  Includes bibliographical references.
  ISBN 1-883052-12-2
    1. Greenhouse plants—Irrigation. 2. Greenhouse management.
  I. Reed, David William, 1952–   .
  SB415.W38 1996
  635.9'823—dc20   96-18929
                                       CIP

Front cover illustration by Bonnie Christiansen, Geneva, Illinois.

Contents

Preface

Producing containerized ornamental crops, either in greenhouses or nurseries, represents the most intensive form of production agriculture. Yield, profit, and loss are not rated on a per acre basis, but rather on a per square foot basis. Capital requirements and production inputs are very high and require an extremely high yield to show financial rewards. There is no room for error! To complicate the picture, the production system is almost entirely artificial or man-made. Growing media, water, fertilizer, temperature, light, etc., are selected, monitored, and manipulated by the grower/manager; very little is left to Mother Nature. Modern container production systems are closer to hydroponics than traditional agriculture production systems. For these reasons, the modern grower/manager must be familiar with a multitude of advanced production practices and specialty techniques.

This book addresses standard topics, such as water, fertility, and growing media. However, this book is unique in that it addresses many of the advanced techniques used in modern production systems. There are chapters on water purification systems, advanced irrigation systems, pH/alkalinity control of irrigation water and growing media, water and tissue testing and interpretation, and recycling and runoff relative to environmental concerns and impending governmental regulations. Until now, no publication brought all these topics together under the same cover. In fact, much of the information presented is not available in print because it represents each author's lifetime experience and has never been formally published.

All of the authors are respected experts from industry and academia. Their diverse backgrounds give a unique personality to the book. The information is not only academically sound and scientifically tested, but it also has been proven effective in practice.

Smaller, inexperienced grower/managers as well as grower/managers of the most modern and sophisticated production operations will find the detailed information presented here invaluable. Beginners will appreciate the basic discussions on irrigation, fertility, and growing media, while master growers will value the data given on cutting-edge systems within each chapter. Although much of the information is technical, even an advanced hobbyist will find the book easily understandable and usable. Horticulture instructors and extension agents will discover that this book replaces the multitude of miscellaneous handouts they once used for most courses and extension presentations.

It is hoped that the book will function as a daily desk reference for the grower/manager, academician, extension agent, and advanced hobbyist.

The editor would like to acknowledge the invaluable assistance of Matthew Kent, Senior Research Associate, for preparation of many of the figures in the manuscript, assistance in gathering background material for the chapters, and proofing for quality control.

Authors

Chapter	Title	Author
1	Irrigation Systems	**J. Heinrich Lieth** Associate Professor and Extension Specialist Department of Environmental Horticulture University of California, Davis Davis, California
2	Water Testing and Interpretation	**Fred H. Petersen** Past President Soil and Plant Laboratory, Inc. Saratoga, California
3	Combating Poor Water Quality with Water Purification Systems	**David Wm. Reed** Professor and Associate Head for Graduate Studies and Research Department of Horticultural Sciences Texas A&M University College Station, Texas
4	Alkalinity, pH, and Acidification	**Douglas A. Bailey** Associate Professor Department of Horticultural Sciences North Carolina State University Raleigh, North Carolina
5	Growing Media: Types and Physical/Chemical Properties	**William C. Fonteno** Professor Department of Horticultural Sciences North Carolina State University Raleigh, North Carolina

6	Growing Media Testing and Interpretation	Harvey J. Lang Assistant Professor Department of Horticultural Sciences Texas A&M University College Station, Texas
7	Macronutrient Fertilizer Programs	Paul V. Nelson Professor Department of Horticultural Sciences North Carolina State University Raleigh, North Carolina
8	Micronutrient Nutrition	David Wm. Reed Professor and Associate Head for Graduate Studies and Research Department of Horticultural Sciences Texas A&M University College Station, Texas
9	Tissue Analysis and Interpretation	Richard P. Vetanovetz Manager, Advanced Technology O.M. Scott and Sons Marysville, Ohio
10	Closed Production Systems for Containerized Crops: Recirculating Subirrigation and Zero-Leach Systems	David Wm. Reed Professor and Associate Head for Graduate Studies and Research Department of Horticultural Sciences Texas A&M University College Station, Texas
11	Total Nursery Recycling Systems	Conrad A. Skimina Research Director Emeritus Monrovia Nursery Co. Azusa, California
12	Water, Fertilizer, Pesticides, and the Environment	Don C. Wilkerson Professor and Extension Horticulturist Department of Horticultural Sciences Texas A&M University College Station, Texas

About the Editor

David Wm. Reed is Professor and Associate Head for Graduate Studies and Research in the Department of Horticultural Sciences at Texas A&M University. He is a native of south Louisiana and obtained his B.S. degree from the University of Southwestern Louisiana. He received both his Master's and Doctor of Philosophy degrees from Cornell University. He has been on the faculty at Texas A&M University since 1978 and has a joint teaching and research appointment. His research ranges from basic to applied and primarily focuses on nutrition, especially iron nutrition, and the effects of water quality and salinity on greenhouse crops. His research findings are routinely published in the scientific literature. However, his first love is teaching, and he teaches to a packed house of about 340 students each semester in his General Horticulture course. As an extension of his desire to teach, he has presented over 70 talks at various industry and professional meetings throughout the country. His presentations incorporate demonstrations and workshops so the participants take home how-to as well as academic knowledge. In fact, this book is a direct reflection of his desire to share horticultural knowledge with others.

Chapter 1

Irrigation Systems

J. Heinrich Lieth

Irrigation is one of the most important practices in greenhouse production. It is the process of providing vital water and fertilizer to the plants. Incorrect or even poor irrigation may result in plants that are not marketable. This chapter provides an overview of irrigation principles, descriptions of irrigation system components, examples of specific systems, an explanation of how irrigation decisions are made, and how such systems are controlled. Nutrition and fertilizer injectors are discussed in later chapters.

Irrigation systems vary by how water is delivered to the crop. Three major irrigation systems or strategies will be discussed. Overhead irrigation systems wet the entire plant, although the primary aim is to provide water to the roots. Surface systems place water directly on the soil surface, avoiding wetting most of the foliage. Subsurface systems introduce water directly into the root zone from below. Understanding the pros and cons of these systems requires some insight into various factors involved in water delivery, water movement within growing media, crop water uptake, and crop water use and loss.

Principles of irrigation

Water inside the plant

Water taken up by the roots of a crop moves through the stems into the leaves. From there, a large percentage of the water is transpired through the stomata of the leaves in the process of transpiration which cools the plant. Without this cooling, a plant in a greenhouse can overheat in full sun. Transpiration is one of the reasons why there is an urgency to irrigating. Water must get to the plant before its water reserves are depleted, particularly on hot, sunny days.

When water is taken up by the plant's roots, many dissolved compounds and solutes are carried into the plant. In greenhouse production, virtually all nutrients needed for plant growth, except carbon and oxygen, enter the plant this way. Fertilization strategies are designed to ensure that proper concentrations of nutrients (not too high or too low) are present at all times. Plants absorb more water than nutrients and have the ability to selectively leave some of the nutrients behind, so when plants remove water from the root zone, these salts become more concentrated. Thus, if the plant is not able to use all the nutrients provided, salts can build up in growing media. Later during a typical dry-down between irrigations, the salts concentrate further, potentially reaching levels that are damaging to the plant.

When testing reveals a salt buildup, apply clear water (no fertilizer) to wash the salts from the root zone. This process is called leaching. Leaching is only able to correct a salt buildup in the root zone; salt damage to the plant is permanent and cannot be corrected once it results in visible symptoms. In the past, when there were no concerns over environmental impacts and water and fertilizer were inexpensive, growers leached at each irrigation, regardless of whether fertilizer salts were dissolved in the irrigation solution. They leached by simply applying 10 to 20% more irrigation solution than was actually needed. This practice is decreasing in popularity because of increasing environmental and competitive pressures.

In addition to water loss through the plant and through drain holes in the container base, water also evaporates from media surface. This can represent a substantial percentage of the total water loss. Initially, when cuttings, seeds, or seedlings are planted into containers, the amount of water taken up by the plant is small compared to the amount lost due to evaporation from the soil surface. As the plant grows, the amount lost from the soil surface remains roughly the same or decreases, while the water used by the plant increases dramatically. Once the plant canopy begins to cover the pot and reduces the amount of light and air currents reaching the media surface, the amount of water lost due to evaporation from the growing media is reduced. The total loss of water through evaporation from media and transpiration from the plant is called evapo-transpiration (ET).

There are many factors that affect the ET rate. As total leaf area increases, so does the potential water loss from the plant. Relative humidity, light, air temperature, and air currents all affect the ET rate. ET increases with decreasing relative humidity, increasing light, increasing temperature, and increasing wind speed. These variables may be quite different at various locations in the greenhouse, resulting in substantial variation in actual ET. Areas of the greenhouse receiving more light have higher ET levels. Plants directly in fan-generated air streams will use more water than those not in such air streams. Also, if relative humidity is at 100%, then actual ET is essentially zero since the air can hold no more water. These factors become important when making irrigation decisions or when diagnosing problems that may have resulted from poor irrigation practices.

Water and the root zone

The root zone is that portion of growing media where the crop's roots are located. In container crops, this is the entire pot. For crops growing in the ground, the root zone is the volume of soil where roots are present. Crops such as cut flowers grown in the ground are produced in ground beds lined with an impermeable layer, and sides are sloped to the middle of the bed. The soil mix of the root zone in such ground beds is generally designed to deal with the plant's need for water, air, nutrients, and physical support. It is rare that the soil where the greenhouse is built will have exactly the desired properties. Generally the soil in the ground beds is either replaced with a specific rooting mix or amended to attain desired characteristics.

Container-grown plants usually have a much smaller root zone than in-ground plants, making the design of rooting media more critical. Container media need to have a high infiltration rate, high water-holding capacity, high hydraulic conductivity, and high air-filled porosity. In general, it is possible to construct these mixes. In this chapter we assume the use of such a mix; if not, then various problems that may appear to be irrigation problems are actually due to using a poorly formulated media.

While irrigation can be viewed as the process of filling a root zone "reservoir" with water, bear in mind that traditionally it has been more of a "flow-through" system. This is because irrigation solution is applied in excess, replacing much of the existing soil solution with a new one. For crops growing in the ground, this means excess water must drain away through drainage lines below the root zone. For container-grown crops, holes in the pot base allow excess water to run off. While this assures that crops are not waterlogged, it does make it possible for a considerable amount of water to bypass the crop and be discharged into the environment. If drainage were blocked, then the resulting waterlogging would deplete oxygen in the root zone, thus killing roots.

Irrigation management involves controlling the moisture content of the root zone. Once water has been placed there, the plant needs to be able to extract it. The force that the plant has to overcome to extract water plays a major role in whether the plant is able to take up adequate amounts. This force can be measured as *moisture tension* (matric tension) and is related to *moisture content* in that high moisture content corresponds to low tension and vice versa. It is possible to generate a curve for this relationship, called the soil moisture release curve (fig. 1.1). This curve is different for every medium (see fig. 5.4), varying in all aspects except that the curve always decreases with increasing tension. Note that low tension corresponds to high moisture content, and high tension corresponds to a lower moisture content. The vertical axis in fig. 1.1 represents the percentage of water in the root zone, and the horizontal line indicates that part of the water that is either readily available or unavailable. The latter category is water that is so tightly bound to the soil particles that it requires great force (perhaps more than the plant can generate) to extract the water. Putting the plant into a situation where the medium is near this line is suboptimal for growth. Most plants will wilt before this situation is reached. Potted plants achieve the highest rates of growth if the root zone is maintained at tensions between 0 and 5 kPa. Note that media whose curves are substantially different from UC Mix (e.g., field soils or rock wool) would dictate substantially different irrigation strategies.

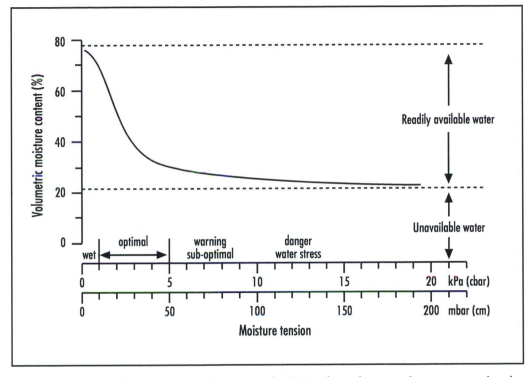

Fig. 1.1   The moisture release curve for typical container media (UC Mix) showing how a greenhouse crop responds to the various conditions.

About irrigation systems

Hydraulics of irrigation systems

Irrigation systems consist of plumbing to move water from a source to the plants. Water from municipal supplies is generally under pressure and comes into the nursery through a main gate valve and, possibly, a water meter. Water from other sources must generally be pumped. Pumping puts water under pressure so that it will move through the pipes of the irrigation system.

Water flowing through pipes is subject to friction, providing resistance to this flow. This means that when water is flowing (i.e., during irrigation) pressure decreases as water travels farther away from the pressure source. It is possible to compensate for this pressure loss by using various sized pipes, since larger diameter pipe means less friction per moving gallon of water. If the system is not designed correctly, the pressure may be so low that the emitters will not perform correctly or so high that emitters or sections of pipe may break, making the entire circuit useless.

When designing and building an irrigation system, consider the following factors: 1) the pressure and maximum flow capacity of the source (after the water meter, if there is one), 2) the distances and pipe diameters from the source to any valve, 3) the distances and pipe diameters from the valves to the points where water will flow out of the system (emitters), and 4) flow rates of the emitters. The effect of pipe diameter and length on pressure loss and flow rate in pipes is detailed in tables that are available from pipe manufacturers or irrigation equipment suppliers. While it might be tempting to use the largest diameter pipe wherever possible, this is the most expensive option. Because large diameter pipe (2-inch) is more expensive, generally it is used to bring water to the various manifolds throughout the nursery; smaller diameter pipe (1.5-inch) carries water from these manifolds or junctions to the valves that control each irrigation circuit. Smaller diameter lines (three-quarter-inch) then carry water to the emitters. Most pipe material used in greenhouse irrigation systems is PVC (polyvinyl chloride) because it is inexpensive and easy to work with.

Irrigation systems that have been assembled without these considerations will invariably cause problems in crop production.

Design of irrigation systems

System criteria. When building, modifying, maintaining, or operating any part of a greenhouse irrigation system, always consider the effect of that part on the entire system. Irrigation that uses any part of the system causes some pressure loss and flow reductions throughout the whole system. The irrigation performance of all concurrently irrigating circuits is affected, thus any design must encompass all of them.

The three most important overall design criteria are: 1) steady availability of water, 2) adequate system capacity, and 3) uniform distribution to individual plants.

Steady water availability. Steady availability means that the water supply is available at all times at some minimum delivery rate. It is particularly important that during high demand periods of summer an adequate supply of high quality water be available at all times during the day. Backup systems and contingency plans should be available in case of pump failure, power outage, etc.

System capacity. An irrigation system's capacity can be defined as the smaller of: 1) the highest rate at which water can be obtained from all usable sources, or 2) the highest rate at which water can be delivered to all plants in the nursery. This rate needs to be high enough so that no plants will run dry during a hot, dry, summer day.

Any greenhouse irrigation system should be capable of irrigating all plants as often as needed on the days of the year with highest potential ET levels. This could easily be twice a day. The best approach is to design the delivery system plumbing so that blocks of the same crop (species and pot size) are on the same irrigation valve. Otherwise, group crops that have roughly the same water and fertilizer requirements.

Distribution uniformity. Uniformity refers to the extent to which all plants in one circuit receive the same amount of irrigation solution. Although it would be ideal to have perfect uniformity, in practice it can't be achieved since such factors as emitter variability, tubing variability, and pressure loss within irrigation circuits contribute to variability in the amount of water for each plant. Also, very high levels of uniformity would require investing in more expensive irrigation equipment (e.g., larger diameter pipes), an investment that may not be justified by the slightly better uniformity than that given by some less expensive alternatives. As systems get older, mineral buildup and plastic deterioration may further reduce uniformity.

Even if a very high level of irrigation system uniformity could be achieved, there is still variability in water demand among individual plants. Thus, there will always be some lack of uniformity, requiring use of media with good drainage and an irrigation approach that delivers water in excess of the average ET. However, the more uniform the irrigation system, the less overirrigation is required.

Monitor the irrigation system uniformity from time to time. To do this with drip systems on containers, set collection containers (cans or bottles) in place of the plants. For overhead or spraying systems, place cans among the plants in a grid. The cans should all be the same size and type, particularly when testing overhead or spray systems. Place cans uniformly throughout the irrigation circuit, including locations close to and far away from the valve. The system is then operated for a duration that assures water delivery to all containers without over-flowing the cans. If this is not possible, then the system is either extremely nonuniform, or larger sample containers need to be used. To get the best information, use durations similar to those used during irrigations and do the test at the same time of day that the irrigation circuit would normally be used.

Once water stops flowing, measure the accumulated volume as accurately as possible with a graduated cylinder. Record the values on paper and use them to compute a coefficient of uniformity (Q). To do this:

1. Compute the average (A) of all the measurements;
2. Subtract this average (A) from each measurement, and drop any negative signs so that all numbers are positive (i.e., compute absolute values of the differences);
3. Sum these positive numbers and divide this sum by A. Divide the result by the number of observations (n). The result of this will be a number between zero and one; and
4. Subtract this number from 1.0.

Mathematically the formula is:

$$Q = 1.0 - \frac{\sum_{i=1}^{n} |x_i - A|}{A \bullet n}$$

where $|x_i - A|$ is the sum of the deviations of each measurement (x_i) from their mean (A), and n is the number of measurements. Q has a maximum possible value of 1, which would indicate perfect uniformity. A Q-value of 0.8 or less indicates a poorly performing irrigation system. The uniformity of subirrigation systems cannot be assessed in this way.

Delivery system components

Irrigation systems consist of pipes that are used to transport water and various other components. The brief description following will familiarize you with the terms and their meanings.

Pumps move water and bring it under pressure. Back-flow preventers stop the irrigation solution from flowing back into the supply lines and causing contamination. Water meters measure how much water has passed through one point (usually where it enters the nursery) in the system. Valves are used to turn on the flow to some section of the system and can be operated manually or automatically with solenoids. Filters prevent particles in the water from reaching portions of the irrigation system where they could clog emitters or valves.

Fertilizer injection systems put dissolved fertilizer directly into the irrigation system at times when the water is flowing. Sometimes it is also necessary to adjust other water quality factors by injecting various chemicals. Place the mixing tank just past the injection point to eliminate any "spikes" in pressure. The resulting mixture is called the irrigation solution. Such irrigation systems should always be equipped with filters to prevent clogging in case of a mistake resulting in chemical precipitation.

EC and pH meters placed past where the injectors are located monitor the quality of the irrigation solution. It would be desirable to have sensors that determine how much of each nutrient is in the irrigation solution, but these are not available yet for use under continual conditions.

Pressure regulators assure that pressures above certain levels are not encountered beyond the point in the system where the regulators are installed. They can be preset to specific pressures or adjustable to a range of pressures. Pressure regulators are particularly necessary where the pump or water source delivers water at pressures much higher than the emitters at the crop can tolerate. Excessive, sudden pressures can damage, or "blow out" emitters. The term "water hammer" refers to a sudden increase in pressure caused by the closing of a valve downstream. Since this happens on the supply side of the valve, it is not likely to affect emitters, but it could cause pipes and valves to burst. This problem is avoidable with proper design.

Control components

At the crop level, each irrigation circuit is controlled by one valve. This can be an electrically activated solenoid valve or one that is manually opened and closed. Solenoid valves must be used if irrigation control is to be automated. Solenoid valves use a low-voltage (24V) electrical signal that causes a solenoid to open the valve. When the voltage is removed, the solenoid returns to its original position, closing the valve.

In automated systems, solenoid valves are activated by controllers that range from electrical timers capable of controlling a few valves to complex computer systems capable of complex decisions. Some allow use of sensors as part of the irrigation control strategy. Controllers should be flexible enough to irrigate several times each day and at intervals of one or more days or on specified days of the week. The system should allow the flexibility to irrigate from 30 seconds to 45 minutes.

Types of irrigation systems

Various types of irrigation systems are used in the greenhouse industry. They can be grouped by the level of automation that is possible (hand watering versus automated irrigation) and by the areas in the crop's microenvironment that the flow of irrigation solution is directed to: overhead systems, surface systems, and subsurface or subirrigation systems.

Hand watering

Irrigation solution can be delivered to greenhouse crops in many ways. One way is manually by a hose. The equipment consists of a standard hose, a hand valve, a wand, and a nozzle to diffuse the stream of water. A diffuser prevents media from washing out of the pot.

Hand watering requires considerable skill and experience to ensure every container is brought to container capacity at each irrigation. If this is not done, dry zones may develop in the root zone of some plants, resulting in plant stress and/or root death. Such stress is almost never optimal and may lead to disease problems and nonuniform crops.

No matter what irrigation control strategy you use in conjunction with hand watering, always water pots fully at each irrigation. Partial irrigation can cause a portion of the root zone to dry out. With most container mixes it is difficult to know whether one has completely rewet the media. Water draining out of the bottom of a pot is not necessarily a good indicator, since in porous media water can rush (channel) through the root zone without adhering to all the soil particles or penetrating the air spaces.

With hand watering there is also a potential problem if too little head space is provided between the top of media and the lip of the pot. Take, for example, a container filled to 80% capacity with media as in fig. 1.1. To replace the water once 50% of the water has been depleted would require replenishment with as much water as half the volume of the pot.

Because the pot is 80% full with media, there is not enough space between the media surface and the lip of the pot to hold that much water. Thus, if the infiltration rate is not fast enough to accept that much water while the pot is being watered, then only a partial amount of the needed water can be supplied. Also a large fraction of this water may run straight through, leaving parts of the root zone dry. Automated systems generally apply water at a slower rate so this problem is reduced or eliminated, provided that the duration of the irrigation is long enough.

In greenhouse production, hand watering is usually not the optimal irrigation method from an economic point of view, due to labor costs and the difficulty in doing it correctly. When hand watering is replaced with an automated system, the change frequently pays for itself through reduced labor costs and more uniform crops.

Overhead systems

Overhead irrigation systems spray water into the air above and around the foliage of the crop. The water droplets should be large enough to fall through the canopy to growing media or run along the foliage and stems to the base of the plant.

The water droplets can leave unsightly residues on flowers and leaves, and wet foliage can be at higher risk for foliar disease problems, particularly when relative humidities are high (at night or during overcast, rainy, or foggy weather).

Sprinkler. Overhead sprinkler irrigation is frequently the least expensive water distribution method because each emitter serves many plants. With potted crops, the major drawback to this type of irrigation is the large quantity of wasted irrigation solution. Because it is difficult to maintain a uniform distribution pattern, extensive overirrigation of most plants is the only way to assure all plants in any block are adequately irrigated.

Various types of emitters are available for sprinkler irrigation (figs. 1.2a, 1.2b). One sprinkler head may throw a stream of water while rotating in a circular pattern (gear driven or impulse sprinklers), while another spray may water in all directions simultaneously (spray heads). Sprinkler heads are available in full circle or in a partial circle pattern. While it is possible to design an overhead system that supplies water to all plants, it is difficult—if not impossible—to achieve a high coefficient of uniformity.

Fig. 1.2a   Spray nozzle that can be used to cover small areas or for mist propagation.

Fig. 1.2b   Impulse sprayer that can cover larger areas.

Many factors including pressure variation, emitter location, and emitter variability conspire against a uniform system. In order to keep all plants alive, significant overirrigation is needed to ensure that plants in the driest spots receive adequate water. If the cost of irrigation solution (water plus any soluble fertilizers) is low, then this type of irrigation may be economically feasible. However, if the wasted irrigation solution is likely to pollute the environment, then select a more efficient system.

While overhead sprinkler irrigation can be used to cool plants on hot days by wetting the plants and allowing the water to evaporate, the effect is a transient one.

Mist and fog. While mist and fog systems dispense water into the air surrounding plants, they are actually cooling systems and are generally not designed to deliver water to the root zone. Mist systems produce smaller water droplets than overhead sprinkler systems. The objective of a mist system is to wet the foliage, either to cool the crop or to prevent or reduce transpiration (as in rooting cuttings).

Fig. 1.3 An overhead boom irrigation system.

Fog systems are similar to mist systems, except water droplets are even smaller. The objective of a fog system is to have the water droplets evaporate in the air before they reach the plants.

Both fog and mist systems must be controlled precisely to avoid disease and algae problems. When using a fog or mist system, greenhouse humidity can become so high that condensation forms. To prevent condensation, be sure to alternate misting with ventilation. Neither fog nor mist systems should be used to dispense fertilizer. Controlling irrigation in greenhouses where such systems are running requires more care—it is possible for the grower to be deceived by water in the canopy and on the soil surface while the root zone may be dry.

Boom. A boom system consists of a rig that moves overhead above the plants (fig. 1.3). Most are suspended from overhead rails, but some ride on concrete aisles, guided by some sort of rail. Arms (booms) extending to both sides over the plants are equipped with nozzles that dispense irrigation solution as the boom travels down the aisle. In some cases, the nozzles generate a spray similar to a sprinkler system. In other instances, water is allowed to flow in a stream to plants below. In the latter case, the plants need to be positioned precisely to receive the water. The stream of water should not be so harsh as to wash media out of the pot or knock plants over.

Hoses deliver irrigation solution from a supply valve to the rig. Some facility is provided for feeding out hose as the boom travels and collecting it when it returns.

Due to the expense of the equipment, one boom must serve several bays to be economically feasible. Booms are moved manually to the starting location. Once started, most can travel unsupervised. Some models allow the grower to program the speed of travel and to even skip over sections.

Boom systems allow for uniform overhead irrigation. The main drawbacks are the expense and the need for manual intervention, which means labor costs. Fully automated systems would require a boom in each greenhouse bay or extensive robotics, raising the cost. In highly automated moving-tray systems, it is possible to mount the boom permanently and have the trays with the plants move underneath. This level of automation is not yet economically feasible in many parts of the United States. Where labor costs are high (as in Europe), this type of automation is sometimes feasible.

Surface systems

Surface systems come in a wide range of schemes that deliver water directly to the soil surface. They can be either low mounted miniature sprinkler heads that deliver a spray, or they can be emitters that deliver a drip or slow flow. These are called drip systems. Note that this does not necessarily mean that water flowing from an emitter appears as a drip: Under pressure with a small orifice in the emitter, even a low application rate can result in a spray.

Drip or spaghetti. Drip systems deliver water directly to the base of each individual plant slowly enough to allow water to move laterally in the root zone before water starts coming out the bottom of the pot (fig. 1.4). If the water is applied too fast to highly porous media, it tends to channel

Fig. 1.4 Surface irrigation systems: a drip or spaghetti tube system.

straight down and is lost from the root zone. A slow application rate allows water to move laterally in typical container media since lateral movement is much slower than the downward flow. Drip systems are designed so that water is applied slowly over a long period allowing for this lateral flow. Other ways to facilitate getting water to all parts of the root zone include using more emitters per plant or pot or using emitters that deliver a spray of water.

Drip systems should always be equipped with filters and pressure regulators. Drip emitters are particularly dependent on adequate pressure (25 to 40 psi). Fluctuations in pressure result in erratic delivery volumes and poor system uniformity. Also, excessive pressure (during surges when valves are opened or closed or due to water hammer at the end of an irrigation cycle) can blow out or destroy emitters. Many emitters have small orifices and small passages so that any undissolved material should be filtered out to prevent clogging.

Much more supply pipe is needed with drip systems than with other irrigation systems to carry the water to the emitters. Near plants the water pipe is generally made of a soft plastic to allow emitters to be attached directly or with drip tubes. Tube or spaghetti systems use small tubes to deliver water from this pipe to each plant. It is also possible to obtain flexible pipe that has emitters built directly into the pipe.

Spaghetti systems can be used with or without emitters. In fact, some emitters actually function only as weights attached at the end of a tube. The tube itself has a small inner diameter, slowing the flow of water. Each tube must be exactly the same length since the flow rate from the tube varies with its length. Another function of an emitter serving as a weight is to diffuse the water from the tube. Some emitters can be shut off when not in use.

In a spaghetti system, the rate of water delivered to each pot depends on the distance to the end of each tube from the main valve. The farther away, the lower the delivery rate. This rate also will vary with pressure fluctuation.

Slightly larger diameter tubes (up to one-quarter inch [6 mm] in diameter) can also be used, but some other means of limiting the flow and maintaining uniform pressure within the circuit must be employed. Emitters with small diameter orifices or pressure-compensating emitters can be used for this. These come in various flow-rate configurations. They are designed so the emitter can be attached directly to the supply pipe or to the end of the small tube.

Giving each individual pot or plant special attention by dedicating a tube and emitter to it has high labor and setup costs. Labor is needed to set and space crops, as well as to maintain the system. For example, throughout the year several crops at various spacings are frequently on the same bench. It is generally too expensive to completely reconfigure an irrigation system for each crop; the originally installed system must serve all subsequent crops. This means that at times there will be too many or too few drip tubes. If there are too few, then new ones are simply added to the circuit. If these are from a different lot from the manufacturer, their delivery rate may not be the same as the others, reducing the uniformity of the system. If there are too many emitters, the unused ones should be turned off or removed, and the resulting hole in the supply line must be plugged. If unused emitters are left lying on the bench or hanging over the edge, they will drain the irrigation system after each irrigation, further wasting water. If they are not removed or disabled, then they should at least be elevated or put in cans on the bench to prevent water waste.

With tube systems it is fairly easy to inadvertently separate the tube from its pot even with the use of weights and stakes. Discovering such an incident is difficult unless the affected plant has already started wilting. Growers with drip systems should always be on the lookout for this.

Drip systems allow the highest degree of precision and uniformity, but the substantial setup and labor costs mean that they may not be feasible for closely spaced plants.

In-line. In-line systems differ from tube systems by being less flexible and less precise in how they place water near the plants. Water is delivered directly from the pipe. For example, pipe that has drippers built in at specific intervals dictates spacing for the crop. Soaker hoses or drip tape lie on top of ground beds and allow water to trickle out at frequent intervals.

Spray emitters. Spray emitters are mainly used on crops (such as cut flowers) grown in growing-media-filled benches. Water is applied as a spray from emitters mounted directly on supply pipe running along the bench perimeter. This focuses the application of irrigation solution to the soil surface immediately surrounding the plants while reducing the amount of water in the aisles.

Subsurface or subirrigation systems

Subsurface or subirrigation systems bring irrigation solution into the root zone from below. Although some attempts have been made to test subirrigation in greenhouse crops growing in the ground, such systems are usually only feasible with container-grown plants. These systems include capillary mats, troughs, and ebb/flood trays, benches, and floors. When subirrigating, the bottom of the pot is put in contact with water. Capillary action in growing media carries the water into and throughout the root zone. While there are advantages to using subirrigation, all subirrigation methods share a drawback: There is a tendency for salts to build up in the upper portion of the root zone. This occurs because irrigation solution (water and fertilizer salts) enters at the bottom. While some water is taken up by the plant, water evaporating from the soil surface leaves salts behind, and they can become concentrated near the media surface. This occurs also in other irrigation systems such as drip systems, but it may more pronounced in subirrigation systems. Monitoring salt concentrations and leaching with overhead irrigation may alleviate some of the salt buildup. No one knows how much leaching is required to remove the salt layer. If insufficiently leached, there is the danger of salt damage as the salts move into the lower regions of the pot where most of the roots will be contacted. Leaching is an extra expense that should not be ignored when comparing various types of irrigation systems.

There is a general impression that subirrigation systems are very uniform, but this is not necessarily the case. Subirrigation systems need to be perfectly level to have optimal uniformity but, paradoxically, they must also be on a slope so that water can be drained off after an irrigation. Ebb/flood tables and trays usually have sloping channels built in, allowing perfectly level tables to drain effectively. Also, plants closest to the flooding valve and drain tend to be exposed to water longer than other plants, so that more water may be absorbed into these pots if the duration of the flooding period is short. Specially designed trays, which constitute a considerable expense, overcome some of these problems to some extent, but they still require precise leveling.

Capillary mat. Capillary action can be used to irrigate by setting pots on a wet mat and allowing the irrigation solution, which is applied to the mat, to be absorbed into the bottom of the pot (fig. 1.5). The mat must be on a level, waterproof surface, and the bases of the pots must have holes so that potting media can make contact with the mat. The basic idea is to saturate the mat with irrigation solution and to keep rooting media in every pot at the same moisture tension (and thus the same moisture content).

Improper leveling can be a substantial problem. If the bench has just a 4-inch (10 cm) drop over its length, plants at the lower level will have moisture tensions 1 kPa lower than those at higher levels. For typical container media (represented in fig. 1.1), this can mean a substantial difference in water content and a resulting lack of uniformity.

Mats are available with a layer of perforated plastic film that is designed to inhibit algae growth and to reduce the incidence of roots growing into the mat.

Do not drape mat over the bench edge since the wicking action will cause water to be drawn off the mat and to be lost as runoff. In

Fig. 1.5 Subsurface irrigation or subirrigation systems: a capillary mat.

fact, for every 4 inches (10 cm) of overhang, tension in each pot is raised by 1 kPa.

When water is applied to the mat slowly, water movement across the bench will be through the mat, and runoff from the bench will be slow until the mat is saturated. If water is applied rapidly, it will travel through as well as on top of the mat. Three sides of the bench perimeter can have the mat edge and watertight plastic under the mat slightly elevated (one-half to 1 inch/1 to 2.5 cm), so that all runoff occurs at the end opposite the water supply. If the edges of the mat are not elevated slightly, then water may run off the bench near the source long before the remainder of the mat is saturated. Some growers also elevate the edge on the fourth side during the irrigation, and then raise the water level above the surface of the mat. Once all plants have absorbed water, the excess water is allowed to drain off by removing the slat elevating one edge or folding down a flap of the mat.

Fig. 1.6 Subsurface irrigation or subirrigation systems: a trough system.

Troughs. Irrigation troughs consist of flat-bottomed channels mounted on a slight slope. Pots are set into the channels (fig. 1.6). Irrigation solution is applied at the elevated end and allowed to run slowly down the trough past the pots. The configuration of the pots, particularly the holes in the bases, is very important since water has to migrate to these holes. Water that reaches drain holes is drawn in via capillary action. During irrigation, water runs in the channel continuously. Unless this water is recycled, trough irrigation can waste a large amount of water.

Take care to place pots into the troughs so that the flow of water comes in contact with the bottom of the pot. Slight warpage of the trough can cause water to miss the pot resulting in poor irrigation of that pot. While it may be tempting to line the trough with matting, that would convert the trough to a capillary mat system. Also, since the trough is on a slope, such a lining is not optimal (as discussed previously).

Fig. 1.7 Subsurface irrigation or subirrigation systems: an ebb-and-flood irrigation system.

Ebb-and-flood trays or benches (flood trays or ebb-and-flow). Ebb-and-flood systems are designed to be flooded with irrigation solution for five to 20 minutes, submerging the bottom of the pots (fig. 1.7). All pots should be submerged to the same depth and for the same length of time for maximum uniformity. Modern trays have grooves for drainage, and they move water rapidly to all parts of the tray at the start of an irrigation.

A typical irrigation cycle starts by flooding the bench or tray. The duration of this phase is dependent on the rate at which water comes onto the tray and the size of the tray. Take care that water coming into the tray does not push pots over. The water level in the tray is raised so that the bottom inch of each pot is submerged. The optimal water level is reached when all holes in the base of the pot are submerged at the start, and the water level has not dropped lower than the bottom edge of the lowest pot by the end of the flooding period.

Once the selected water level is reached, the plants stand long enough for water to be drawn up into the top portions of the root zone by capillary action. The time required is usually short, ranging from 15 to 30 minutes. Note that during this time a significant portion of the root zone is above container capacity. As the tray is drained, the excess water in the pots also leaves the pots. This can have significant consequences if some pots are infected with water-borne pathogens. However, usually disease is not spread, probably because most of the water that enters the pot stays there.

In an ebb-and-flood system there usually will be a lot of water that needs to be drained. This water can be either recycled in a separate recycling system or pumped directly onto the next bench. There is a risk that pathogens—from diseased plants or from plant material lying on the bench—may be transmitted from bench to bench if the irrigation solution is not disinfected between applications. This also means that growers must typically be more diligent about roguing infected plants and sanitation of benches.

Flooded floors. Another approach is to subirrigate on a larger scale by lining large sections of the greenhouse floor with concrete (fig. 1.8). Water supply lines and drainage pipe are incorporated directly into the concrete. Low walls (curbing) are used to section the system into functional irrigation circuits. The operation is the same as with ebb-and-flood benches.

Proper design and construction is critical since even small mistakes can have extensive consequences. Flooded floors are on a slope to allow drainage. Incorporating sloped channels into a perfectly level pad (like ebb and flood trays) would be prohibitively expensive and/or weaken the concrete pad to the point of cracking easily. Also, since the surface is shaped by human hands, the concrete is likely to have some areas where puddles will form. Cut drainage grooves to drain puddles. Otherwise the plants in these areas will be at saturation much longer than others, and the continual moisture can cause disease problems.

Another potential problem is that it is very difficult to pour a large pad of concrete on most soils without some cracking occurring in the concrete after it has been put into use. During the design phase it is important to verify how large a pad can be poured so that the floor will not crack later. Once a crack has occurred, allowing water to seep through it will exacerbate the situation. Driving forklifts or other heavy equipment onto the pad may also contribute to cracking. Obviously, design and installation of flood floors should be done by an experi-

Fig. 1.8 Subsurface irrigation or subirrigation systems: a flooded concrete floor system.

enced concrete contractor—and only after the soil has been tested and prepared to assure that concrete pads will not be susceptible to cracking.

Sanitation on flooded floors is very important since workers will carry pathogens on their shoe soles directly into the irrigation system. Once disease symptoms appear in one area, it is likely that workers walking on the floor will already have transmitted the problem throughout the nursery.

Irrigation control

Regardless of which delivery system is used, how do you decide when and for how long to irrigate? Water use of the plant, container size, and water-holding capacity of media dictate irrigation frequency. Plants should never be allowed to run out of readily available water since this will delay the crop or, at worst, cause root or tissue death or even death of the entire plant. Also, many media, particularly those that include peat, are very difficult to rewet once they have dried out.

Another consideration in deciding when to irrigate relates to the high levels of relative humidity resulting from some types of irrigation. In situations where irrigation is likely to be followed by a period of no ventilation while the air cools off (late afternoon or evening), relative humidities can rise to levels where condensation will occur. Since the leaves and greenhouse glazing are generally slightly cooler than the air in the greenhouse, that is the first place where condensation will occur. For many crops, water on foliage should not be allowed for any extended period of time, since this is likely to result in increased foliar disease problems.

There are several approaches to making irrigation decisions in the nursery: 1) look-and-feel, 2) gravimetric method, 3) timer-based method, 4) sensor-based irrigation, and 5) model-based methods.

Look-and-feel method

The look-and-feel irrigation method involves close inspection of the plant, paying particular attention to any drooping foliage or slight color changes that occur in some crops just prior to wilting. In containerized production, this might be accompanied by picking up one or two pots to gauge their weight or sticking a finger into the growing media to attempt to feel whether a significant amount of water has been removed from the pot. To do this accurately requires a substantial amount of experience in relating these "human sensor readings" to moisture content and moisture tension and is virtually impossible to do reliably and consistently, especially in a large-scale operation.

While this approach can be fine-tuned to be superior to scheduling irrigation based solely on time, there are numerous problems. One problem is that human touch is not a particularly good measure of moisture tension or content. As long as there is any amount of readily available water, one will feel its presence—while its absence is generally felt only at fairly high moisture tensions that are not good for plant growth. In general, moisture tensions far below those coinciding with wilting or color changes prior to wilting should be maintained for optimal growth. If irrigation is based solely on the appearance of the plant or the feel of the soil, the plants will be consistently subjected to stress. As the plants adapt to this stress it will become less noticeable even though it is still suboptimal for growth.

Judging the weight of pots by lifting a few representative pots is a better approach. However, it too is subject to problems if you are not aware of the moisture release characteristics of the media and if you have not formally learned how various water contents relate to how heavy the pot feels. Also, when judging a pot's weight, a grower has to somehow subtract the weight of the plant and be aware of the percentage of sand, which is relatively heavy, in the media. The fresh weight of the plant also varies dramatically and has to be subtracted.

Gravimetric method

One way to determine how much water is in a pot is to weigh it, remove the water, and then weigh it again. Unfortunately, this is not possible while a plant is growing in the pot since the procedure would kill the plant. In fact, the only way to remove all the water is to place the soil in a drying oven. While this method is useful for determining the properties of media, it cannot be used to precisely measure water content during crop production.

It is possible, however, to use weighing as a tool in irrigation scheduling. Generally, weight changes due to plant growth are much smaller than weight changes due to loss of water from the pot. Thus, it is possible to weigh the pot day to day and determine how much water is lost from the pot. Since the container volume and water-holding capacity of media are known, it is possible to approximately track water use. There are, however, possibilities for inaccuracies. For example, as the roots fill in the pot they take over some of the space that would otherwise be occupied by water. Thus the volume of readily available water decreases as the plant grows. In root-bound plants this can be substantial.

Scales specifically designed for use with irrigation control are available. They are, however, not commonly used due to frequent adjustments and inaccuracies.

Timer-based control

Time-based irrigation involves using a timer to program when to irrigate, how long to irrigate, or both. This works because growing media used in greenhouse production consist of amended soils with high infiltration rates, which allow excess water to readily drain away. Under these circumstances it is possible to water on a fixed schedule so watering always occurs sooner than actually needed by the crop and for longer than is needed. While this generates a lot of wasted irrigation solution, many growers currently consider the waste a small price to pay for the insurance that plants will always be watered and fertilized adequately. The price, however, is likely to rise as government regulations controlling runoff and public pressure force growers to eliminate the pollution caused by waste.

Timed irrigation is easy with the use of electrical or electronic timers specifically designed to control irrigation valves. Seasonal adjustments to irrigation timing are necessary to reflect changes in climate or season. Timers can also be used when the decision to irrigate is made by other methods such as look-and-feel or sensors, and a timer is then used to irrigate for some duration.

Sensor-based control

It is possible to use sensors to measure the moisture content or related characteristics of growing media, and then use this information to control the irrigation schedule. A number of different sensor types exist, but currently the most feasible sensor for moisture measurement is the tensiometer. Tensiometers are relatively low cost, and they are not affected by salts (fertilizer) in the irrigation solution.

Tensiometers consist of a tube fitted with a ceramic tip on one end and a gauge on the other end. In automated systems, the gauge is supplemented with, or replaced by, a transducer to convert the tension (suction) to an electrical signal that can be sensed by control computers. The tube is filled with water, and the device is sealed and inserted in the soil so the ceramic tip is in the root zone. Tensiometers with "high-flow" ceramic tips should be used for greenhouse applications rather than field tensiometers designed for field soils.

Once the tensiometer is inserted into the root zone, take a reading at saturation. The low and high tension set points should be 1 and 5 kPa above this point, respectively. The high tension set point represents the tension at which an irrigation is initiated. During irrigation the tension drops. If the irrigation is through a drip system, then the tensiometer can be used to monitor the tension as it drops. Once the tension is 1 kPa above the saturation point, the system is shut off.

Control devices generally also need safety features: minimum and maximum time between irrigations, alarms, and minimum and maximum irrigation durations.

Tensiometer placement and location of the plant where it is installed are very important (fig. 1.9a, 1.9b). The guiding principle is that the tensiometer needs to provide a representative reading so that no plants in the crop are extensively exposed to water stress. Thus, the ceramic tip should be inserted well into the root zone, and the selected plant should be a specimen with higher-than-average water use (a bigger plant, more leaf area, in a sunny location, at the edge of the bench, within air currents, etc.).

With many automated systems based on simple controllers, it is possible to use tensiometers to override irrigation systems to prevent timer-controlled solenoid valves from coming on unless a specific level of moisture tension has been reached. Greenhouse environmental control computers are available that provide irrigation control using tensiometers.

Model-based control

It is possible to compute how much water a crop has used and then to irrigate to replace this water. One way to accomplish this in the greenhouse is to set out a pan of water (evaporation pan) and track the water level in it. The water evaporation from the evaporation pan can be related to the evapotranspiration (ET) of the crop, and irrigation schemes can be developed based on this measurement. Evaporation pans can be purchased for precisely this use.

Greenhouse environmental control computers can control many characteristics of the crop environment. Many schemes to irrigate crops have been devised using data recorded by these computers. As scientists develop models for water use in crops, computer manufacturers implement these models in their systems, providing growers with a continually wider array of choices of model-based irrigation strategies. These methods attempt to relate the amount of water that has been lost by the plant and from the soil to one or more environmental variables (temperature, light, etc.), so that irrigation can be scheduled to replace lost water.

Various methods exist for approximating how much ET has occurred since the last irrigation. These methods are only feasible with computerized irrigation since the estimation requires extensive

Fig. 1.9a A standard tensiometer with its ceramic tip inserted in the root zone. The gauge is read manually.

Fig. 1.9b High-flow ceramic tip tensiometer, which is wired to and read by a computer, and irrigation spitter inserted in a pot.

computation using sensor data. One method sums light measurements at regular intervals. Once a specified light-sum level is reached, irrigation is initiated. The light-sum level set points are refined by the individual grower for each crop.

Another method estimates the vapor pressure deficit (VPD) of the air and relates this to ET rate. VPD essentially measures how much water can be taken up by the air. In conjunction with other variables, VPD can be used to estimate the rate of ET over time. However, when implemented without the use of light, temperature, wind speed, and leaf area, the calculations can only serve as a rough approximation requiring frequent set point modifications.

When using a particular method it is important to understand how calculations are being made and which variables are being used in the computations. Using a method that bases ET calculations on measurements of temperature, light, relative humidity, and wind speed has the greatest potential for success, but frequent grower intervention is still required as the crop grows.

In summary, there are circumstances under which any of the irrigation systems and control strategies are appropriate. However, for any one crop and cropping system, there is generally one system that is best. The main variables determining which is best include labor and installation costs as well as the degree to which each system is able to keep the crop at optimal moisture conditions.

Prior to the 1990s, water was readily available at relatively low cost, and growers faced little pressure to prevent pollution and water waste. Thus, simple irrigation systems with inherent waste were the most feasible. Today, however, it is frequently cost-effective to modify an existing irrigation system by replacing overhead irrigation with drip for example, particularly for containers that are not spaced pot tight. As governmental regulation and public pressure to reduce runoff continue, the cost of overhead irrigation will increase through fines so that overhead irrigation may no longer be feasible, even for pot-tight crops. Furthermore, irrigation schedules will have to be more tightly controlled to prevent excess irrigation. Even in situations where water is recycled, there will be an incentive to minimize overwatering since that will reduce pumping costs and problems associated with having to process too much reclaimed water to allow proper blending or cleanup.

Water Testing and Interpretation

Fred H. Petersen

nderstanding irrigation water quality thoroughly is a prerequisite to successful plant production. Water quality often impacts the selection of the nursery site, which crops to grow, irrigation systems, and fertilization programs.

Evaluating water quality ━━━━━━━━━━━━━

Before considering a new nursery site, thoroughly evaluate your water quality. When a site is supplied water from a municipal vendor, you need to ensure that the quality of delivered water is constant and, if not, that the variation in quality is within desired limits. Many vendors of domestic potable water deliver water that has been blended from different water sources. Vendors are required by government mandate to maintain analytical test result records, and vendors should make those records available. While these records are sometimes far more comprehensive than required for horticultural evaluation, in some cases they may not be sufficient for meaningful conclusions. In all cases have test results reviewed by a competent person or agency.

Many plants respond satisfactorily when irrigated with water of wide ranging chemical composition. Some plants, however, are particularly sensitive to specific water quality parameters. In such cases, production might still be attainable by avoiding some irrigation methods, pretreating water with chemicals, diluting water as necessary, and selecting specific fertigation programs.

After water has been analyzed, you can select pretreatment and fertigation programs to help you deal with any problems that test results may have uncovered. For example, if you must dilute primary source water with water of more favorable quality to reduce soluble salts, electrical conductivity meters are frequently necessary upstream at the primary source and downstream to ensure appropriate correction.

Making the choice of which irrigation system to use is frequently dictated by water quality. Retaining a licensed and registered engineer is sometimes necessary, especially if one is storing, handling, or injecting acids for bicarbonate reduction. Water with sodium or chloride toxicity may be hazardous to apply through an overhead system, but it is significantly less hazardous when applied to growing media. Likewise, water with the potential to cause unsightly mineral deposits on foliage from overhead irrigation may be best applied to media. Water high in calcium, magnesium, manganese, iron, and bicarbonate frequently falls into this category.

Fertilizer programs must also take into account water quality. Low mineral water may not supply sufficient sulfur as sulfate. Other water may not contain sufficient levels of boron. Still others may contain significant levels of metallic ions such as copper, zinc, manganese, and iron, yet once exposed to air, the ions may oxidize, becoming unavailable to plants as nutrients.

Without reliable data and interpretation of your irrigation water quality, you may obtain unpredictable growing results. If you have not tested your irrigation water, then make testing your first step.

Water sampling and sample handling

Test results, to be valuable, must represent the quality of water in use or the water being considered for use. Exercise care when obtaining samples of well water. Before obtaining samples the well must be operated at normal flow, and the sample must be taken as close to the well head as possible after upstream piping has been purged of standing water. Test results will be grossly misleading if water is from the casing of a well that has not been in normal use. Using a portable conductivity meter is helpful to ensure that the sample is representative of water from the source, since conductivity should be stable prior to sampling.

For determining horticultural quality, samples can be placed in any container of inert material. Polyethylene and polypropylene are preferred over glass because some glass can contaminate the sample with boron. When it is necessary to have the sample tested for organic constituents such as herbicides and/or pesticides, do not use plastic containers because some plastics will absorb some organic compounds. To avoid absorption problems, use only specially pretreated glass containers available from many testing laboratories. Most laboratories request one pint or 500 ml water samples, and containers should be filled to the brim.

Unless the sample is to be tested also for potability, you don't need to refrigerate the sample during shipment to the testing laboratory.

Testing and test parameters

Partial testing for electrical conductivity (EC) should be within the in-house capability of all nurseries through the use of hand-held, portable "conductivity meters," sold by many horticultural and laboratory supply houses. Determining pH in-house is desired when using acidification to reduce carbonate and bicarbonates. For some in-line acid injection systems, pH must be measured in-line. Nurseries treating their water with acid should also have the capability to measure alkalinity in-house. Alkalinity is primarily due to concentrations of carbonate and bicarbonate; its levels are determined by titration. To measure alkalinity you need to purchase and use specialized laboratory grade glassware and supplies. Kits are available for quick tests of approximate alkalinity.

Whenever you perform in-house testing, proper equipment calibration with standards is prerequisite to success. Standards for pH and conductivity are frequently available from equipment suppliers. Unfortunately, some very misleading data can be generated from using equipment that is later found to be seriously out of calibration. Maintain an inventory of fresh standards that have been appropriately stored to calibrate equipment prior to use.

Whenever comprehensive data are required, obtain a water analysis from a qualified testing laboratory. Laboratory testing is available through some vendors of horticultural supplies, some university extension services, and private agencies. The names and addresses of testing laboratories are available from the Soil and Plant Analysis Laboratory Registry for the United States and Canada published by the Council of Soil Testing and Plant Analysis. The testing laboratory you select should use only approved, standard methods such as those used for examining waste water. Note that while accurate data are not difficult to obtain, you must be confident of the test data interpretation by either the data vendor or another party.

Comprehensive evaluation

Critical parameters

Critical element parameters are either determined by the laboratory or are calculated by the laboratory or by others using laboratory data. The minimum required determined parameters include the concentrations of the *cations*: calcium (Ca), magnesium (Mg), sodium (Na), ammonium (NH_4), and potassium (K); and the *anions*: chloride (Cl), sulfate (SO_4), carbonate (CO_3), bicarbonate (HCO_3), nitrate (NO_3), and phosphate (PO_4). These must be reported in terms of milliequivalents per liter (me/l). When reported in terms of parts per million (ppm) or milligrams per liter (mg/l), appropriate conversion is necessary (see Appendix 2.1). When possible to do so, it is helpful to have results reported both in terms of me/l and in ppm to simplify some calculations.

The final required determinations include values for pH and electrical conductivity of the water (EC_w). Electrical conductivity of the water (EC_w) should be in the units deciSiemens per meter (dS/m). Some testing laboratories and conductivity meters still report conductivity as millimhos per centimeter (mmhos/cm, $EC \times 10^{-3}$ mho/cm) or micromhos per centimeter (μmho/cm) at 25C (77F). One deciSiemen per meter equals one millimhos/cm (i.e., dS/m = mmhos/cm).

For comprehensive evaluation, results should include the concentrations in parts per million (ppm) of elements—copper (Cu), zinc (Zn), manganese (Mn), iron (Fe), boron (B), fluoride (F), and lithium (Li).

The minimum required calculated parameters are those for the equilibrium reaction (pHc) and the adjusted sodium adsorption ratio (Adj R_{Na}).

Data evaluations and predictions

Table 2.1 summarizes the various chemical properties of water tested and their evaluation. How each of the chemical properties should be interpreted will be discussed below.

Total anions and cations. A complete analysis should give the total anions and cations expressed as milliequivalent/liter (me/l). The me/l for anions and cations should be approximately equal. If the two are not equal, it indicates either a significant cation or anion present in the water was not tested or that the analysis was faulty.

Calcium and magnesium. Plants can tolerate high levels of calcium and magnesium, and their concentrations are seldom high enough in irrigation water to cause salinity damage. Therefore, acceptable limits of calcium and magnesium in irrigation water usually are not published. Calcium and magnesium still must be determined, because their concentrations are used in the calculation of the adjusted sodium adsorption ratio for sodium water. In addition, irrigation water high in calcium and magnesium results in hard water. Hard water may warn that unsightly precipitates of calcium and/or magnesium carbonates may occur on leaves with sprinkler irrigation or that scaling may impair irrigation lines, valves and orifices.

Sodium absorption ratios. The status of sodium (Na) is one of the most common concerns. If the concentration is less than 3 me/l (69 ppm), overhead irrigation is usually fine. Higher values suggest increasing the hazard of foliar absorption, with leaf burn a frequent consequence.

Potential toxicity from root assimilation and impact upon soil permeability and drainage are best judged from the adjusted sodium adsorption ratio (Adj R_{Na}). An Adj R_{Na} below 3 is considered ideal. Other terms that are often used to express the sodium hazard include residual sodium carbonate, sodium percentage, exchangeable sodium percentage (ESP), sodium adsorption ratio (SAR), and the adjusted sodium adsorption ratio (SAR_{adj}). There is, however, some potential for confusion because the term "adjusted sodium adsorption ratio" now describes parameters with different symbols, Adj R_{Na} and SAR_{adj}. In this text we will use Adj R_{Na} as the measure for sodium.

The effect of sodium on soil permeability and drainage is of negligible concern in ornamental horticulture container production because so little production occurs in nonamended mineral soils. Where production occurs in such soils, as is the case for most field production and in some ground beds used for cut flower production, permeability impact is important. In general, there should be no significant adverse impact if the Adj R_{Na} is below 6. Higher values suggest potential limitations that can frequently be mitigated by supplemental calcium. Note that when evaluating the impact of water chemistry on permeability, the use of Adj R_{Na} rather than any other sodium related term is preferred because derivation of Adj R_{Na} takes into account the water's electrical conductivity (salinity). This is important because low mineral content water does not percolate as well as higher mineral content water. Potential toxicity from root assimilation isn't a concern if the Adj R_{Na} is less than 3. Higher values suggest an increasing potential hazard which, like permeability concerns, frequently can be mitigated by supplemental calcium.

Sulfate. Sulfate is measured for possible deficiency problems as opposed to excesses. If the sulfate concentration is less than 1 me/l (48 ppm), assume that the water might not supply all the required sulfur as sulfate. In such cases, supplemental sulfate can be applied through the fertigation program.

Chloride. If chloride concentration is less than 3 me/l (108 ppm), there is usually no concern from excessive foliar absorption under overhead irrigation. With higher values, you should consider avoiding wetting foliage. If the concentration is less than 4 me/l (144 ppm), there is usually no concern about toxicity by root assimilation.

Bicarbonate, carbonate, and alkalinity. Bicarbonate concentration less than 3 me/l (183 ppm) is unlikely to present a problem. There even are instances where a low level of bicarbonate is desirable (see Chapter 4 on alkalinity). Higher concentrations suggest potential problems involving the soil pH and micronutrient nutrition. Water's carbonate content is seldom a concern because water rarely contains high carbonate concentrations. In most irrigation waters, the main contributor to alkalinity is bicarbonate, and to a lesser degree, carbonate. Some analytical testing labs report alkalinity as the sum of bicarbonate and carbonate. Chapter 4 on alkalinity discusses this topic in greater detail and gives suggested alkalinity ranges.

Ammonium, nitrate, phosphorus, and potassium. These are not tested to determine acceptable upper limits of tolerance, but rather to determine possible contamination of water sources. Their concentration (if present in significant amounts) needs to be taken into account in the fertility program. In production facilities where the water is captured and recycled on the premise, these nutrients must be monitored closely since the recycled water may supply a significant, but variable, portion of the fertilizer requirement. Chapter 11 on recycling systems addresses this in greater detail.

Micronutrients and trace minerals. The most important micronutrients are **copper**, **zinc**, **manganese**, **iron**, and **boron**. Of these, boron is frequently a concern relative to potential excess or deficiency. Water containing less than 0.3 ppm boron is a candidate for supplemental boron. Water containing more than 1.5 ppm can be troublesome in terms of excess. Plants vary in their sensitivity to boron, so account for the boron tolerance of particular plants being grown when you plan corrective actions.

Copper, zinc, manganese, and **iron** are usually determined by testing a portion of the sample that has been acidified in the laboratory. The values reported might or might not reflect the water's true nutrient availability. The status of iron and manganese is important when the concentration of either is much above 1 ppm. At concentrations higher than 1 ppm, there may be problems from precipitation of compounds of these elements after they oxidize from air exposure. Precipitates can cause unsightly rust and/or blackish colored deposits on foliage with overhead irrigation. Deposits of manganese compounds within metal pipe and valves can also impair proper operation of valves and increase friction losses within piping.

Fluoride and **lithium** can be excessive in some areas. Fluoride can be hazardous if the concentration is greater than 1 ppm. The concentration of lithium should be less than 2.5 ppm, except for the production of citrus and other known sensitive plant material where the concentration should be less than 0.075 ppm.

Removal of copper, zinc, manganese, iron, boron, and fluoride is discussed in Chapter 3 on water purification systems.

Electrical conductivity (EC$_w$). This is sometimes referred to as specific conductance, salinity, or salt content. Total dissolved solids (TDS) are expressed as parts per million (ppm) or in the metric equivalent term milligrams per liter (mg/l). TDS can be estimated by multiplying the electrical conductivity (EC) value by 640 or 700. However, this provides only a rough estimate, and 10 to 20% errors are possible with this rough conversion. Conductivity meters that read ppm use the approximate conversion.

The calculated impact of electrical conductivity upon soil salinity (Ec_e) is of more value. This is the electrical conductivity of the soil saturated paste extract. Dissolved salts can typically increase by a factor of about 1.5 under "normal" irrigation intensity.

To estimate soil salinity, add the conductivity of water (EC_w) to that predicted from the addition of conductive fertilizer salts, and multiply the result by 1.5. The product will predict soil salinity (EC_e). This soil salinity, EC_e, needs to be compared to interpretation tables. If the EC_e value is lower than the table, there should be no problem from soil salinity. If the value is greater, a more aggressive than normal irrigation intensity might be required for optimal plant response; you may have to accept some yield or quality reduction. At the extreme, you may have to find alternate irrigation water. By far the simplest solution is to increase irrigation intensity and leaching. By calculating the leaching requirement (LR), irrigation intensity can be precisely determined as a function of acceptable soil salinity.

pH and the equilibrium reaction. The pH is frequently an overemphasized and inconsequential parameter, except in special circumstances. The normal pH range for most water is between 6.0 and 8.0. Values in the basic range, above 7.0, are frequently incorrectly assumed to be undesirable. However, unless the high pH is coupled with high alkalinity and the presence of significant calcium, magnesium, carbonate and bicarbonate, such water might not impact at all upon the soil pH. Many excellent quality, low mineral content waters might have pH values in excess of 8.0.

Water with unusually low pH values might be of concern because of its corrosive nature, since continuous use can deplete the irrigated soils of calcium and magnesium with resulting pH decline. Low pH water can also corrode metallic pipe and fittings. Of most value is the relationship between the pH value and the calculated equilibrium reaction value (pH_c).

The equilibrium reaction (pH_c) is a better indicator of water quality due to alkalinity. Since most labs do not report the equilibrium reaction, you may chose to calculate it yourself using the following equation: $pH_c = (pK_2' - pK_c') + p(Ca + Mg) + pAlk$. (See Appendix 2.1.)

The terms pK_2' and pK_c' are the negative logarithms of the second dissociation constant for H_2CO_3 and the solubility constant of $CaCO_3$, respectively, both corrected for ionic strength. The terms $p(CA + Mg)$ and $pAlk$ are the negative logarithms of the molal concentrations of Ca and Mg and of the equivalent concentration of titratable base (CO_3 + HCO_3), respectively. For convenience, the tables prepared by L.V. Wilcox from the U.S. Salinity Laboratory at Riverside, California, can be used rather than making exacting calculations. Edited portions of these appear in Appendix 2.1 if you wish to calculate the pH_c from laboratory data.

If the pH is greater than the equilibrium reaction (pH_c), you can assume that precipitates of calcium and magnesium will form. These precipitates accumulate on wet foliage and can become unsightly, detracting from plants' salable quality. These same precipitates can form within parts of small orificed irrigation and propagation mist and fog equipment and can impair the system's optimal operation.

Note how important alkalinity (due to concentrations of carbonate and bicarbonate) becomes in calculating the pH_c.

Interpreting results

Test results, while of significant value, are frequently insufficient to categorically define water quality. To form meaningful conclusions, you need to evaluate test data in terms of cultural management, including crop selection, irrigation practices, environmental control, and the willingness to accept an adverse level of plant performance when water quality may be a limiting factor.

Many authorities in academia, private consulting, and industry have attempted to develop and publish interpretation tables from observing the relationships between crop response and analytical data (table 2.1). Though valuable, these tables frequently lack the specificity necessary to evaluate data in any more than a broad sense.

The most valuable water quality parameters are those involving salinity, specific ion toxicity, alkalinity, and some miscellaneous aspects

Table 2.1 Quality of irrigation water as evaluated from chemical properties

Chemical property	Relative hazard				
	None	Little	Moderate	High	Severe
	me/l[a]				
Bicarbonate	<2	2–3	3–4	4–6	>6
Chloride, foliar	<3				
Chloride, root	<4		4–6	6–10	>10
Sodium, foliar	<3				
Sodium, root	<3		3–9		>9
	ppm[a]				
Bicarbonate	<122	122–183	183–244	244–366	>366
Chloride, foliar	<108				
Chloride, root	<144		144–216	216–360	>360
Sodium, foliar	<69				
Sodium, root	<69		69–207		>207
Lithium	<2.5				
Zinc	<2				
Iron	<1				
Manganese	<1				
Fluoride	<1				
Boron	<0.3	0.3–0.5	0.5–1.0	1.0–2.0	>3
Copper	<0.2				
	dS/m[b]				
Electrical conductivity (EC$_w$)	0.2	<0.7	0.7–2	2–3	>3
Adjusted sodium	unitless				
Absorption ratio(Adj R$_{Na}$)	<3	3–6	6–8	8–9	>9

Source: Adapted from: Ayers and Wescott [1], and Soil and Plant Laboratory, Form 112.

[a] Micronutrients and trace minerals usually are reported in ppm; nutrients and minerals present in larger quantities are often reported in ppm and/or milli-
equivalents/liter (me/l); the following conversions can be used:
    sodium: ppm = (me/l) (23)
    chloride: ppm = (me/l) (36)
    bicarbonate: ppm = (me/l) (61)

[b] The trend is to report electrical conductivity as deciSiemens/meter (dS/m). Some labs still report milliSiemens/centimeter (mS/cm) or millimhos/centi-
meter (mmhos/cm). There is no need for conversion because they are all equal, i.e., 1 dS/m = 1 mS/cm = 1 mmhos/cm.

as they impact crop selection, irrigation, fertilization, soil mix, and the overall design of an efficient production program.

Salinity

The salinity of water is expressed as its electrical conductivity (EC_w) in deciSiemens per meter (dS/m). This value is useful in estimating the salinity of the irrigated soil/media (EC_e). Under "normal" irrigation management, soil salinity will typically be about 1.5 times that of the water. If the water has an electrical conductivity EC_w of 2.0 dS/m, the estimated salinity of the soil (EC_e) will be about 3 dS/m. Though many ornamentals perform well with elevated salinities, a useful guide is to maintain soil salinity below 4 dS/m for crops with moderate salinity tolerance and below 2 dS/m for ornamentals that are not as salt tolerant.

Salinity tolerance tables for many commonly produced ornamentals are available in various publications. For floriculture crops, the work of Kofranek, Kohl, and Lunt from the University of California includes 10% yield decrement predictions in decreasing tolerance from chrysanthemum (EC_e 4.0) to azalea (EC_e 1.0). There are more exacting tolerance references for agricultural crops, including yield decrement predictions resulting from salinity stress over wide ranges. Yield decrement predictions are very helpful in evaluating water quality and the extent to which a crop may tolerate poor quality as a compromise from otherwise stress-free conditions.

Since many ornamentals are produced under constant liquid fertilization, the contribution of nutrient salts to the salinity of the irrigation water must be taken into account. When fertilizer companies do not supply such data it can be obtained on site empirically by referring to publications or from testing laboratories. A note of caution: The presence of urea or other nonconducting salts in fertilizers can lead to underestimating soil salinity. For example, urea is a nonconducting salt, but the first product of urea hydrolysis is the ammonium ion, which is conductive. To be conservative in estimating the impact upon soil salinity, an equivalent concentration of nitrogen from ammonium nitrate can be substituted for the nitrogen supplied from urea.

Leaching requirement for salinity

Sometimes salts can build up soil salinity under normal irrigation resulting in higher than desired soil salinity. By increasing the amount of water applied at each irrigation, thus increasing the amount leached, salinity levels can be lowered. In such situations, it is useful to calculate a leaching requirement (LR).

A formula used frequently with success is that from Rhoades in 1974 and from Rhoades and Merrill in 1976 (given in the reference by Ayers and Wescott, 1989). Though their work involved mineral field soil chemistry, experience has confirmed the usefulness of applying this work in ornamental horticulture, where the soil is frequently synthetic in composition.

$$LR = \frac{EC_w}{5(EC_e - EC_w)}$$

For example:
$EC_w = 2.5$
EC_e desired $= 3.0$
$LR = 0.2$

This indicates that 20% of the irrigation water applied must pass through the active root zone to maintain a soil salinity value of 3.

To illustrate an extreme condition, assume an EC_w of 5 and a desired EC_e of 3. The calculated leaching requirement LR in this case is 0.5, indicating the need to irrigate with greater intensity so that 50% of the water passes through the root zone. The water to achieve this degree of leaching might not be available or economical. In that case, sometimes salinity can be reduced by blending high- and low-salinity waters. If a low-salinity water is not readily available for blending then it must be produced by some form of water purification to dilute the adverse water to the degree necessary. (See Chapter 3 on water purification systems.)

Specific ion toxicity

When the concentrations of specific ions are potentially excessive, they may be reduced by diluting the adverse quality water with water of better quality. When that is not possible, select a form of water purification to produce mineral-free water for dilution. To calculate the degree of dilution necessary, use the following formula:

$C_{BW} = (C_A)(P_A) + (C_B)(P_B)$
where:

C_{BW} = Concentration in blended water
C_A = Concentration in water A
C_B = Concentration in water B
P_A = Proportion of water A used
P_B = Proportion of water B used

and concentration units are the same, i.e., me/l or ppm.

When the concentration of sodium is not excessive, but when the adjusted sodium adsorption ratio (Adj R_{Na}) is unfavorably high, adding calcium and/or magnesium is helpful unless the addition excessively increases the electrical conductivity.

Bicarbonate is frequently a concern. There does not appear to be agreement as to what might be considered clearly "excessive." When bicarbonate is present at a concentration of 4 me/l (244 ppm) or higher, managing soil pH is troublesome, and many plants develop chlorosis, suggesting a micronutrient deficiency. In cases where neither pH nor chlorosis problems can be avoided from liming and/or fertilizer adjustments, consider reducing bicarbonate by introducing an acid. Because of the complexities that may arise from using concentrated acids, including safety aspects, consider acidification with hazardous mineral acids in the last resort category of possible solutions. This topic is addressed in detail in Chapter 4 on acidification.

Alkalinity

Alkalinity is the concentration of soluble alkalis (often called bases) in irrigation water and is a measure of the water's capacity to neutralize acids. Bicarbonate and carbonate are the main contributors to the alkalinity of water, with hydroxides, ammonia, borates, organic bases, phosphates, and silicates being minor contributors. For practical purposes, the sum of bicarbonates and carbonates is often reported as the alkalinity of a water. Chapter 4 on alkalinity, pH, and acidification addresses this topic in detail. Table 4.3 gives the recommended alkalinity limits for irrigation water for different production systems.

Irrigation: method and management

Water containing potentially excessive concentrations of sodium and/or chloride that is applied through overhead irrigation systems can frequently be used with less concern when applied by surface application or if applied at night when temperatures are typically lower and winds are frequently less intensive.

Successfully using small orifice irrigation systems such as drip emitters requires particular attention to the relationship between the pH of the water and the calculated equilibrium reaction (pH_c), which you know from interpreting your test results. If the pH is greater than the pH_c, carbonates of calcium and magnesium may form and appear as deposits and can often interfere with optimal equipment operation. Reducing bicarbonate as discussed above is one solution.

Fertigation and fertilizer management

Deficiencies are somewhat easier to combat than excesses. Deficiencies frequently involve sulfur and micronutrients and can be overcome by modifying the fertigation program. Magnesium sulfate and ammonium sulfate are commonly used sulfur sources. The most efficient sources for copper, zinc, manganese, and iron are chelates. The most common sources for boron are borates. These are addressed in Chapter 8 on micronutrients.

Excesses, except for bicarbonate, can not be dealt with by manipulating fertilization. There are no materials to "neutralize" salts or similar excesses. An increase in soil pH caused by high bicarbonates can frequently be avoided by reducing the quantity of lime in prepared soil mixes to the minimum and by applying ammonium fertilizers to the maximum. Use caution when depending on acidification by ammonium because ammonium toxicity can occur. Since one impact of high bicarbonate is to limit root assimilation of metallic micronutrients, aggressive fertilization with iron and manganese chelates often helps to avoid chlorosis. Of the two elements, manganese seems most sensitive to bicarbonate and is frequently underemphasized in preference to iron. Unfortunately, these elements are frequent antagonists, and where the problem might be a water quality induced manganese deficiency and where only iron is supplemented, the chlorosis problem might be aggravated rather than corrected. In such cases using leaf tissue analysis is frequently helpful in devising your best corrective action.

In summary, plant material frequently contains 90% water, and water is the common conveyer of nutrients to the roots for nutrient assimilation. Understanding water quality is a prime factor in successfully producing all economic crops. Having accurate data competently evaluated cannot be overemphasized.

References

Ayers, R.S., and D.W. Wescott. 1989. *Water quality for agriculture.* FAO Irrigation and Drainage Paper 29, Rev.1. Food and Agriculture Organization of the United Nations.

Clesceri, L.S., A.E. Greenberg, and R.R. Trussell, eds. 1989. *Standard methods for the examination of water and wastewater.* 17th ed. Washington, D.C.: American Public Health Association.

Ludwick, A.E., ed. 1990. *Western fertilizer handbook—horticultural edition.* Soil Improvement Committee of California Fertilizer Association. Danville, Ill.: Interstate Publ. Inc.

Salinity Laboratory Staff, Riverside, California. 1954. *USDA handbook 60: diagnosis and improvement of saline and alkali soils.*

Soil and plant analysis laboratory registry for the United States and Canada. 1992. Council on Soil Testing and Plant Analysis, Athens, Georgia.

Appendix 2.1 Equations and Factor Tables

Milliequivalents per liter (me/l):

This is the preferred unit for expressing the concentration of the major cations and anions in water. The equivalent weight of an element is its atomic weight or formula weight divided by its valence. The following table is sufficiently accurate for day-to-day use in converting concentration units from ppm or mg/l to me/l:

Ion	Symbol	Equivalent weight
Sodium	Na^+	23
Calcium	Ca^{++}	20
Magnesium	Mg^{++}	12
Potassium	K^+	39
Chloride	Cl^-	36
Sulfate	$SO_4^=$	48
Bicarbonate	HCO_3^-	61
Carbonate	CO_3^-	30
Nitrate	NO_3^-	62
Ammonium	NH_4^+	18

To convert from ppm (or mg/l) to me/l, divide ppm (or mg/l) by the equivalent weight of the ion:

$$me/l = \frac{ppm\ (or\ mg/l)}{equivalent\ weight}$$

Parts per million (ppm):

Parts per million is a weight relationship used to express concentration. For irrigation water the term is assumed to be equivalent to milligrams per liter since the specific gravity of such water is approximately 1. The ppm is the unit weight of salts in a million units of water.

pH

The pH is a measure of the hydrogen ion and hydroxyl ion concentration in water. pH is used to describe the degree of acidity or alkalinity of water. pH is defined as the common logarithm of the reciprocal of the hydrogen ion concentration. A pH of 7 is neutral.

Equilibrium reaction (pH$_c$)

The equilibrium reaction is calculated using the formula in Ayers and Wescott in 1976, which was a modification of that proposed by Wilcox from the U.S. Salinity Laboratory, Riverside, California, in 1966.

Though no longer necessary to calculate the adjusted sodium absorption ratio (Adj R_{Na}), the pH_c is important relative to the actual pH of the water and should be determined when not included in laboratory test results.

The formula for the equilibrium reaction is:

$$pH_c = (pK_2' - pK_c') + p(Ca + Mg) + pAlk$$

where:

1. pK_2' and pK_c':   are the negative logarithms of the second dissociation constant for H_2CO_3 and the solubility constant of $CaCO_3$, respectively.
2. $p(Ca + Mg)$:   is the negative logarithm of the molal concentration of Ca + Mg.
3. pAlk: is the negative logarithm of the equivalent concentration of titratable base $(CO_3 + HCO_3)$.

In practice, each of the three terms can be approximated from the following tables using laboratory data:

1. The sum of cations from water analysis results for the term pK_2' and pK_c'.
2. The sum of calcium and magnesium concentrations in me/l for the term $p(Ca + Mg)$.
3. The sum of carbonate and bicarbonate for the term pAlk:

Sum of cations	$(pK_2' - pK_c')$
0	2.03
1	2.13
2	2.16
3	2.18
4	2.20
5	2.21
6	2.23
7	2.24
8	2.25
9	2.26
10	2.12

Sum of Ca + Mg	p(Ca + Mg)
0.1	4.30
0.5	3.60
1.0	3.30
1.5	3.12
2.0	3.00
2.5	2.90
3.0	2.86
3.5	2.76
4.0	2.70
4.5	2.65
5.0	2.60
6.0	2.52
7.0	2.46
8.0	2.40
9.0	2.38
10.0	2.30

Sum of CO_3 + HCO_3	pAlk
0.1	4.00
0.5	3.30
1.0	3.00
1.5	2.82
2.0	2.70
3.0	2.52
3.5	2.46
4.0	2.40
5.0	2.30
6.0	2.22
7.0	2.15
8.0	2.10
9.0	2.05
10.0	2.00

Adjusted sodium absorption ratio (Adj R$_{Na}$)

The latest procedure to estimate sodium hazard is to determine the value by following the procedure by Suarez. When laboratory data does not include this term, it can be approximated from the following using data from your laboratory results.

$$\text{Adj } R_{Na} = \frac{Na}{\sqrt{\dfrac{Ca_x + Mg}{2}}}$$

wherein sodium (Na) and magnesium (Mg) are in me/l, and the term Ca$_x$ is taken from the following abbreviated table of Ayers and Wescott.

Values for Ca$_x$ for varying me/l HCO$_3$/Ca and EC$_w$:

HCO$_3$/Ca (me/l)	EC$_w$ (dS/m)				
	0.10	0.50	1.00	1.50	2.00
0.10	8.31	9.07	9.62	10.02	10.35
0.25	4.51	4.92	5.22	5.44	5.62
0.50	2.84	3.10	3.29	3.43	3.54
0.75	2.17	2.37	2.51	2.62	2.70
1.00	1.79	1.96	2.09	2.16	2.23
1.25	1.54	1.68	1.78	1.86	1.92
1.50	1.37	1.49	1.58	1.65	1.70
2.00	1.13	1.23	1.31	1.36	1.40
3.00	0.85	0.94	1.00	1.04	1.04
4.00	0.71	0.78	0.82	0.86	0.88
5.00	0.61	0.67	0.71	0.74	0.76
7.00	0.49	0.53	0.57	0.59	0.61
10.00	0.39	0.42	0.45	0.47	0.48

Combating Poor Water Quality with Water Purification Systems

David Wm. Reed

Many regions of the country are plagued with poor water quality. The most common water quality problem is high total dissolved solids (TDS), which are the total of the nonvolatile solutes dissolved in water. TDS are mainly composed of soluble salts. High TDS may decrease plant growth and cause salt burn on leaves. Hard water high in calcium and magnesium and water high in iron or manganese often cause unsightly salt deposits and stains on leaves. Water high in fluoride can cause leaf chlorosis or necrosis in some tropical foliage plants. Boron also reaches damaging toxicity levels in some irrigation water. Chapter 2, Water Testing and Interpretation, addresses many of these problems.

The problem of poor water quality likely will become progressively severe. Ground and surface water depletion is forcing agricultural production to use irrigation water of increasingly poor quality because of salt intrusion and accumulation of salts from runoff. Future regulations concerning on-site irrigation water recycling will dictate the use of even poorer quality water.

For these reasons, many growers use water purification systems to improve irrigation water quality. Purified water is primarily used to irrigate salt sensitive crops, during mist propagation, and for holding solutions for cut flowers.

This chapter is somewhat technical by the nature of the subject matter covered. Water purification technology and chemistry can be

Table 3.1   Water purification methods for removing total dissolved solids (TDS) and selected salts from water

		Reverse osmosis	Distillation	Deionization (cation and anion exchange)	Electro-dialysis	Anion exchange	Water softener or cation exchange
Total dissolved solids (TDS)		X	X	X	X		
Aluminum	Al^{+3}	X	X	X	X		X
Bicarbonate	HCO_3^-	X	X	X	X	X	
Borate	$H_2BO_3^-$	X	X	X	X	X	
Calcium	Ca^{+2}	X	X	X	X		X
Carbonate	CO_3^{-2}	X	X	X	X	X	
Chloride	Cl^-	X	X	X	X	X	
Copper	Cu^{+2}	X	X	X	X		X
Fluoride	F^-	X	X	X	X	X	
Iron (ferric)	Fe^{+3}						
Iron (ferrous)	Fe^{+2}	X	X	X	X		X
Magnesium	Mg^{+2}	X	X	X	X		X
Manganese (manganous)	Mn^{+2}	X	X	X	X		X
Manganese (oxidized)	$Mn^{+3,4}$						
Nitrate	NO_3^-	X	X	X	X	X	
Sodium	Na^+	X	X	X	X		X[a]
Sulfate	SO_4^{-2}	X	X	X	X	X	
Zinc	Zn^{+2}	X	X	X	X		X

Source: Water Quality Association Bulletin R27, R28, and S9a; Council of Better Business Bureaus Publication 24-236 HBL 400290; Faust and Aly.
[a]The resin is charged in the potassium (K^+) form.

confusing. This discussion will simplify water purification for the novice, while covering the topic in enough detail so that the involved owner/manager can "talk shop" with companies that sell, install, and/or maintain water purification units.

The first section addresses the systems available for water purification. (See also table 3.1.) The next section discusses pretreatments used to prepare raw water for purification. The last sections deal with removal of specific contaminants, waste water disposal, blending, and finally, costs will be examined.

Activated carbon	Activated alumina	Chlorination/ filtration	Sequestration (chelation)	Oxidation/ filtration	Aeration/ filtration	Filtration	Acid injection
							X
							X
X	X						
						X	
		X	X	X	X		
		X	X	X	X		
						X	
	X						

Water purification systems to remove total dissolved solids

Reverse osmosis

Reverse osmosis (RO) water purification systems are the most commonly used water purification systems in container crop production. Usually, RO is the most cost-effective. A moderate-sized unit (5,000–15,000 gal./day [20–60 kl]) should produce water at $0.01 to $0.02

per gallon (4 l). The purified water has 95 to 99% of the salts removed, which is sufficient for most horticultural applications.

RO systems work by osmosis. When two solutions that have different solute (salt) concentrations are separated by a membrane, water will move from the solution of lower solute concentration to the solution of higher solute concentration. This process is called osmosis. If pressure is applied to the solution with higher solute concentration, then water can be forced to move from the solution of higher solute concentration to the solution of lower solute concentration. This is pressure-induced reverse osmosis.

Reverse osmosis water purification systems rely on this principle. Irrigation water is pressurized on one side of a semipermeable membrane, which causes water to cross the membrane by reverse osmosis, leaving the solutes behind. Relatively pure water accumulates on the other side of the membrane. The membrane must be very fine with pores small enough to filter out solutes. This process is sometimes called hyperfiltration.

Most RO systems require pressures of 150 to 400 psi, which makes energy one of the most significant costs of operating the system. Membranes are another significant cost. The two major types of membranes used are cellulose acetate membranes and polyamide membranes (thin film composite and hollow fiber membranes). Maintenance and replacement of membranes contribute significantly to the system's cost. Less efficient membranes that are less expensive to operate are available, and they deliver about 50 to 70% purification. They work at lower pressures (100–300 psi), and this can result in considerable energy cost savings. Cost savings, however, must be balanced with efficient solute removal.

The rate of water production and degree of TDS removal by an RO system depend on the pressure of the system, membrane type, TDS of the water being purified, and temperature. Commercial units should yield in excess of 95% salt removal, with removal above 99% possible on well-maintained units. One of the disadvantages of RO systems is that brine waste water is produced. RO units vary from 20 to 75% recovery as purified water and 25 to 80% loss as waste brine water (from Culligan International Co. personal communication). Governmental regulations may impact the brine water disposal, and users should investigate this for their own localities.

RO systems are very effective in removing most TDS, some organic compounds, and some microorganisms. RO removes virtually all the sol-

PHOTO: Culligan International Company

Fig. 3.1 An example of a reverse osmosis water purification system. The long tubes contain the cylindrical membranes that purify the water.

uble salts commonly found in irrigation water. Even though TDS removal should exceed 90%, individual salts are removed at varying efficiencies. In general, divalent cations (calcium, magnesium) and anions (sulfate) are removed more efficiently than monovalent cations (sodium, potassium, lithium) and anions (nitrate, chloride, borate).

Whether or not an RO system operates at 20 to 80% efficiency is totally dependent on the integrity and cleanliness of the membranes. Membranes must be protected from compounds such as chlorine and sediment in the water which can cause them to deteriorate or clog. For these reasons, water is usually pretreated before injection into the RO unit. Commonly used pretreatments include suspended solid removal, antiscaling treatments, pH control, dechlorination, and softening.

An example of a moderate-sized reverse osmosis system with a capacity of 6,000 gallons (22.7 kl) per day is shown in fig. 3.1. The actual RO unit is compact and is made up of several long tubes (approximately 4 inches [10 cm] by 6 feet [2 m]) that contain the membranes to purify the water and associated pressure pumps. The bulk of the system is composed of various filters and tanks.

Deionization

Water is often called the universal solvent because more substances dissolve in water than any other liquid. Water is especially effective at dissolving ions, which are charged particles. When an ionic compound dissolves in water, it dissociates into a positively charged ion called a cation and a negatively charged ion called an anion. The soluble salts in irrigation water are all cations and anions. Examples of cations are: sodium (Na^+), calcium (Ca^{++}), magnesium (Mg^{++}), potassium (K^+), ammonium (NH_4^+), lithium (Li^+), iron (Fe^{++}), manganese (Mn^{++}) and copper (Cu^{++}). Examples of anions are: chloride (Cl^-), sulfate ($SO_4^=$), carbonate ($CO_3^=$), bicarbonate (HCO_3^-), nitrate (NO_3^-), phosphate ($H_2PO_4^-$, $HPO_4^=$), fluoride (F^-), and borate ($H_2BO_3^-$). Deionization is a process that removes ionic compounds from water. It is sometimes called demineralization.

Deionization uses ion exchange resins to remove the ions. The ion exchange resins are usually solid beads that are covered with fixed positive or negative charges. Cation exchange resins remove cations (such as sodium, Na^+) from the water. Anion exchange resins remove anions (such as chloride, Cl^-) from the water.

The ion exchange resin replaces its exchangeable ions for ions of the salts in the water. For example, a cation exchange resin contains fixed negative charges that are neutralized by hydrogen ions (H^+) on the resin's surface. When water passes over the resin, the positively charged soluble ions (cations) in the water replace the hydrogen ions on the resin. The ions of the salts are retained on the resin, and hydrogen ions are released. Anion exchange resins remove negatively charged soluble ions (anions) from the water and replace them with hydroxyl ions (OH^-). The hydrogen and hydroxyl ions released by the resin neutralize each other by combining to form water. A deionization unit will contain both anion and cation exchange resins so that the ions of all salts are removed.

Deionization is very effective and can produce very pure water. In normal container production, water of such high purity is not needed. However, deionized water is used for holding cut flowers in the cut flower trade.

The cost of deionization increases as the soluble salt content of the irrigation water increases. Major costs associated with the system are the resins and their maintenance. The higher the soluble salt content of the irrigation water the more frequently the resins have to be regenerated or replaced. Deionization can be five to six times more expensive than reverse osmosis. Thus, deionization is most practical when: 1) high purity water is needed, or 2) when the soluble salt content of the water is relatively low.

If high purity water is required and the soluble salt content of the irrigation water is high, a combination of reverse osmosis and deionization can be used. The water is first treated by reverse osmosis to remove the vast majority of the salts, and then the water is further purified by deionization. Often this is more economical than deionization alone.

Distillation

Distillation relies on evaporation and condensation of water. The water is heated to the boiling point to cause rapid water vapor formation. The salts, particulate matter, and non-volatile organic compounds are left behind. The water vapor passes over cooled coils and that causes condensation. Condensed water is of very high purity.

If irrigation water is highly alkaline or hard, it may cause scaling in the distillation unit boiler, which may require extensive cleaning to keep the unit functioning efficiently. To reduce scaling, pretreat the water with acid injection to remove carbonates and bicarbonates or soften the water to remove calcium and magnesium.

Distillation is seldom used to produce purified water for horticultural applications. It is rather expensive, maintenance may be a problem, and the volume output is lower than other methods. I know of one greenhouse operation that used a steam still, but after a couple of years it was abandoned.

Electrodialysis

Electrodialysis (ED) is a water purification process in which water is passed between alternating cation-permeable and anion-permeable membranes. A direct current (DC) is applied across the membranes that causes the cations and anions to migrate through the membranes toward electrical poles. This leaves purified water between the membranes. Several hundred sets of cation permeable and anion permeable membranes form a stack that is positioned between a set of electrodes.

The current is reversed periodically in a process called electrodialysis reversal (EDR) to prevent scale buildup on the membranes. Each stack of membranes may remove 30 to 55% of the salts, and a series of membrane stacks is used to achieve increasing water purification.

Electrodialysis effectively removes soluble salts and short chain organic molecules from water. One of the ED's advantages over other membrane purification processes (such as reverse osmosis) is its tolerance of contaminates found in some irrigation water. The process is less affected by many organic, inorganic, colloidal, and biological contaminates, so less water pretreatment (pH control, softening, anti-scalant chemicals, dechlorination) is needed compared to reverse osmosis systems.

Electrodialysis has had limited use in the past. There are only a few manufacturers that use the technology, and the costs can be high (capital outlay and replacement parts). However, it has been used for desalination of brackish water.

Pretreatment systems

Usually, raw water must be pretreated before it can be fed into a water purification system. Necessary pretreatments depend on the type of water purification system and the quality of the water to be purified. A complete water analysis is required to determine necessary pretreatments. A pretreatment system is best designed by a professional to maximize efficiency and longevity and to minimize costs.

Suspended solids removal

Suspended solids are particulate materials that are suspended in water. When present in high counts, water may appear turbid. Water analysis should test for turbidity, which is reported as a silt density index (SDI) or nephelometric turbidity units (NTU). Suspended solids may be from colloids, silica, bacteria, or mineral precipitates, such as calcium/magnesium bicarbonate or ferric iron. They can clog membranes and resins reducing their efficiency and life. When suspended solids are coagulated to form larger particles, they may be filtered out by sand, anthracite, micron and, to a lesser degree, ultra filtration filters. Coagulation of the particulate material depends on the contaminant. Iron and manganese may be: 1) precipitated by oxidation using either air (aeration filter) or chemicals (permanganate filter) and then removed by filtration, 2) removed by lime softening at high pH, or 3) removed by zeolite ion exchange. Colloidal material is coagulated with polymers or alum, then filtered out by sand or depth filtration.

Scaling prevention

Brine water may cause scaling, which is the buildup of deposits of calcium and magnesium carbonate, hydroxide, and hemihydrate. Scale is usually controlled by injecting antiscalant chemicals, such as sodium hexametaphosphate, or acids, such as sulfuric acid.

pH and alkalinity control

If the water to be purified has high alkalinity, acid may be injected to reduce the alkalinity and pH to slightly acid levels. Acid injection also helps prevent scaling. Sulfuric acid is commonly used. Cellulose acetate membranes used in RO systems are sensitive to alkaline pH, so acid injection is essential for RO systems using these membranes. Thin-film composite membranes are used more commonly than cellulose acetate membranes, however, and do not require pH control.

Dechlorination

Polyamide and thin-film composite membranes used in RO systems are pH resistant, but they are attacked by chlorine. If these membranes are used, chlorine must be removed, especially from chlorinated municipal water. Removal usually is by carbon filtration or injection of sodium sulfite.

Water softening (cation exchange)

Hard water is high in calcium and magnesium. It may be treated with a water softener to replace the calcium and magnesium with sodium. Sodium also causes fewer problems with scaling in membrane systems. However, never use sodium-softened water on plants.

Correcting specific ion problems

Total dissolved solids are removed by reverse osmosis, deionization, distillation, or electrodialysis. These processes also solve most of the problems associated with individual salts. There are situations, however, where the TDS are not high enough to justify total salt removal, but individual salts may pose a problem.

Table 3.1 lists the salts found in some irrigation waters and the water purification techniques that can be used to correct the problem.

Iron and manganese

Iron and manganese occur in irrigation water in two forms: a reduced, more soluble form and an oxidized, less soluble form. Underground water may be high in the more soluble reduced form of iron (ferrous) and manganese (manganous) because of the lack of oxygen. However, when the water is pumped to the surface and exposed to air, the iron and manganese are oxidized to the less soluble form. These oxidized forms are responsible for the black, brown, or rust-colored stains that develop on leaves of plants irrigated with high iron or manganese water.

The problem can be solved with large oxidation/sedimentation tanks or ponds. The ground water is pumped into the tanks as a spray, which causes rapid oxidation of the iron and manganese to the insoluble forms. The oxidized iron and manganese gradually settle to the bottom of the tank or pond, and the surface water is used for irrigation. The problem with this method is that rather large ponds or tanks are required to let the water stay in the tank long enough for the iron and manganese to settle. If the turnover of water in the tank is too rapid, the suspended iron will settle in irrigation lines and on plants.

Oxidation filters yield the same effect by oxidizing the iron and manganese through aeration, potassium permanganate, or chlorine. Filters remove the precipitated iron or manganese and must be periodically back-flushed to remove the accumulated precipitates. If a chemical oxidant is used (potassium permanganate or chlorine), the unit must also be regenerated with new oxidant. Sand filtration may be used after oxidation to remove precipitated iron. Oxidation by aeration followed by reverse osmosis was used by a Michigan grower to reduce iron residues in propagation houses.

Manganese is much slower to oxidize than iron, and the precipitates are much slower to settle. Chemical coagulation, sedimentation, and filtration may be required to remove manganese from water.

Water softeners (cation exchange type) and zeolite softeners can also be used to remove iron and manganese. A water softener removes the soluble form of iron (ferrous) and manganese (manganous) by ion exchange. The insoluble forms occur as fine, suspended precipitates in the water and are filtered out by the softener. However, backwashing the resin is required to prevent buildup of precipitated iron. Sand filtration before water softening will remove suspended iron and prevent clogging of the water softener.

Another approach is to sequester or chelate the iron or manganese. The chelated iron or manganese remains soluble and is resistant to oxidation-induced precipitation. Therefore, the chelated forms pass through the irrigation system and are not precipitated on plants. Polyphosphate compounds (hexametaphosphate) are commonly used chelates and are injected into the water line. Polyphosphates are good for water with relatively low soluble iron and manganese content (less than 1 to 2 mg/l). They do not react with oxidized iron (ferric) or manganese (+3 and above) that are suspended in the water. Do not heat polyphosphate-treated water because heating causes the polyphosphates to break down and release the iron and manganese.

Calcium and magnesium

Hard water is due to excessive amounts of calcium and magnesium. Plants have a very high tolerance to calcium and magnesium, so hard water is seldom directly injurious to plants. However, irrigating overhead with hard water may contribute to unsightly salt deposits on leaves.

Calcium and magnesium are removed with a water softener. Most water softeners replace the calcium and magnesium with sodium. Soft water high in sodium should not be used on plants because it is very damaging. However, a water softener charged with potassium to replace calcium and magnesium will function as a fertilizer source. If the irrigation water is very hard, overfertilization with potassium can occur. Also, you must take into account the economics of recharging a water softener with the more expensive potassium chloride. Since the calcium and magnesium are exchanged with potassium, the water's total TDS does not change appreciably with softening.

Carbonates and bicarbonates

Carbonates and bicarbonates are the major contributors to water alkalinity, but they seldom cause direct salt damage to plants. However, there are many secondary effects caused by high carbonates and bicarbonates, such as: 1) accumulation of unsightly salt deposits from overhead irrigation, 2) precipitation of nutrients in a liquid feed program, especially micronutrients, 3) increase in the pH of growing media over time, and 4) induction of iron and/or manganese deficiency.

Carbonates and bicarbonates can be removed with acid injection. Acidification causes carbonates and bicarbonates to convert into dissolved carbon dioxide, which then diffuses out of the water. Carbonates and bicarbonates are replaced by the anion associated with the acid used, i.e., sulfate, if sulfuric acid is used or phosphate if phosphoric acid is used. Because of this, the TDS does not change appreciably with acid injection. This process is discussed extensively in Chapter 4, Alkalinity, pH and Acidification.

Fluoride

Fluoride causes leaf burn in some tropical foliage plants and Easter lilies. Fluoride contamination comes from fertilizers (especially superphosphate), growing media (especially perlite), and irrigation water. Usually irrigation water is the least likely cause of the problem because most irrigation water contains 1 mg/l or less of fluoride, the level usually found in fluorinated municipal water. This level of contamination usually is not injurious to plants. However, some irrigation waters contain damaging fluoride levels (up to 67 mg/l).

Activated alumina or activated carbon can be used to remove fluoride. Both of these processes absorb the fluoride to remove it from water. Adsorption by activated alumina is pH dependent, and adjustment of the water to pH 5.5 before treatment is necessary. This is done by an ion exchange process and is reversible. The system can also be regenerated with a strong base such as sodium hydroxide and reused. Activated carbon is usually replaced once its capacity is exhausted.

Fluoride is insoluble at high pH. A common way to control fluoride toxicity is to raise the growing media's pH instead of purifying the water. Maintaining a pH of 6.0 to 6.5 will prevent most fluoride toxicity.

Boron

Boron occurs in many irrigation waters. A small amount (0.3 to 1.0 mg/l) is desirable because it will fulfill the plant's boron requirement (see Chapters 2 and 8 on water analysis and micronutrient nutrition). Higher levels may cause problems. Boron occurs in water as negatively charged borates, so it can be removed by anion exchange. Anion exchange resins used are similar to those used in deionization systems discussed earlier. The resins will not be selective for boron, however, and the expense of such a system may make boron removal impractical.

Reverse osmosis systems will remove boron at 70 to 75% efficiency. For maximum efficiency, the pH needs to be adjusted to slightly alkaline levels (pH 7.5). Due to the requirement for a higher pH, thin-film composite type membranes are used that tolerate the higher pH. Since the cellulose acetate type membranes are usually accompanied by acidification, they are not as effective for boron removal.

Waste water disposal

All water purification methods produce either liquid or solid waste. For reverse osmosis, electrodialysis and distillation, the waste water is a concentrated brine, and some of the systems produce large volumes of brine. For example, a reverse osmosis system may produce 20 to 75% purified water and 25 to 80% brine waste. For systems that can be regenerated, such as ion exchange resins and activated alumina, the regeneration process produces liquid waste that may be very acid or very alkaline. For filters and adsorbents that usually are not regenerated, such as activated carbon, you must dispose of the spent filter, and you need to make proper provisions for waste disposal. In some areas, there may be regulations, and permits may be required.

Costs

Seldom is 100% removal of TDS and contaminants required in horticultural operations. Instead, decide the highest level of TDS that can be tolerated for each given application, and then take one of these two approaches: 1) purify the water to that level and use it directly, or 2) purify the water to a very high level and then blend it back with untreated water. Economics will determine which of these two options is best for you.

The cost associated with water purification systems is determined by two major factors: 1) the initial water quality, and 2) the degree of purification required. The initial water quality can only be determined through water analysis. Among the factors to determine are TDS, concentrations of individual ions, presence of toxic ions, colloidal or suspended solids, turbidity, organic matter, microorganisms, hardness, alkalinity, and pH. All of these factors must be taken into account in designing a water purification system.

The degree of purification needed is determined by the situation. For example, a holding solution for cut flowers may need greater purification, while water for a propagation mist system may need partial purification, and irrigation water for moderately salt-sensitive plants may require only limited purification.

Once initial water quality and degree of purification are known, a system can be designed. Costs to be considered include land and construction costs, the purification unit, pretreatment systems required, energy for operation, chemicals, maintenance materials, labor, and waste disposal. Because of the individualized nature of water purification systems, even generalizations about costs are difficult to make.

The following example shows the water purification costs for a typical greenhouse production facility. The operation is a foliage plant production facility in south Texas. Most of the nursery's foliage species are salt tolerant, but some species in their product line are salt sensitive (spathiphyllum, dieffenbachia, and some ferns). Their water source is surface water from the Rio Grande River that has been treated for municipal use. The soluble salt content varies from 1.0 to 1.75 dS/m (approximately 700 to 1,225 ppm), and the water has a high degree of submicron particles causing high turbidity. The water purification system used is detailed in table 3.2.

The system is leased and maintained by a local major brand name water purification company. The water is variously pretreated and then purified by reverse osmosis. The system yields about 6,000 gallons (23 kl) of purified water per day, which is then blended with untreated water at a ratio of 40% purified water to 60% untreated water. The blend rate varies seasonally to yield a blended water soluble salt content of 0.75 dS/m (approximately 500 ppm). This is sufficient purity for their application.

Table 3.2   Example of a commercial water purification system[a]

Initial water quality

Salinity:	1.0 to 1.75 dS/m (700 to 1,225 ppm)
Silt Density Index (SDI):	very high
Chlorine:	added by municipality

Water purification system

Pretreatments:	1) Polymer injection due to high SDI	to coagulate submicron particles
	2) Depth filter	to remove coagulated particles
	3) Charcoal filter	to remove municipal chlorine
	4) Ion exchange	to remove residual polymer
Purification system:	Reverse osmosis	using Filmtec thin-film composite polyamide membranes (pH resistant, chlorine sensitive)
Storage tanks:	32,000 gal. (2@ 16,000 gal. each)	
Purified water production capacity:	5,760 gal. per day	
Blended water production capacity:	14,400 gal. per day (40% purified/60% untreated water)	
Water blended to maintain minimum salinity	0.75 dS/m (approximately 500 ppm)	

Monthly costs (excludes cost of plumbing and pumps to irrigation system, storage tanks):

Lease and service		$900 per month
Water ($1.09/1,000 gal.)		$700 per month
Electricity		$200 per month
	Total	$1,800 per month
Purified water costs:		$0.01 per gal.
Blended water costs:		$0.004 per gal.

Production space irrigated

80,000 to 135,000 sq. ft. of 6-in. pot production space (at 12–20 oz./6-in. pot/day and 0.9 sq. ft. production space/6-in. pot)

Purified water used for

Salt-sensitive foliate plants (spathiphyllum, diffenbachia, some ferns)
Mist propagation

[a] This system was designed for a large foliage plant facility in south Texas. Water salinity here can be as high as 1.75 dS/m (1,225 ppm) and can cause salt burn on some sensitive crops.

The blended water is used to irrigate 6-inch (1.5 cm) spathiphyllum, dieffenbachia, and some fern species. It is also used for mist propagation of salt sensitive species. The volume of blended water produced is sufficient to irrigate 80,000 to 135,000 square feet (7,500 to 12,500 m²) of production space. The total costs (lease and service, water and electricity) is $1,800 per month. This translates into a cost of approximately $0.01 per gallon ($0.0025/l) of purified water or about $0.004 per gallon ($0.0013/l) of blended water.

Sources for equipment

The Water Quality Association, Lisle, Illinois, publishes the *Validated Water Treatment Equipment Directory and List of Manufacturers and Suppliers*. NSF International (formerly National Sanitation Foundation) publishes the *NSF Listing of Drinking Water Treatment Units* that contains a listing of certified manufacturers. These publications are valuable in locating reputable equipment dealers across the country. Since water purification systems are individualized to each user and are technical in nature, it is often best to have a system designed by professionals in the field. Also consult OSHA and other regulations.

Be sure to obtain multiple bids. Sometimes the best option is to lease a system that is designed, installed, and maintained by the dealer. Also consider that a local dealer can ensure prompt attention and correction when needed.

References

Aschoff, A.F., Sargent and Lundy. 1993. Ensure the best performance from membranes and demineralizers. *Power*, March.

Deionized water doubles vase life of cut flowers. *Culligan Job Report No. 182*. Northbrook, Ill.: Culligan International.

Deionized water benefits florists in many ways. *Culligan Job Report No. 190*. Northbrook, Ill.: Culligan International.

Council of Better Business Bureaus. 1988. *Tips on water quality improvement*. Publication 24-236 HBL 400290. Arlington, Va.

Eisenberg, T.N., and E.J. Middlebrooks. 1986. *Reverse osmosis treatment of drinking water*. Stoneham, Mass.: Butterworths Publ.

Faust, S.D., and O.M. Aly. 1983. *Chemistry of water treatment*. Woburn, Mass.: Butterworths Publ.

Gumerman, R.C., B.E. Burris, and S.P. Hansen. 1986. *Small water system treatment costs*. Park Ridge, N.J.: Noyes Data Corp.

Heitmann, H-G. ed. 1990. *Saline water processing*. New York: VCH Publ.

Kren, L. 1994. Beating the bad water blues. *Greenhouse Grower*, 12(12):14–15.

NSF International. 1994. *NSF Listings—Drinking water treatment units*. Ann Arbor, Mich.: NSF International.

Poole, R.T., C.A. Conover, R.W. Henley, and A.J. Pate. 1978. Fluoride toxicity of foliage plants—A research review. *Foliage Digest* 1(7):3–6.

Solt, G.S., and C.B. Shirley. 1991. *An engineer's guide to water treatment*. Hants, England: Avebury Technical Academic Publishing Group.

Validated water treatment equipment directory. 1994. Lisle, Ill.: Water Quality Association.

Recognized treatments techniques. 1993. Bulletin R28. Lisle, Ill.: Water Quality Association.

The stainers—iron and manganese. 1993. Bulletin S9a. Lisle, Ill.: Water Quality Association.

Chapter 4

Alkalinity, pH, and Acidification

Douglas A. Bailey

Water is essential for plant production, and the importance of testing water sources prior to use in irrigation has already been emphasized. However, the alkalinity and pH of irrigation water need further discussion. The pH of a media solution (the water solution in the pores of growing media) controls the relative availability of nutrients, especially micronutrients, to plants (table 4.1). The pH and alkalinity of irrigation water are dominant factors affecting the pH of the media solution. Controlling media pH is essential for a successful crop fertilization strategy and may involve modifying the pH and alkalinity content of your irrigation water.

pH and alkalinity

Media solution pH can be a limiting factor in greenhouse crop production. Nutrient availability and subsequent plant growth can be affected severely by high media and irrigation water pH. Since irrigation water quality can have a great effect on media solution pH, understanding both water pH and water alkalinity content is necessary to accurately treat water with a high pH.

Table 4.1 Effects of media pH on nutrient uptake in plants

Low pH	High pH
increased uptake:	**increased uptake**
iron	molybdenum
manganese	
zinc	**decreased uptake**
copper	iron
	manganese
decreased uptake	zinc
molybdenum	copper
calcium	boron
magnesium	

pH: definition and recommendations

A pH reading is a measurement of the hydrogen ion concentration of a solution (how acidic or basic a solution is). Readings are reported as the negative logarithm of the hydrogen ion concentration, expressed in moles per liter. Solution pH ranges from 0 (most acidic; highest concentration of [H+]) to 14 (most basic; lowest concentration of [H+]). Although pH 7 is considered neutral (not acidic or alkaline), 7 is not the optimum pH for irrigation water or media solutions (figs. 4.1 and 4.2).

There are two main categories of greenhouse crops with respect to proper media pH. Most crops grow best when the media pH is slightly acid, 6.2 to 6.8 for media containing a significant proportion of mineral soil and 5.6 to 6.2 for soilless media. However, some species such as azaleas, gardenias, and blue hydrangeas perform best with a media solution pH of 4.8 to 5.8. A few species fall outside these two groupings. For example, Easter lilies in soilless media are best grown at higher pHs of 6.5 to 6.8, because high pH reduces availability of fluoride and, subsequently reduces the possibility of fluoride toxicity leaf scorch. Other examples are seed geraniums and marigolds. Both species are susceptible to toxicities of iron and manganese. Many growers grow these plants in soilless media at pH 6.2 to 6.5 to reduce iron and manganese availability and avoid the toxicity problems.

Recommendations for proper irrigation water pH differ quite a lot, but most authors agree the maximum pH should be 6.5. If acidification

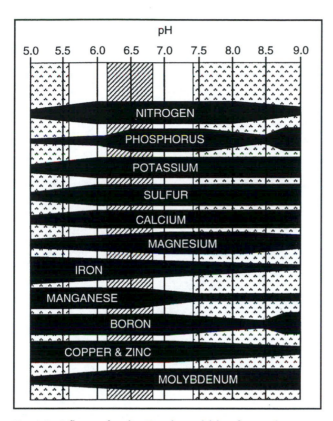

Fig. 4.1   Influence of media pH on the availability of essential nutrients in a mineral soil. The recommended optimum pH range for nutrient uptake is indicated by slashed lines (pH 6.2 to 6.9). The white and figured zones indicate increasing problems with nutrient uptake.

is necessary to reduce water alkalinity and pH, an end point pH of 5.8 to 6.0 should be sufficient.

Water pH can vary quite a lot, depending on the amount of dissolved gases, mainly carbon dioxide (CO_2), that are present (table 4.2). You can demonstrate this yourself by measuring your water pH directly out of the tap. Allow it to sit overnight (covered with a piece of paper to prevent debris from falling into the water), then measure the pH. Next, collect a sample from the tap, bubbling air through the sample via a straw for 30 seconds, and measure that sample for pH. The samples measured will more than likely vary in pH similar to the samples shown in table 4.2. Fortunately, the water's CO_2 content has little effect on the

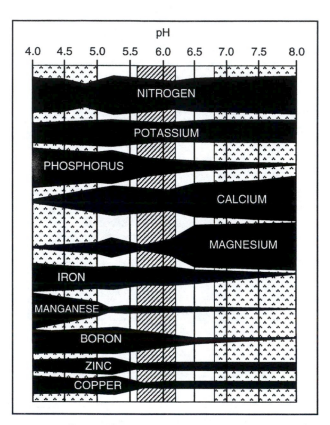

Fig. 4.2 Influence of media pH on the availability of essential nutrients in soilless media. The recommended optimum pH range for nutrient uptake is indicated by the slashed region (pH 5.6 to 6.2); the white and figured zones indicate increasing problems with nutrient uptake.

alkalinity and electrical conductivity measurements that laboratories perform. To get a consistent pH water reading, allow the sample to sit overnight, covered with paper to prevent contaminants from entering the sample. The key, however, to irrigation water effects on media pH is not the water pH, but the alkalinity content of the water.

Alkalinity

Water alkalinity is a measure of a water's capacity to neutralize acids—that is, the concentration of soluble alkalis in a solution that can neu-

Table 4.2 Effect of dissolved carbon dioxide on the pH of three irrigation waters

Water and treatment	pH	Alkalinity (me/l)	Electrical conductivity (dS/m)[a]
Sample A (Raleigh, N.C.)			
directly out of tap	6.8	0.80	0.21
equilibrated overnight	7.1	0.81	0.22
bubbled for 30 seconds	6.5	0.79	0.21
Sample B (Plymouth, N.C.)			
directly out of tap	6.7	5.20	0.70
equilibrated overnight	6.8	5.19	0.71
bubbled for 30 seconds	6.3	5.20	0.71
Sample C (W. Lafayette, Ind.)			
directly out of tap	6.9	6.39	0.72
equilibrated overnight	7.0	6.39	0.72
bubbled for 30 seconds	6.3	6.38	0.73

[a] A deciSeiman (ds/m) equals millimhos/cm (mmhos/cm).

tralize acid. The term alkalinity is different from the term alkaline. Alkaline simply means any pH above 7.0. The two terms should not be confused with each other.

Laboratory test results should express alkalinity as milligrams per liter of calcium carbonate equivalents (mg/l $CaCO_3$) or milliequivalents per liter of calcium carbonate equivalents (me/l $CaCO_3$). You can convert between these two units using the following conversion: 1.0 me/l $CaCO_3$ = 50.04 mg/l $CaCO_3$. The term total carbonates (TC) may also be used by some labs to refer to a solution's alkalinity, and the units reported are usually calcium carbonate equivalents of alkalinity. Alkalinity has also been expressed as ppm bicarbonate (mg/l HCO_3^-). To convert from ppm bicarbonate to the preferred me/l $CaCO_3$, divide the ppm HCO_3^- by 61.

Alkalinity is related to pH because alkalinity establishes the buffering capacity of water. Buffering is a term used to describe how resistant a solution is to a change in pH. Alkalinity is the main cause of buffering in water and affects how much acid is required to change the pH of water. The greater the alkalinity, the more buffered the water, and

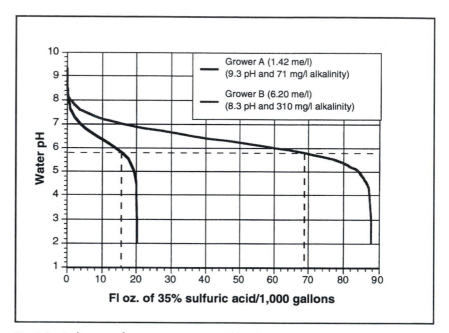

Fig. 4.3 Acid titrations for two irrigation waters. Although Grower A's water is one pH unit above Grower B's water, it takes only one-fourth the amount of acid for Grower A to reach pH 5.8 than it takes Grower B. Grower B's water requires more acid due to its increased alkalinity.

more acid is required to lower water pH as compared to a lower alkalinity water.

The following example (adapted from an article by Peterson and Ludwig in *GrowerTalks* magazine) may help explain the importance of alkalinity when trying to acidify water: Grower A has water with a pH of 9.3 and an alkalinity of 71 mg/l $CaCO_3$ (TC = 1.42 me/l $CaCO_3$) (fig. 4.3). To reduce the pH of this water to 5.8, it takes 15.76 fluid ounces (466 ml) of 35% sulfuric acid per 1,000 gallons (3.8 kl) of water. In contrast, Grower B has water with a pH of 8.3 and an alkalinity of 310 mg/l $CaCO_3$ (TC = 6.20 me/l $CaCO_3$). To reduce this water to a pH of 5.8, it takes 68.64 fluid ounces (2 l) of 35% sulfuric acid per 1,000 gallons (3.8 kl) of water. Despite the fact that Grower B's water is a full pH unit lower than Grower A's, it takes more than four times more acid to lower the pH to 5.8. Both alkalinity and pH are important to consider when attempting to adjust the pH of water, and both should be tested when evaluating the quality of a water source.

Chemical properties of alkaline water. Dissolved bicarbonates and carbonates are the major chemicals contributing to alkalinity in irrigation water. Dissolved hydroxides, ammonia, borates, organic bases, phosphates, and silicates also increase alkalinity, but they are usually minor contributors to the alkalinity of most irrigation water. Since bicarbonates and carbonates are the major components of water alkalinity, most laboratories assume that carbonates + bicarbonates (total carbonates or TC) equals alkalinity, and in most cases, this is a safe assumption with respect to water acidification calculations.

Carbonate reactions are among the most important chemical reactions that occur in an irrigation water system. The relative concentration of the three carbonates [carbonates ($CO_3^=$), bicarbonates (HCO_3^-), and carbonic acid (H_2CO_3)] is the main buffering system controlling irrigation solution pH, and it also controls the media solution pH to a very large degree. Dissolved carbon dioxide (CO_2) in irrigation water can also affect the pH of the water, but its effects on the pH of media is relatively small. When you use water with high concentrations of bicarbonates and carbonates, the pH of the media solution can increase over time. As plants use the water in the media or as water evaporates, the carbonates and bicarbonates are left behind. These ions neutralize hydrogen, reducing the hydrogen concentration of the media solution, and thus increase the pH. This is why it is important to neutralize or remove bicarbonates and carbonates from irrigation water prior to use to prevent undesirable increases in media pH.

Carbonate and bicarbonate ions reportedly have toxic effects on root growth of plants. The toxic effects of bicarbonates are believed to be due to interference with plant root uptake of essential elements and an associated increase in media solution pH, rather than direct uptake of bicarbonate by plants. Whether carbonates and bicarbonates reduce plant growth directly or indirectly is unknown. It is known that neutralization of alkalinity in irrigation water can prevent the detrimental effects of irrigating plants with high alkalinity water.

Optimum alkalinity levels for irrigation water. Some fertilizers contain small amounts of carbonates such as potassium carbonate (K_2CO_3), potassium bicarbonate ($KHCO_3$), dissolved malachite ($Cu_2 (OH)_2O_3$), manganese carbonate ($MnCO_3$), and zinc carbonate ($ZnCO_3$). However, the main sources of carbonate in media are limes, such as calcium carbonate (calcitic limestone, $CaCO_3$), magnesium carbonate ($MgCO_3$), and calcium-magnesium carbonate (dolomitic limestone, $CaMg(CO_3)_2$). If too much lime is used in media, or if the irrigation water contains a high concentration of carbonates and bicarbonates, the media solution pH will rise to undesirable levels during plant production.

How much alkalinity is too much? Unfortunately, there is little information available on acceptable levels of alkalinity, nor are there established thresholds for toxicity. Farnham reported that concentrations of alkalinity above 1 me/l in an irrigation water are high enough to cause pH increases in the media solution. Traditional recommendations for acceptable upper limits of alkalinity in irrigation water range from 1.3 me/l to 2 me/l for plugs and from 2.6 me/l to 3.6 me/l for plants in 6-inch (15 cm) pots. For both container sizes, the recommended thresholds vary quite a lot.

More than likely, the upper acceptable limits for alkalinity vary for species, media, irrigation method, and fertilization program used. Research is needed to more precisely measure the effects of alkalinity and of neutralizing alkalinity on plant growth. In the meantime, generally recommended normal ranges are given in table 4.3 for irrigation water alkalinity.

Ironically, the carbonate buffer system in an irrigation solution can prevent significant changes in the media solution pH, and subsequently, prevent sudden changes in nutrient availability due to pH changes. Therefore, using very pure water for irrigation may result in a gradual decrease in media pH, especially if acid-forming fertilizers are used. For this reason, some growers with very pure water that lack carbonates and bicarbonates may actually benefit from adding potassium bicarbonate ($KHCO_3$) to their irrigation water if media pH decreases over time. Suggested minimum levels of alkalinity range from 0.66 me/l to 0.8 me/l for plugs and from 1.2 me/l to 1.98 me/l for plants in 6-inch (15 cm) pots. Table 4.4 gives rates of potassium bicarbonate to use to increase the carbonate buffer capacity of pure water along with the concentration of K supplied for each treatment.

Neutralizing alkalinity

The only economical way to eliminate alkalinity in water is to neutralize it with acid. Consider acid injection for all water used on plants to control alkalinity. However, even if you choose not to acidify irrigation

Table 4.3 Recommended irrigation water alkalinity limits for different production systems

Product/container size	Suggested minimum alkalinity[a]	Suggested maximum alkalinity[b]
	me/l	me/l
Plugs and/or seedlings	0.75	1.3
Small pots and shallow flats	0.75	1.7
4- to 5-inch pots and deep flats	0.75	2.1
6-inch pots and long-term crops	1.25	2.6

[a] Consider adding potassium bicarbonate to the irrigation water to at least this level if media pH tends to decline during production.

[b] Consider acidifying the irrigation water if alkalinity is above this level and if media pH tends to rise during production.

Table 4.4 Amount of potassium bicarbonate ($KHCO_3$) to add to irrigation water to supply 0.10, 0.25, 0.50, and 1.0 me/l alkalinity and the corresponding amount of potassium added

Amount of alkalinity to add	Amount of potassium bicarbonate needed	Amount of potassium supplied
me/l	oz. per 1,000 gal.	ppm
0.10	1.3	4
0.25	3.3	10
0.50	6.7	20
1.00	13.4	39

water, you should neutralize alkalis in water used to create fertilizer stock solutions to help avoid fertilizer precipitation.

Acidifying irrigation water

Injecting sulfuric, phosphoric, or nitric acid into irrigation water improves the quality of high pH/high alkalinity water by reducing the amount of bicarbonate and carbonate to prevent a rise in media pH over time. To

Table 4.5 Alkalinity reduction to an end point pH of approximately 5.8[a]

Acid used	Amount of acid to add to 1,000 gals. of water for each me/l of alkalinity[b]	Concentration of nutrient provided by 1 fl. oz. of acid per 1,000 gals. of water[c]
Nitric acid (67%)	6.6 fl. oz.	1.64 ppm N
Phosphoric acid (75%)	8.1 fl. oz.[d]	2.88 ppm P
Sulfuric acid (35%)	11.0 fl. oz.	1.14 ppm S

[a] The values indicate the amount of acid to inject to neutralize approximately 80% of the alkalinity and drop the irrigation water pH to approximately 5.8 and the resulting concentrations of nutrients provided by 1 fluid ounce of each acid per 1,000 gallons of water.

[b] Add this amount of acid to 1,000 gallons for each me/l of alkalinity present to neutralize approximately 80% of the alkalinity. For example, if your water report indicates an alkalinity of 3 me/l and you choose to use sulfuric acid, you would need to add 33 fluid ounces of 35% sulfuric acid per 1,000 gallons of water (11 fl. oz./me/l × 3 me/l = 33 fl. oz.).

[c] In the above example, the acidification treatment would supply 38 ppm S at each irrigation (33 fl. oz. × 1.14 ppm S/fl. oz. = 38 ppm S).

[d] Assumes an effective dissociation rate of 1.02 me/l H+ per 3 me/l of phosphoric acid.

accurately predict the amount of acid required to acidify water to a given pH, you must know the pH and alkalinity of the irrigation water.

Should you neutralize alkalinity to an end point pH or to an end point alkalinity concentration? This question has not been conclusively decided. The goal of reducing irrigation water alkalinity and pH is not to reach an end point in the water, but to reach a level where the water has little effect on the pH (by either raising or lowering the pH) of the media solution. As mentioned earlier, this optimum end point (whether a pH or a me/l alkalinity concentration) will vary with the crop, watering technique, fertilization program, and media. Keep precise crop records with respect to media solution pH changes over time to fine-tune water acidification requirements for your particular greenhouse situation.

Table 4.5 outlines starting amounts of acid to inject per 1,000 gallons (3.8 kl) of water to drop pH to approximately 5.8. However, this table takes only alkalinity into account (and does not account for the starting pH of a water sample). Adjusting the amount of acid added will be necessary. Targeting an end point pH allows growers to monitor their

Table 4.6   Complete alkalinity reduction[a]

Acid used (%)	Amount of acid to add to 1,000 gals. of water for each me/l of alkalinity[b]	Concentration of nutrient provided by 1 fl. oz. of acid per 1,000 gals. of water[c]
Nitric acid (67%)	8.477 fl. oz.	1.64 ppm N
Phosphoric acid (75%)	9.62 fl. oz.[d]	2.88 ppm P
Sulfuric acid (35%)	14.18 fl. oz.	1.14 ppm S

[a] The values indicate the amount of acid to inject to completely neutralize 1 me/l of alkalinity and the resulting concentrations of nutrients provided by 1 fluid ounce of each acid per 1,000 gallons of water.

[b] Add this amount of acid to 1,000 gallons for each me/l of alkalinity present. For example, if your water report indicates an alkalinity of 3 me/l and you choose to neutralize only 2 me/l using nitric acid, you would need to add 16.95 fluid ounces of 67% nitric acid per 1,000 gallons of water (8.477 fl. oz./me/l × 2 me/l = 16.95 fl. oz.).

[c] In the above example, the acidification treatment would supply 27.8 ppm N at each irrigation (16.95 fl. oz. × 1.64 ppm N/fl. oz. = 27.8 ppm N).

[d] Assumes an effective dissociation of 1.1 me/l H^+ per 3 me/l of phosphoric acid.

irrigation water and acidification with a pH meter. Remember to allow samples to sit overnight prior to taking a pH reading so the CO_2 concentration will come to equilibrium, thus minimizing dissolved CO_2 effects on pH.

When acidifying water, an end point of 5.8 should be adequate to prevent a rise in media solution pH due to alkalinity in the irrigation water, and it should be high enough to prevent a slow decline in media pH if alkaline fertilizers are rotated with acid-forming fertilizers. Table 4.6 was designed for growers who would rather target an end point alkalinity content. To monitor the effectiveness of acidification, use an alkalinity test kit, available from most supply companies. Table 4.6 indicates how much acid should be added per 1,000 gallons (3.8 kl) of water to neutralize each milliequivalent of alkalinity in the water and also indicates the corresponding ppm of nutrient supplied. Use it to decide your target end point alkalinity concentration (pick a level between the minimum and maximum suggested for the container sizes you are producing). As with table 4.5, table 4.6 takes only alkalinity into account and does not account for the starting pH of a water sample or the end point pH of the water. Therefore, the end point pH cannot be predicted for any of the acids. The phosphoric acid recommendation will not result in the exact targeted alkalinity end point due to the pH-related dissociation of hydrogen from phosphoric acid.

For exact calculations of either end point pH or end point alkalinity concentrations, acquire a copy of an acidification spreadsheet developed by Hammer and Bailey (see citation in References at end of chapter under Whipker, Bailey, Nelson, Fonteno, and Hammer). This spreadsheet accounts for starting pH, starting alkalinity, and the pH variable due to the dissociation rate of phosphoric acid. It allows users to more exactly calculate the amount of acid needed to achieve an end point pH or alkalinity concentration. It also allows you to estimate acidification costs for your water using the three acids discussed in this section.

Growers who acidify their water should adjust their fertilization program for the nutrient supplied by the acid used (tables 4.5, 4.6). For example, if using phosphoric acid, make sure to reduce your phosphorus feed accordingly to account for the P supplied from the acid. When attempting to acidify waters very high in alkalinity, phosphoric acid may not be feasible. For example, if your water supply contains 6.0 me/l of alkalinity and you wish to target an end point pH of 5.8, over 328 ppm P_2O_5 (143 ppm P) are supplied at each irrigation; this would result in too high a level of phosphorus. If using nitric acid, account for the additional N supplied from the acid. Using 67% nitric acid to acidify water containing 6.0 me/l of alkalinity to a pH of 5.8 would supply 67 ppm N at each irrigation, which is a significant quantity of nitrogen. Sulfuric acid treatment for 6.0 milliequivalent of alkalinity would supply 75 ppm S, which is more than sufficient sulfur for plant production.

The 75% phosphoric acid and the 35% sulfuric acid are relatively safe to work with compared to the 67% nitric acid. However, care should be taken when handling any acid, and protective eyewear and clothing are required.

The sulfuric acid recommended is a battery electrolyte product named Qual, which can be purchased from most auto supply stores for about $10 per 5 gallons (19 l). At this price, a grower would spend $0.172 on sulfuric acid per milliequivalent of alkalinity per 1,000 gallons (3.8 l) of water. For example, if your water had an alkalinity of 4 me/l and you targeted pH 5.8, you would need to add 44 fluid ounces (1.3 l) of 35% sulfuric acid per 1,000 gallons (3.8 l) of irrigation water, and this amount of acid would cost $0.69. We recommend sulfuric acid over nitric and phosphoric acid due to its relative ease and safety of use, cost, and availability.

Acidifying fertilizer concentrates

Control of alkalinity is also crucial to avoid precipitation of fertilizer salts from stock tank concentrates. Neutralizing of alkalinity and lowering pH to about 5.8 should be considered for fertilizer stock tank water prior to adding fertilizer salts. This can be done by using the three acids described above or using commercially available organic acids such as citric acid. Using citric acid (and other weak organic acid) products is usually not economically feasible for bulk acidification of irrigation water, but it is better suited to neutralize stock tank alkalinity than sulfuric and phosphoric acids. Citric acid does not supply a carrier ion, such as phosphate (as would phosphoric acid) or sulfate (as would sulfuric acid), that can precipitate out salts in a stock tank fertilizer concentrate.

One final warning about water acidification: Acidic water will corrode galvanized piping and fittings over time. Also, the injector used to add acid into your water should be designed by the manufacturer for acid injection.

Highly acid fertilizers

There are specially formulated, highly acid fertilizers on the market (Peters Excel Fertilizer, O.M. Scott & Sons Co.) that use urea phosphate to create a very acid (pH 1.0 to 2.0) fertilizer stock solution to be used in a continuous feed program with a fertilizer injector. When injected into the irrigation line, these fertilizers have the same effect as injecting acid into the irrigation water. The main function of this type of fertilizer is to supply plant nutrients; irrigation water acidification is a secondary effect. The amount of acidification is dictated by the level of fertility maintained. For a standard fertility program, these high acid fertilizers are most applicable for waters with an alkalinity between 0.8 to 4.1 me/l (50 to 250 ppm) alkalinity. For waters above 4.1 me/l (250 ppm) alkalinity, the high acid fertilizers will only cause partial neutralization and additional acid may need to be injected. For waters below 0.8 me/l (50 ppm) alkalinity, the highly acid fertilizers may cause too much acidification, especially if the N level applied is above 150 ppm. In addition, it is not always desirable to acidify water with alkalinity below 0.75 to 1.25 me/l (45 to 75 ppm) (table 4.3). Consult the label for the specific high acid fertilizer used.

Fertilizer effects on media pH

Fertilizers used during crop production can affect media solution pH. Most fertilizer salts have an effect on pH, either by having an acidic or basic residual effect. The acidifying effect of acid forming fertilizers (their use lowers media solution pH) is largely due to the ammonium nitrogen content. Acid forming fertilizers are those that contain ammonium, ammonia, and urea. During the nitrification process of converting ammonium to nitrate in the media, hydrogen is released causing a decrease in pH. In addition, plants secrete hydrogen into media when they absorb any ammonium present in media. Other principal acid-forming nutrients are sulfur (S), chlorine (Cl), and phosphoric oxide (P_2O_5).

The pH rise caused by basic fertilizers (their use raises media solution pH) is largely due to nitrate (NO_3^-), calcium (Ca), magnesium (Mg), potassium oxide (K_2O), and sodium (Na) content of the mixed fertilizer.

A nonacid-forming or neutral fertilizer is one that leaves neither an acidic or basic residue in media. Potassium salts, except for potassium nitrate, are examples of neutral fertilizers. The acidic and basic nutrients in common potassium salts neutralize each other to form physiologically neutral compounds. Superphosphates have no permanent effect on media solution pH for the same reason.

Fertilizer labels contain a potential acidity or potential basicity on the bag in terms of pounds of calcium carbonate ($CaCO_3$) per ton of fertilizer. The acidic residue of any fertilizer in media, measured in terms of the calcium carbonate required to neutralize it, is sometimes called physiological, equivalent, residual, or potential acidity. Likewise, the basic residue of any fertilizer, in terms of its calcium carbonate equivalent, is called the physiological, equivalent, residual, or potential basicity of that fertilizer.

If you are irrigating with water low in alkalinity and pH, continuous use of acid-forming fertilizers can result in a reduction in media solution pH over time, while constant use of basic residue fertilizers can cause the pH to rise over time. Alternating between the two types helps to maintain a stable media pH. Growers can partially adjust media pH through fertilizer selection, based on relative acidity and basicity (table 4.8). One word of caution when selecting fertilizers—make sure you are maintaining the proper ratio of ammonium-N to nitrate-N as described in Chapter 7 on macronutrient nutrition. Most acid residue fertilizers have a high ammonium-N content; take care to keep ammonium-N plus urea-N at or below 40% of the total nitrogen supplied.

Note that brands of blended fertilizers with identical analyses can differ dramatically in potential acidity and basicity, depending on the salts used in deriving the formulations. For example, various formulations of 21-7-7 reported potential acidity of 362 to 1,560 pounds of $CaCO_3$ per ton of fertilizer (180 kg to 780 kg per 1,000 kg)! Make sure to check the label of the fertilizer you are using for correct estimates of residual acidity and basicity.

Adjusting media solution pH

Although it is probably the most important factor affecting media solution pH, the alkalinity content of the irrigation solution is not the only factor capable of modifying media solution pH. There are actually four major components of production that can ultimately affect media pH: 1) media components in the mix (tables 4.7, 4.8); 2) the liming materials added to media during blending; 3) fertilizers used during plant production; and 4) irrigation water quality (pH and alkalinity). Most media are pH-adjusted to a desired level with lime added during media mixing, but cultural practices used during plant production can change the pH of the media solution.

Postplanting methods to raise media pH

Figures 4.1 and 4.2 indicate the optimum media pH ranges for soil-containing and soilless mixes. If the pH is out of the optimum zone, take corrective measures. For small increases in pH (media pH is just below the optimum zone), follow these three steps: 1) discontinue irrigation water acidification, if you are currently acidifying your water; 2) if the pH does not begin to rise within seven to 10 days after step one, or if you are not currently acidifying your water, then discontinue the use of acid-forming fertilizers (containing ammonium, ammonia,

Table 4.7 Media component pH and subsequent influence on pH of growing media

Component	Initial pH	Influence on final media pH
Coarse aggregates		
Calcined clay	5.0 to 9.0	small
Perlite	7.0 to 7.5	small
Polystyrene	inert	none
Rock wool	7.0 to 7.5	small
Sand	variable	moderate
Vermiculite	6.0 to 6.8	small
Organic matter		
Composted pine bark	3.5 to 6.5	large
Hypnum peat moss	5.0 to 5.5	large
Peat humus	5.0 to 7.5	large
Sedge-Reed peat moss	4.0 to 7.5	large
Sphagnum peat moss	3.0 to 4.0	large
Soil		
Loam	variable	moderate

and urea), and use basic-forming fertilizers (containing nitrate) such as calcium nitrate to raise the media pH, and 3) if you are already using basic-forming fertilizers, or if the pH still does not rise within seven to 10 days after step two, then add potassium bicarbonate as outlined in the optimum alkalinity levels for irrigation water section (table 4.4).

If the above procedures do not correct a falling pH, or if your media pH is in the far-below-optimum zone, then implement one or more of the following procedures.

Limestone. Limestone can be applied to the media surface to raise the pH. Use dolomitic limestone instead of calcitic limestone since dolomite supplies both calcium and magnesium and is less likely to result in a high-calcium-induced magnesium deficiency. The rate of dolomite typically recommended to raise the pH by 0.5 to 1 unit is 3 to 5 pounds of dolomite per cubic yard of media (1 kg to 1.7 kg per m^3) or per 100 square feet (7 m^2) of ground bed area. Using tables 4.9 and 4.10, you can

Table 4.8 Acidity and basicity of principal fertilizer materials and common fertilizer formulations[a]

Fertilizer (nutrient analysis)	Effect of fertilizer on pH	
	Alkaline reaction	**Acidic reaction**
	lb. of CaCO$_3$ equivalent in 10 lbs. of material	**lb. of CaCO$_3$ needed to neutralize 10 lbs. of material**
Ammonium nitrate (34-0-0)	–	5.9
Ammonium sulfate (21-0-0)	–	11.2
Calcium nitrate (15.5-0-0)	2.0	–
Diammonium phosphate (18-46-0)	–	6.4
Diammonium phosphate (21-53-0)	–	7.4
Magnesium nitrate (10-0-0)	1.96	–
Monoammonium phosphate (11-48-0)	–	6.5
Monocalcium phosphate (0-55-0)	neutral[b]	neutral
Monopotassium phosphate (0-53-35)	neutral	neutral
Nitric acid, 67% (15-0-0)	–	2.7
Phosphoric acid, 75% (0-54-0)	–	5.3
Potassium chloride (0-0-60)	neutral	neutral
Potassium nitrate (13-0-44)	2.3	–
Potassium sulfate (0-0-50)	neutral	neutral
Sodium nitrate (16-0-0)	2.9	–
Sulfuric acid, 35% (11.5% S)	–	3.6
Superphosphate (0-20-0)	neutral	neutral
Treble superphosphate (0-45-0)	neutral	neutral
Urea (44-0-0)	–	8.4
15-0-15	1.6 to 2.1	–
15-16-17	–	1.0 to 1.1
20-10-20	–	2.0 to 2.1
20-20-20	–	2.4 to 3.0
21-7-7	–	1.8 to 7.8

[a]Alkaline fertilizers tend to raise the media pH over time, while acidic fertilizers tend to lower media pH over time.

[b]Neutral means the fertilizer has no significant long-term effect on soil pH.

convert weight per volume recommendations into volume per pot recommendations. For example, 5 pounds of limestone per cubic yard (1.7 kg/m³) converts to approximately 1 level teaspoon (5 ml) per standard 6-inch (15 cm) pot. Due to its low solubility, it takes six weeks for surface applied ground limestone to have a full effect on media pH.

There are flowable suspensions of limestone that are more effective (faster reacting) than simply placing ground limestone on the media surface and watering. Suggested rates for Limestone-F, a flowable dolomite product containing 6 pounds of limestone per gallon (3.6 kg/5 l), range from 2 to 4 quarts per 100 gallons (2.5 l to 5 l per 500 l) applied as a media drench. Consult the label of commercial products for precise rates based on existing and desired pH. The increase in pH achieved can be quite variable. Depending on media components and initial pH, pH will rise between 0.5 to 1.5 pH units two to three weeks after application.

Hydrated lime. Hydrated lime [Ca(OH)₂; calcium hydroxide], sometimes referred to as builder's lime or quick lime, can also be used to raise media pH. Calcium hydroxide is very caustic, and handlers and applicators should wear protective clothing, gloves, and a respirator when working with the powder. Hydrated lime reacts much more rapidly than ground agricultural limestone. It should not be used on media containing a large quantity of ammoniacal nitrogen, including slow-release fertilizer products. The ammonium nitrogen absorbed on the soil complex can be rapidly released by calcium hydroxide, which in turn releases ammonia gas that can burn roots and foliage. Also, very rapid changes in soil pH are seldom desirable. Consider using hydrated lime only in a situation where the media pH is extremely low, and a rapid increase is needed to salvage the crop.

There are two ways to apply hydrated lime. It can be applied as a liquid by dissolving 1 pound of calcium hydroxide in 5 gallons (0.5 kg/20 l) of water; stir approximately five minutes; allow the mixture to settle overnight; and then apply only the liquid portion (the supernatant) to the media at 1 quart per square foot (10 l/m²) (a "normal" watering; equals 8 fluid ounces per 6-inch pot [250 ml per 15 cm]). The undissolved sediment is not used; do not stir the solution prior to use. The second method is a surface application of calcium hydroxide at 1.5 pounds per 100 square feet (750 g/10 m²) of ground bed or 0.75 pounds per cubic yard of media (250 g/m³). Using tables 4.9 and 4.10, this equals approximately one-third teaspoon (2 ml) calcium hydroxide per standard 6-inch (15 cm) pot.

Table 4.9   Approximate volume of various pot sizes and the number of pots filled per cubic yard of media[a]

Pot size (inch diameter)	Approximate pot volume (fluid ounces[b])	Number filled by 1 cubic yard
2-inch standard	2.6	9,943
2¹/₄-inch standard	3.7	6,987
2¹/₂-inch standard	5.3	4,878
3-inch standard	8	3,232
4-inch standard	20	1,293
4-inch azalea	16	1,616
5-inch standard	36	718
5-inch azalea	29	891
5-inch low pan	23	1,124
6-inch standard	65	397
6-inch azalea	56	462
6-inch low pan	30	861
7-inch standard	108	239
7-inch low pan	69	375
8-inch standard	147	176

[a] These numbers can vary, depending on the brand of pot being used and the depth of media placed in each pot. If you are unsure of the volume of the pots you are using, tape the holes shut, fill the pot with water to the height pots are usually filled with media (after watering plants in), then measure the volume with a cup measure. There are 957.506 fluid ounces per cubic foot and 27 cubic feet per cubic yard (25,852.67532 fl. oz./cu yd).

[b] Containers were filled to the top of pots without packing. (Once watered in, media compacts and leaves space for subsequent waterings.)

Postplanting methods to lower media pH

If the media pH rises out of the optimum zones shown in figs. 4.1 and 4.2, follow these steps: 1) Acidify your water to pH 5.8, or neutralize all but 20% of the alkalinity in your water; or 2) if the pH does not begin to fall within seven to 10 days after step one, or if you are already acidifying your water to this degree, then discontinue use of basic-forming fertilizers such as calcium nitrate, and use acid-forming fertilizers to lower the pH of the media (maintain 60% or more of the N supplied in the nitrate form).

Table 4.10 Approximate weight equivalents of common media pH amendments[a]

Material	Approximate fluid ounces per pound	Approximate teaspoons per pound
Aluminum sulfate	22	132
Calcium hydroxide	32	192
Dolomitic limestone	12	72
Ground sulfur	30	180
Iron sulfate	21	126

Source: Adapted from recommendations by the Clemson University Cooperative Extension Service, Clemson, South Carolina, and the Cooperative Extension Service of the Northeast States.

[a] These are given to assist in volume per pot recommendations. *Use only when no scales are available.* These numbers can vary, depending on the manufacturer, the moisture content, and the compaction of the material. A fluid ounce is a volume measure and an ounce is a weight measure; 1 fluid ounce does not equal 1 ounce. You should weigh out 1 pound of the material just prior to use, then measure how many fluid ounces are contained per pound for more accurate calculations.

If the above procedures do not correct a rising pH, or if your media pH is far above the optimum zone, then implement one of the treatments described in table 4.11.

Sulfur. Sulfur or sulfur-containing compounds (elemental sulfur, not sulfates) can be applied to lower pH if needed. If you have a history of rising pH during production, then preplant soil incorporation as outlined in the second column of table 4.11 may be beneficial. However, a more likely scenario is a rise in pH during production, making surface applications necessary.

Finely ground sulfur is the slowest reacting of the three materials because microorganisms must first oxidize it before it can become sulfuric acid. This process can require two to three weeks before any response is measurable. Sulfur can be applied as a top dressing when only a small pH change or a slow decline in pH is desired. The rate given equates to approximately one-third teaspoon (2 ml) finely ground sulfur per standard 6-inch (15 cm) pot.

There are flowable suspensions of sulfur that can be applied as a media drench. Suggested rates for Sulfur-F, a flowable product containing 6 pounds of sulfur per gallon (3.5 kg per 5 l), range from 0.28 to 3.8 quarts

Table 4.11 Materials and rates for lowering media pH 0.5 to 1.0 units

Material	Amount to incorporate in lbs./cubic yard	Amount to dissolve in 100 gal. of water[a]	Rate of change in pH
Aluminum sulfate	1.5	6.0	rapid
Iron sulfate	1.5	6.0	moderate
Finely ground elemental sulfur	0.75	—	slow

[a]Apply this drench as a normal watering, about 1 quart per square foot or 8 fluid ounces per 6-inch pot.

per 100 square feet (0.3 kg to 4 kg per 7 m²), applied as a media drench. Consult the label of commercial products for precise rates based on existing and desired pH. The decrease in pH achieved can be quite variable, and depending on the media components and initial pH, pH will fall between 0.5 to 1.5 pH units in two to three weeks after application.

Aluminum sulfate and iron sulfate. For a more rapid decrease in media pH, use aluminum or iron sulfate. Aluminum and iron sulfates are faster reacting because they are already in the oxidized state. As a surface application, rates in table 4.11 equate to about one-half teaspoon (2.5 ml) of either aluminum or iron sulfate per 6-inch (15 cm) standard pot.

Both of these salts dissolve readily in water and can be applied as a media drench using the rates in table 4.11. If applying these materials as a media drench, lightly syringe plants immediately after application to avoid burning the leaves. Iron deficiency often accompanies adversely high pH. In this situation iron sulfate would be a wise choice because it would correct the deficiency and lower the pH.

References

Arent, G.L. 1984. Down-to-earth differences: choice of media matters in bedding plant production. *Florists' Rev.* 175:32–38.

Bailey, D.A., and P.A. Hammer. 1986. Growth and nutritional status of petunia and tomato seedlings with acidified irrigation water. *HortScience* 21(3):423–425.

Biernbaum, J. 1992. Water and media testing essential to managing the root zone with minimal leaching. *PPGA News* 23(6):2–5.

———. 1994. A delicate balance. *Greenhouse Grower* 12(1):88, 90, 93–94.

Brady, N.C. 1974. *The nature and properties of soils*. New York: Macmillan Publishing Co.

Brown, J.C. 1960. An evaluation of bicarbonate-induced iron chlorosis. *Soil Sci.* 89(5):246–247.

Farnham, D.S., R.F. Hasek, and J.L. Paul. 1985. *Water quality: its effects on ornamental plants*. Univ. of Calif. Coop. Ext. Ser. Lflt. #2295.

Grace-Sierra. 1991. *Solution analysis*. Grace-Sierra testing laboratory, Allentown, Penn.

Hammer, P.A. 1983. Adding phosphoric acid to your water. *Focus on Floricult*. Purdue Univ. 11:3–4.

———. 1985. Growing ideas. *GrowerTalks* 48(12):14.

Kelly, J., and G. Heusel. 1990. *Conversion charts*. Clemson Coop. Ext. Serv. Lflt. #EB134.

Koths, J.S., R.W. Judd, Jr., J.J. Maisano, Jr., G.F. Griffin, J.W. Bartok, and R.A. Ashley. 1980. *Nutrition of greenhouse crops*. Coop. Ext. Serv. of the Northeast States. Bul. #NE 220.

Koranski, D.S. 1983. Growing plug annuals. *GrowerTalks* 46(11):28–32.

Lindsay, W.L., 1979. *Chemical equilibria in soils*. New York: John Wiley and Sons Inc.

Lindsay, W.L., and D.W. Thorne. 1954. Bicarbonate and oxygen as related to chlorosis. *Soil Sci.* 77:271–279.

Ludwig, L.S. 1985. Influences of water pH, alkalinity and acid additions upon floral crop growth and nutrient relationships. Master's thesis, The Ohio State University, Columbus.

Lunt, O.R., H.C. Kohl, and A.M. Kofranek. 1956. The effect of bicarbonate and other constituents of irrigation water on the growth of azaleas. In *Proceedings*. Amer. Soc. Hort. Sci. 68:537–544.

Matkin, O.A., and F.H. Petersen. 1971. Why and how to acidify irrigation water. *Amer. Nurseryman* 13(12):14, 73.

Nelson, P.V. 1991. *Greenhouse operation and management*. 4th ed. Englewood Cliffs, N.J.: Prentice-Hall, Inc.

Peterson, J.C. 1984. Current evaluation ranges for the Ohio State floral crop growing medium analysis program. *Ohio Florists' Assoc. Bul.* 654:7–8.

Peterson, J.C., and L.S. Ludwig. 1984. The relationship between water pH and alkalinity. *GrowerTalks* 46(8):30, 32, 34.

Standard methods for the examination of water and wastewater. 1966. New York: Amer. Public Health Assoc., Inc.

Tisdale, S.L., W.L. Nelson, and J.D. Beaton. 1985. *Soil fertility and fertilizers.* New York: Macmillan Publishing Co.

Wadleigh, C.H., and J.W. Brown. 1952. The chemical status of bean plants afflicted with bicarbonate induced chlorosis. *Bot. Gaz.* 113:373–392.

Whipker, B.E., D.A. Bailey, P.V. Nelson, W.C. Fonteno, and P.A. Hammer. 1996. A novel approach to calculate acid additions for alkalinity control in greenhouse irrigation water. *Comm. Soil Testing and Plant Analysis.* (In Press).

Chapter 5

Growing Media: Types and Physical/Chemical Properties

William C. Fonteno

Change has always been a part of the greenhouse business, but today the rate of change and areas of change are increasing at an alarming pace. The only thing changing faster than the problems facing growers is the amount of information available to help solve them. Twenty years ago, growers could count on the fact that once they learned something, the information would be useful for years to come. Today, the longer growers use the same piece of information, the greater their chances are of becoming obsolete, or of missing marketing opportunities, or being "caught" with serious environmental problems.

Facts about media

The ground water issue has brought into focus the relationships of media, irrigation, and fertility. In order to combat possible chemical contamination of water supplies, media are changing with the goal of reducing water and nutrient runoff from the greenhouse. Reductions are accomplished by using less water and nutrients and capturing the excess. Media will be redesigned to hold more water and nutrients, and these media will be harder to manage because growers will have to adjust their water and fertility practices.

One of the hurdles to overcome in learning how to water is understanding plant—soil—water relationships. All three aspects must be considered when determining when and how much to irrigate. Also, there are misconceptions among growers about media. A major misconception is that media are responsible for setting up the air and water relations for the root system of their crop. Actually, media account for only about 25% of this responsibility. Seventy-five percent of the air and water relations for a plant in a container sitting on a greenhouse bench is controlled by the grower.

Media components

Part of the confusion is that many growers think media and media components come with certain physical and chemical properties that are built in. This causes them to focus on the components themselves instead of the properties they produce. One of the first questions a grower wants answered when confronted with a new medium is, "What's in it?" Many growers also think that these properties do not change. This is a holdover from thinking about field soils. Most field soils have certain properties that are attributed to them. In fact, they are classified according to these attributes. Therefore, when a farmer examines a piece of land for potential production, he can be relatively assured that once these properties are known, this soil will behave in a particular manner, practically forever. This is not true for container media.

Most media today are blends of two or more components. The chemical and physical properties of the resulting medium are not always equal to the sum of its parts. Making media is similar to making soup. When the ingredients are first added, all of the flavors of the ingredients can be identified. But after cooking for awhile, the flavors combine to add to the others. When greenhouse media are blended, the chemical and physical properties of the components are "married" to each other to form new properties that are different from the individual components.

Learn to shift your thinking from ingredients and components to properties and parameters. By doing this, you begin to think about the plant's needs, and you open up a world of material for use in media for the next century.

Media aeration

Another question often asked about a new medium is, "How much aeration does it have?" or, "How much water does it hold?" Indeed, some recommendations in industry literature state fixed values for these properties. However, according to the laws of soil physics, this is physically impossible in media used in the greenhouse industry today. The amount of air and water held in a medium is determined by at least three other factors: the container in which it is grown, how the medium is handled (compaction, moisture content, pot filling technique) prior to placing the plant/seed into the container, and the watering practices used by the grower.

Media functions

A medium serves four functions: 1) to provide water, 2) supply nutrients, 3) permit gas exchange to and from the roots and 4) provide support for the plants. Unfortunately, this has been misconstrued to mean that these properties are immediately present after blending the components. The only function that is guaranteed after blending is plant support. The other three are grower controlled.

A more successful approach to media is to think about creating and managing the plant's subsurface environment (fig. 5.1). The subsurface environment is created in three major steps: 1) blending selected components and additives, 2) filling flats and/or pots, and 3) initial watering of containers after transplanting.

The subsurface environment is not set until the plants are placed in the greenhouse and watered in. And once the environment is created, it is not constant but changes as roots grow into media. During a typical production day, the environment can change hourly as water is removed by the plant and replaced by the grower.

Properties of media

Chemical properties

pH. The pH is a measure of the concentration of hydrogen ions (H^+) found in the media solution, and it controls the availability of all essential plant

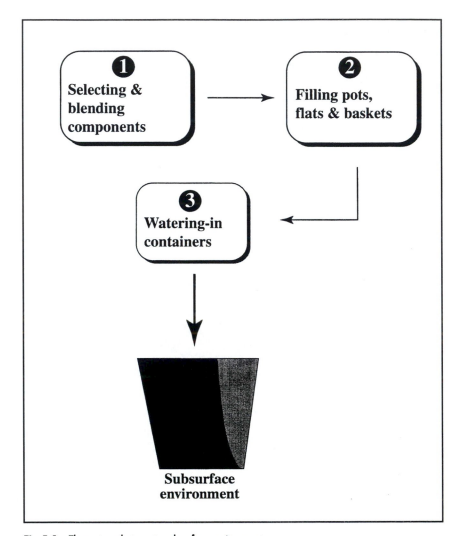

Fig.5.1   Three steps that create subsurface environment.

nutrients. A pH of 7 is neutral, below 7 is acid, and above 7 is alkaline or basic. The pH range should be between 5.4 to 6.0 for soilless media and 6.2 to 6.8 for media that contain mineral soil at volumes of 20% or greater.

Cation exchange capacity (CEC). The cation exchange capacity is a measure of media's nutrient holding capacity. It is defined as the sum of the exchangeable cations (positively charged nutrients) that media can retain per unit weight. For field soils this is usually expressed as milliequivalents per 100 grams (me/100 g) of media, but for soilless media it is expressed as milliequivalents per 100 cubic centimeters (me/100 cc). Cation exchange capacity should be high for ample nutrient reserves (6–15 me/100 cc).

Soluble salts. Soluble salts are dissolved mineral salts found in media. They come from fertilizers, impurities in irrigation water, and organic matter, such as manure and media components. All the nutrients in the soil available for absorption are called soluble salts. Initial nutrient content (soluble salts) should be low, so that sensitive young plants and seedlings are not damaged.

Physical properties

A medium is any material or combination of materials used to provide support, water retention, aeration, or nutrient retention for plant growth. A component is a single material that is combined in volumetric proportions with other components to achieve a desired air, water, and nutrient ratio for plant growth. Common components are mineral soil, sand, sphagnum peat moss, vermiculite, pine bark, perlite, styrofoam beads, and rock wool.

Bulk density. Bulk density is the ratio of the mass of dry solids to the bulk volume of media. The bulk volume includes the volume of solids and pore space. The mass is determined after drying to constant weight at 105C (220F), and volume is that of media in containers. Values are expressed as pounds/cu ft or grams/cc. Media should have a light bulk density to ease handling and shipping. For this reason, organic matter is usually a large percentage of final media. Yet it should have high enough bulk density to stabilize the plant.

Total porosity. Total porosity is the percent volume of media or media component that is comprised of pores. This is the volume fraction that provides media water and aeration. The total porosity + the percent solids = 100% of media volume. The major difference between soil-based and soilless media is total pore space (fig. 5.2). Most mineral soils have approximately 50% solids and 50% pore space by volume. Most organically based media have between 75 and 85% pore space. This increased

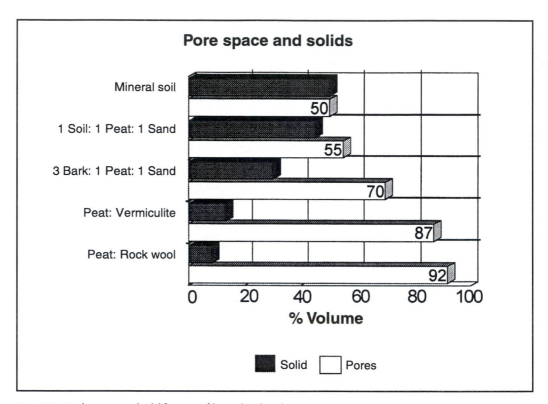

Fig. 5.2 Total porosity and solid fractions of horticultural media.

pore space improves the water and air holding capacities of container media. It also makes soilless media more susceptible to mishandling during blending and flat or pot filling.

Container capacity. Container capacity is the percent volume of media or media component that is filled with water after saturating media and allowing it to drain. It is the maximum amount of water (or capacity) media can hold. Since drainage is influenced by media height, this property is dependent on container size. The taller the container, the more drainage and the less capacity media will have to hold water.

Air space. Air space is the percent volume of media or media component that is filled with air after media has achieved container capacity. It is the minimum amount of air the material will have. Air space is affected by container height in reverse fashion to container capacity; i.e., the taller the container, the more drainage and therefore more air space. For a given bulk density, moisture content, and container size, air space is equal to the total porosity minus container capacity.

Unavailable water (PWP). Unavailable water is the percent volume of media or media component that contains water unavailable to the plant. This is also called the permanent wilting percentage (PWP). This water is actually a thin film that binds so tightly to particles of media that the roots cannot pull it away. PWP is usually measured as the amount of water remaining at a tension of 1.5 MPa (megaPascals or approximately 15 atmospheres). This is a measure of the media's inefficiency to provide water to the plant. Mineral soils and soil-based media generally have only 5 to 10% of their volume filled with water that is unavailable to the plant. However, soilless media have 20 to 25% of their volume filled with water the plant cannot use (fig. 5.3).

Available water capacity (AWC). Available water capacity is a measure of the amount of water in media that can be used by the plant. It is calculated by subtracting the unavailable water (PWP) from the container capacity. The actual availability of any quantity of water to the plant depends on the root distribution throughout media, the hydraulic conductivity of media, and the moisture content.

Moisture content. Moisture content is the percent moisture found in media on a wet mass basis. This is calculated by: [(wet weight – dry weight) / wet weight] × 100. This is the common format for most data. It denotes how much of a particular sample is comprised of water.

Media, air, and water relations

Subsurface environment

Air and water relations of the subsurface environment are affected by the size of the container used. After irrigation, most of the water applied becomes "suspended" in the pores of media through a combination of hydrogen bonding, capillary action, and gravity. Gravity tries to pull water through and out of the bottom of media. Water is held in the

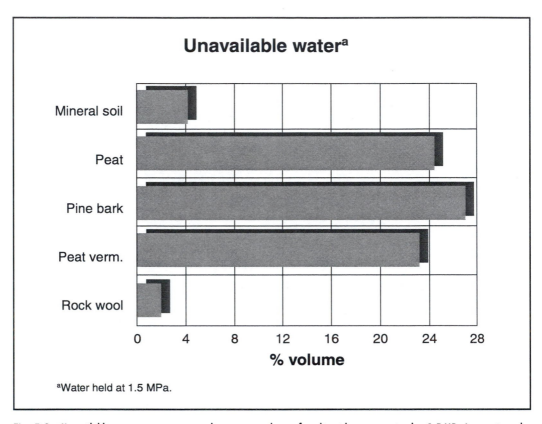

Unavailable water[a]

Mineral soil

Peat

Pine bark

Peat verm.

Rock wool

0   4   8   12   16   20   24   28

% volume

[a]Water held at 1.5 MPa.

Fig. 5.3 Unavailable water content measured as percent volume of media with water retained at 1.5 MPa (approximately −15 atmospheres).

pores of media against the force of gravity by capillary action and absorptive and adsorptive forces that generate a negative suction pressure in media. This negative suction pressure is called the matric tension and is measured in Pascals (Pa). Plants obtain water from media by developing a negative suction pressure (water potential) in their roots lower than that at which water is held by media matric tension, effectively pulling water out of the pores.

During production, most growers irrigate plants by experience, and when the medium is dry and it is measured, it usually reveals a matric tension between 10 and 30 kPa (0.1 to 0.3 bar). A moisture retention curve characterizes the media's ability to retain water under various tensions from 0 to 30 kPa (fig. 5.4). Media components vary widely in their

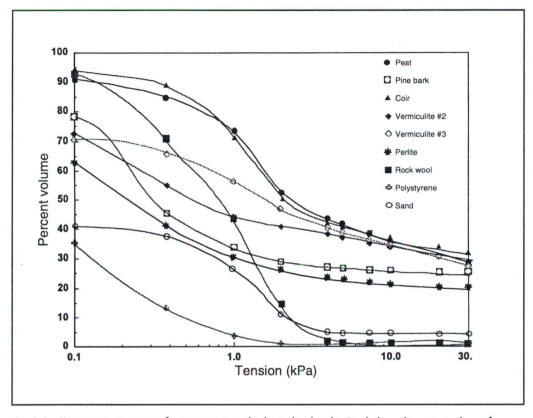

Fig. 5.4 Moisture retention curves for components used in horticultural media. Graph shows the percent volume of a material filled with water in a range of tensions from saturation (0 tension) to 30 kPa (−0.33 atmospheres).

ability to hold and release water. Components with similar moisture retention curves may supply similar physical properties for aeration, drainage, and water holding capacity.

For example, in the 1980s many people thought rock wool could be a substitute for peat moss, because both had high total porosity (see fig. 5.4 for percentage volume at 0 kPa). However, moisture retention curves reveal that the moisture retention patterns of these two materials are very different. Subsequent research has shown rock wool to be a useful addition to, but not a substitute for peat. Conversely, coir fiber (composted coconut husk fiber) has a similar moisture retention curve to peat, provides much of the same physical properties, and is therefore a better peat substitute when considering aeration, drainage, and water holding capacity.

The force of gravity exerted in media is increased as the height of media increases. Therefore, the taller the container, the more gravitational pull. The more gravitational pull, the more media will drain and the less water media will hold. Figure 5.5 shows the relationship between height and the amount of water held at that height. Gravity has the least effect near the bottom, so the moisture content is the greatest. As you move up in the container, gravity increases so less water is held. Therefore, in most containers a water gradient is formed with the most water in the bottom and the least in the top of the container.

As less water is held, more air diffuses into media. Taller containers drain more, and consequently have more aeration. Figure 5.6 shows the air and water content of a peat:vermiculite (1:1) media in five different containers. As container height decreases, air space drops from 20% in a 6-inch (15 cm) pot to 0.5% in a 648-cell plug tray. Air space and container capacity are not fixed values but change with container height.

Recommendations of air and water values necessary for good plant growth *must* be specific to container size. For example, table 5.1 lists the percent water and percent air for four media in 6-inch (15 cm) pots, 4-inch (10 cm) pots, a 48-cell bedding plant flat and a 512-cell plug tray. In 6-inch pots, soil-based media have only 7% air space while soilless media have 19 to 23%. As container size decreased, all media dropped in air space and increased in water content. Air space in bedding plant flats should range from 5 to 10%, while plug flats should range from 2 to 5%. As air space decreases, the chance of plant damage due to over watering increases. Generally, the higher the air space in these ranges, the better root growth and the better start for seedlings and transplants.

Handling media

Pot and flat filling also influences media air and water relations. Table 5.2 shows the effects of compaction on peat:vermiculite media. For a 6-inch (15 cm) pot, air space dropped from 23 to 9% with increasing compaction and density, while the 48-cell bedding plant flat dropped from 9 to 2%. Not only does air space decrease, but unavailable water content increases with filling density (21 to 30%). Media compaction reduces air space, increases the chance of overwatering, and reduces the ability of media to provide water and nutrients to the plant.

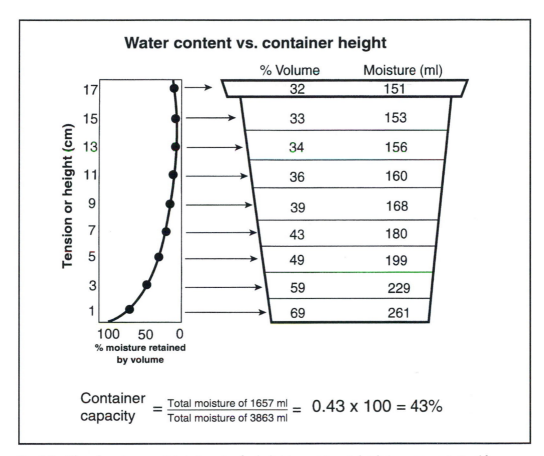

Fig. 5.5 Effect of gravity on media's drainage in a freely draining container. As height increases, gravitational force increases, causing less water to be retained (left). This creates a gradient of moisture content within the container (right).

Whether filling by hand or by machine, fill pots and flats to excess, then brush or scrape them level at the top of the container. Take care not to stack pots or flats directly over one another, as this also increases compaction. Excessive shrinkage in the container after initial watering is caused by low moisture content in media and not from light container packing.

If excessive shrinkage is a problem, increase the water content in media prior to filling the container, but do not pack more media into the container. For best results moisten media and allow media to equilibrate overnight, then agitate just prior to filling containers.

Chapter 5

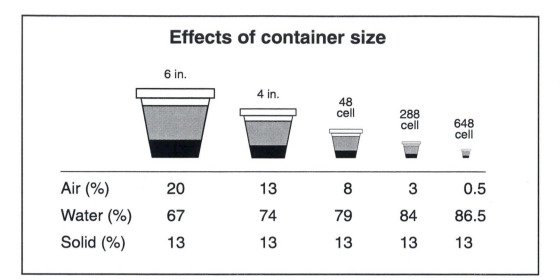

Fig. 5.6 Effect of container size on air-water relations of peat:vermiculite (1:1) media. Note as container height decreases, air space decreases, and water content increases.

Determining physical properties of media

Total porosity, air porosity, water holding capacity, and bulk density can be determined using a number of procedures.

Using a porometer for accurate measurements

The following procedure uses the porometer developed at the North Carolina State University Horticultural Substrates Laboratory, Raleigh, N.C. The porometer consists of three parts—an aluminum base plate with an inner and outer plate with eight holes in each (fig. 5.7). The plates fit together as one unit and can be rotated so that the holes are aligned in the open position to allow drainage through the plates. Also, the plates can be rotated so the holes are covered in the closed position to prevent water seepage. The second part is a 3-inch (7.5 cm) aluminum core that is packed with a media sample and then is placed onto the base

Table 5.1   Percentages of container volume occupied by water and air (at container capacity) for four media in pots, flats, and plugs

	Container			
	6 in. standard	4 in. standard	48 cell flat	512 plug tray
1 peat moss: 1 vermiculite				
Water (%)	67.9	75.2	79.5	84.8
Air (%)	19.0	11.7	7.4	2.1
1 peat moss: 1 rockwool				
Water (%)	68.4	76.0	80.5	86.9
Air (%)	23.4	15.7	11.2	4.9
3 pine bark: 1 sand: 1 peat moss				
Water (%)	51.5	57.6	61.4	66.9
Air (%)	18.9	12.9	9.1	3.6
1 soil: 1 peat moss: 1 sand				
Water (%)	47.2	51.2	52.9	54.3
Air (%)	7.4	3.4	1.7	0.3

Table 5.2   Effects of container filling/packing method on media, water, and air space

	Container		
Peat:vermiculite (1:1)	6-in. standard	4-in. standard	48 cell flat
Filled and brushed			
Available water	43%	51%	58%
Unavailable water	21%	21%	21%
Air space	23%	15%	9%
Filled, tapped twice on bench			
Available water	44%	52%	56%
Unavailable water	26%	26%	26%
Air space	15%	9%	4%
Filled, pressed, and refilled			
Available water	45%	49%	52%
Unavailable water	30%	30%	30%
Air space	9%	4%	2%

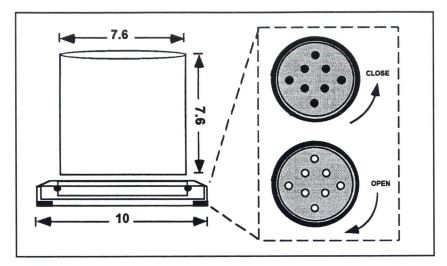

Fig. 5.7 Aluminum core and base plate for the NCSU Porometer.

plate. The third part is a funnel into which the base plate with the core is placed to saturate and drain the sample.

For each sample, attach a base plate to each of the aluminum cylinders used for testing. Place each unit (cylinder with attached base plate) in a modified Buchner funnel that keeps the unit in a fixed position so the outside plate does not move. Insert rubber stoppers into the bottom of the funnels to prevent drainage (fig. 5.8).

Rotate the base plate into the open position, and add distilled water in between the aluminum cylinder and the Buchner funnel walls to allow water to be absorbed through the bottom of the open base plate. Add water slowly in a step-wise fashion to prevent trapped air. The water level comes to the top of the sample where it is allowed to equilibrate for an additional 15 minutes before draining.

Then close the base plate. Next, remove rubber stoppers and allow excess water to drain. Place a graduated cylinder under each funnel to catch drain water for 60 minutes. The amount of water that drains from the saturated sample is the drained volume.

After draining, remove the base plate from the core. Record wet weights of the sample. Then place the sample in a forced-air drying oven at 105C (220F) for 24 hours and record dry weight. Some samples (particularly samples with high peat moss content) may require 48 hours to dry.

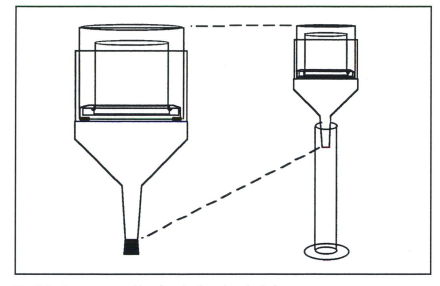

Fig. 5.8 Porometer assembly in funnel with graduated cylinder.

Approximate method for growers

A simpler method can be used by growers to determine porosity and density. This procedure will yield less accurate results, but provide growers with a good approximation of how a mix will drain. Fill a container of known volume with the medium. The container must have holes in the bottom that are taped closed and covered on the inside by nylon screen. A standard growing pot can be used. Record the volume of medium used, i.e., the volume of the container if it is filled level with the top. Add water slowly until the medium is saturated to the surface. Make sure the medium does not rise or float, or that the water level is higher than the surface of the medium. Allow the sample to equilibrate for 15 minutes, adding more water if needed. Record the volume of water added. Remove the tape from the bottom of the container and collect the drained water for 60 minutes. Weigh the wet sample, then dry and reweigh.

Calculations

The values from the above procedures are used to calculate total poros-ity, container capacity, air space, and bulk density.

In the equations:

wet weight   = weight of media sample after draining
dry weight   = weight of media sample after drying
drained volume   = volume of water that drained from the satu-rated sample
media volume   = volume of media in cylinder/container (equals volume of cylinder/container if it was filled level with the top)

Total porosity. Percent total pore space on a volume basis (v/v).

$$\frac{(\text{wet weight} - \text{dry weight}) + \text{drained volume}}{\text{media volume}} \times 100$$

or, if using the approximate method

$$\frac{\text{volume of water added}}{\text{media volume}} \times 100$$

Container capacity. Percent moisture on a volume basis (v/v) after satura-tion and drainage.

$$\frac{(\text{wet weight} - \text{dry weight})}{\text{media volume}} \times 100$$

Moisture content. Percent moisture on a weight (as opposed to volume) basis (w/w) after saturation and drainage.

$$\frac{(\text{wet weight} - \text{dry weight})}{\text{wet weight}} \times 100$$

Air space. The percent volume of drainable pore space on a volume basis (v/v).

$$\frac{\text{drained volume}}{\text{media volume}} \times 100$$

or

total porosity – container capacity

Bulk density. Dry bulk density (g/cc) is a measure of the oven-dry weight of the sample per unit volume.

$$\frac{\text{dry weight (g)}}{\text{media volume (i.e., cc)}}$$

To convert density from g/cc to pounds/cu. ft., multiply the answer (g/cc) by 62.427961.

Interpreting results

The values in table 5.3 are a compilation of over 1,000 samples tested in our laboratory using the NCSU porometer. These data are offered as guidelines and are not to be considered standards for these media. There are no standards, and to define standards for these materials would be inappropriate. However, it is useful to have these values as guidelines.

The values for total porosity, air space, bulk density, and moisture content are not averages but values that we expect to see from particular media. The Max/Min values are the total range we have found for that material—not acceptable ranges. Container capacity and air space numbers are not fixed values and are valid for a 3-inch-tall (7.5 cm) container only. The air:water ratio would grow larger as container depth increases. Conversely, air content decreases and water content increases as container depth decreases. Total porosity is not container dependent. However, the values are valid for the listed bulk density and moisture content.

Media components

There are a number of materials that can be used separately or in various combinations to make media. The choice is determined by availability, cost, shipping, and local experience in their use. Following is a brief description of the most commonly used components of horticultural media.

Table 5.3   Physical properties of various media and components[a]

Media	Total porosity (% vol.)	Total porosity (max/min)	Air space (% vol.)	Air space (max/min)	Bulk density (g/cc)	Moisture content (%)
Coir fiber	92 – 94	95 / 89	9 – 12	14 / 4	0.07 – 0.08	70 – 80
Grower media (Peat-lite)	85 – 88	92 / 84	9 – 10	13 / 9	0.14	70
Peat:Vermiculite (1:1, v/v)	88	90 / 82	9 – 10	13 / 6	0.14	65 – 75
Peat:Perlite (1:1)	78	82 / 76	15 – 18	27 / 14	0.12	60 – 70
Peat:Rock wool	88	92 / 74	13 – 17	28 / 9	0.16	60 – 70
Pine bark (< 0.5")	75 – 80	83 / 73	19 – 24	41 / 6	0.2	60
Peat (Canadian sphagnum)	89 – 94	97 / 87	12 – 20	27 / 6	0.06 – 0.10	75 – 80
Perlite	68	82 / 65	28 – 32	46 / 14	0.15 – 0.17	50
Rock wool (medium grade)	90	94 / 87	20	25 / 19	0.2	50 – 60
Sand	38	38 / 36	3	4 / 2	1.4	10
Vermiculite (hort. grade, #2 US)	78 – 80	85 / 74	6 – 10	26 / 4	0.16 – 0.18	60 – 65

[a] Numbers represent the minimum and maximum values determined for numerous samples tested. They are not recommended standards, but rather are offered as guidelines to interpret test results.

Organic components

Peat. Peat is the most widely used material to make media for 6-inch (15 cm) and smaller pots, flats, and hanging baskets. Good quality peat has low bulk density, high container capacity, and good air space properties, along with adequate cation exchange capacity and manageable pH. Peat is defined as largely organic residues of plants, incompletely decomposed through lack of oxygen. They are formed by partial decomposition of mosses, reeds, and sedges, found mainly in Canada, northern Europe, and Russia. The quality and usefulness of peat is determined by: 1) species of plant residue, 2) level of decomposition, 3) variations in local climate, 4) method of harvesting, and 5) moisture conditions during harvest.

The vast majority of peat used in the United States comes from Canada, with lesser amounts from Michigan and Florida.

The American Society for Testing Materials has proposed a system of classifying peat based on generic origin and fiber content (values on an oven-dry weight basis). **Sphagnum moss peat** can be composed of several *Sphagnum* species and must contain over 75% sphagnum moss fiber and a minimum of 90% organic matter. **Hypnum moss peat** is composed of leaves and stems from various *Hypnum* species, with a fiber content of over 50% and an organic matter content of at least 90%. **Reed-sedge peat** must contain a minimum of 33% reed, sedge, or grass fibers. **Peat humus** has a total fiber content less than 33%. **Other peat** is a classification of peats that does not fit into the above categories.

In commercial horticulture, degree of decomposition is often used to classify peats into light and dark or black. Light peats are found on the tops of bogs, have loose, coarse structure, are the least decomposed, and are light or blonde in color. Most sphagnum peats from Canada and sold in the United States are of this type. Beneath the light peat is usually more highly decomposed peat called dark or black. These peats generally have poor structure for aeration, but have increased cation exchange and nutrient content. Dark peat structure can be improved by blending with light peat. In Europe, black peat is harvested and left in the field to freeze. Freezing expands the peat and improves drainage.

Originally, peat was harvested by cutting blocks from a drained bog. This method still provides the best structure for peat. Today, many peat companies in Canada first rake or till a layer of peat 1 to 3 inches (2.5 to 7.5 cm) thick and then vacuum up the loose peat. This is less costly, but it reduces the particle size of the peat. While this method still provides useful peat, it changes the way peat is used in media. For example, the majority of media used in greenhouses in Europe is comprised of only peat. This peat is block harvested and then screened into three to four fractions. The air and water relations desired by an individual grower are generally accomplished by blending various ratios of these peat fractions. In the United States, peat is a major component, but it must be mixed with other components such as vermiculite and perlite because the harvested peat is finer.

Bark. Bark is a byproduct of saw mills and was regarded as a waste product until the 1950s. Now it is used extensively in the nursery industry. In greenhouse media, bark functions to improve aeration or reduce the cost of media. Bark can yield excellent results provided it is prepared properly. Bark is a generic term encompassing several species of hardwood or softwood trees. Since shipping costs can add significantly to media cost, local bark sources are often used. On the U.S. West Coast, fir bark and redwood bark are commonly used. Hardwood bark is used in several other states. Pine bark is the most prevalent and widely used bark source. Bark variability can be due to the type of wood, species of tree, age of tree, method of bark removal, and degree of bark decomposition.

Bark is removed from logs by drum or ring debarkers. This process also removes varying amounts of cambium and wood. If the bark is in large strips, it must be broken by hammer milling and/or screening before being composted. Some form of composting is recommended to reduce the possibility of nitrogen tie-up associated with biological decomposition.

Several companies now process bark for media. Processing bark generally begins with raw bark acquired from mills that make lumber, pulp, or paper. This raw bark may be allowed to dry for four to eight weeks to make screening easier. The bark is then passed over a series of screens to separate the large decorative bark nuggets from the bark mulch. The mulch contains bark (<0.5 inch [1 cm] diameter), cambium, and wood. Mulch may be further processed through a cambium extractor. This mulch can be sold as green or fresh bark, or it can be further processed by composting.

Composting is generally performed in two ways. The bark may be aged by placing it in windrows for three to 12 months. Windrows are monitored for temperature, pH, and soluble salts and are turned periodically to maintain decomposition conditions. Composting bark is similar to aging, but nitrogen is added first (approximately 3 pounds N per cubic yard) (1 kg/m^3) to speed up decomposition. A good source of N is ammonium nitrate used at 9 pounds per cubic yard (3 kg/m^3). The additional nitrogen increases the decomposition rate significantly and requires close monitoring and frequent turning of the bark piles. This rapid phase of composting can be completed in four to six weeks and produces a more satisfactory product often used for greenhouse media. Both systems can result in wood degradation, reduction of particle size, and destruction of toxins and other growth inhibiting compounds found in fresh bark.

Take care not to build windrows or piles over 12 to 15 feet (3.5 to 4.5 m) tall, and keep heavy equipment such as front-end loaders off of the piles. Taller piles and compaction reduce oxygen content in the row interior and trap heat generated by the composting process. This results in slower decomposition or even fire outbreaks.

Once aging or composting is finished, the bark may be used as is or further screened into final products. Particles between three-eighths and three-quarters of an inch (10 to 20 mm) may be used as organic matter additions for greenhouse fresh flower and vegetable beds. Particles ≤ three-eighths of an inch (10 mm) are preferred in greenhouse media for pots and flats, while particles ≤ one-eighth of an inch (3 mm) are used for soil conditioners, golf greens, and mass market bag products.

The bark processing industry is largely unregulated, and the quality of products is highly variable among processors. Use caution when choosing a bark source.

Wood products. Sawdust is similar to bark, but it decomposes at a much faster rate. Avoid using fresh sawdust because it will tie up nitrogen in media. Locally, piles of old sawdust may be available for the cost of transportation. Well-decomposed sawdust can be used in greenhouse media. However, old piles may be extremely variable, having dry spots or areas that have fermented and contain volatile organic acids that may injure plants. Old piles may be made useable by adding nitrogen and composting like barks or perhaps by aerating and leaching the pile, leaving it to age another season. Sawdust is considered too variable for use in commercially available media.

Processed sludges/composts. Since 1990, many municipalities have altered their waste processing systems to reduce the amount of materials they must landfill. Consequently, many new products are being offered to the plant growing industry, including composted sewage sludges, composted yard waste, and composted garbage. While these materials have been steadily improving, they generally do not offer the performance found in more traditional components for greenhouse media. Composted sludge is high in CEC, but it generally is heavy and has reduced aeration. Composted yard wastes are variable and more suitable for landscape and urban soil uses. Composted garbage is too variable and needs much more work before it can be recommended.

Coir. Coconut processing produces large quantities of husk fiber. This fiber can be composted, screened, dried, and compressed into bricks for easy shipment. Bricks can be rehydrated, and the resulting coir fiber is used in media. Coir has shorter fiber length than peat and has the general consistency of coffee grounds. Well-processed and composted coir has physical properties similar to peat (fig. 5.4) but has a pH around 7 and slightly less aeration. Coir is sometimes used as a peat substitute. Coir can also be used in combination with peat to extend peat supplies. As with most media components, properties of coir can vary with the source. Some sources may contain excessive levels of soluble salts.

Other organic residues. Straw, peanut hulls, bagasse (sugar cane fiber), and rice hulls are occasionally used in media. These materials have high carbon:nitrogen ratios and can cause nitrogen tie-up in media. Composting or additional nitrogen reduces this problem. All of these materials can be used successfully, but they may require experience, knowledge, and special handling. Manure has a high CEC and is a good nutrient source. Manure was regularly added to fresh flower beds and media until the 1950s. Cow manure is most often used in one of two forms: 1) solids from a farm manure slurry, separated and dried, or 2) old bedding from cow stalls (combination of sawdust bedding and manure) that is aged and screened. Manure is generally high in soluble salts and should be incorporated into media no more than 10 to 15%. Manure can supply substantial levels of nutrients, which must be accounted for when determining a crop nutritional program.

Inorganic components

Sand. Sand is used in media to change bulk density. Sand that is washed and free of clay and calcium carbonate will generally have little effect on chemical characteristics. Sand is very heavy (100 lbs/ ft^3 [1.5 kg/l]) and is useful in stabilizing tall plants and nursery stock. Coarse concrete-grade sand is most commonly used. While this material generally has good drainage and aeration properties on its own, the combination with peat or bark often has the opposite effect, reducing aeration and increasing water retention in final media. Finer sand particles clog the pores of the coarser peat or bark.

Perlite. Perlite is a volcanic rock (alumino silicate) that is mined, crushed, and heated rapidly to 1,800F (~ 1,000C). The rock expands to form a white, lightweight aggregate with a closed cellular structure. Water is retained on the surface or in the pore spaces between the aggregates. Media with a high proportion (>25%) of perlite are generally well drained, making perlite a good lightweight substitute for sand. Perlite is stable, sterile, chemically inert, has virtually no CEC (0.15 me/100 cc), and is almost neutral pH (7.5). Perlite does contain small amounts of fluoride (17 ppm). Certain plants such as dracaena and chlorophytum have been shown to be fluoride-sensitive. However, liming peat-perlite media to increase pH to 6.0 to 6.5, leaching the perlite prior to use, and reducing the use of superphosphate in the media can reduce risk of fluoride injury.

Vermiculite. Vermiculite is a micalike ore found principally in the United States and Africa. This aluminum-iron-magnesium silicate is mined, graded, and heated in a process similar to that used for perlite. The heating process turns the water trapped between the mineral layers to steam, expanding the ore to 15 to 20 times its volume. The resulting latticelike structure is highly porous with good water retention properties. Vermiculite is available in a number of grades, ranging from a fine grade for seed germination to a coarse grade with particles up to one-quarter-inch (6 mm) in diameter. The large surface area provides good CEC (1.9 – 2.7 me/100 cc). The pH can vary depending on the source of ore. U.S. vermiculite is slightly alkaline (6.3 to 7.8), while African vermiculite is very alkaline (9.3 to 9.7). Vermiculite also provides some nutrients such as calcium, magnesium, and potassium. Because of its high nutrients, water retention, and low bulk density, vermiculite is a commonly used component in greenhouse media. The particles are soft and easily compressed, so handle vermiculite gently. Particles of dry vermiculite often separate easily causing the finer particles to migrate to the bottom of the bag. Take care when blending to assure structural uniformity within media.

Styrofoam. Flakes and beads of expanded polystyrene foam are inexpensive, lightweight aggregates that improve aeration and drainage in media. They are white plastic products with no nutrients, virtually no CEC, no water holding capacity, and a practically neutral pH. Styrofoam is extremely light and will float. However, styrofoam can migrate to the tops of containers in long-term crops, and can become a nuisance in windy outdoor production areas. Due to its movement by wind and water, some local ordinances restrict the use of styrofoam along beaches, waterways, and landfills.

Rock wool. Mineral or rock wool slabs are the media of choice for cucumber, tomato, and sweet pepper greenhouse production in Europe and increasingly in Canada and the United States. Smaller cubes and blocks are used for stock plants, cut flower production of gerbera, young starter plants, and for propagation. Rock wool, a basic product in the commercial insulation industry, is made from basalt rock, steel mill slag, or other minerals that are liquefied at 1500C (2700F) and spun into fibers, similar to the way that sugar is melted and spun into cotton candy. These fibers are either formed into board stock for slabs and cubes or granulated into small nodules for use as a component in horticultural media. The granules have high total porosity, air space, and water holding capacity, as well as very low unavailable water content. Rock wool is slightly alkaline and has little or no buffering capacity. It has a low CEC and no nutrient content. In production, rock wool performs best in relatively dry growing situations such as subirrigation, pulse irrigation, and reduced leaching systems. Rock wool increases the available water capacity of media, helping to reduce water stress in the marketing/retail sales areas. Granular rock wool rewets easily, making it a good component for hanging baskets.

Calcined clay. Clay aggregates can be fired (calcined) at high temperatures to form large (8 to 45 mesh), stable, hardened particles. These aggregates have a relatively low bulk density (0.3 to 0.7 g/cc) with an internal porosity of 40 to 50%. This translates to 13 acres of surface area for each pound of aggregate (100 g/ha). Their main purpose in media is to increase percolation, drainage, and air space, although the aggregates have a CEC of 3 to 12 me/100 cc.

Formulating and mixing media

Mixing options

Growers can prepare their own media formulation or buy a commercially prepared one. The decision to mix your own or purchase is a management and economic decision. In addition to the cost of mixing equipment and raw materials, growers must add the costs of skilled labor, the consequences of mixing errors, and quality control testing. When looking at commercial media, it is more important to choose a reputable company with a well-developed quality assurance program and technical assistance for trouble shooting, rather than a particular product.

Generally, it is less expensive for growers with less than 50,000 square feet (5,000 m^2) of greenhouse space to purchase commercial media than to mix their own. Growers with over 100,000 square feet (10,000 m^2) and a willingness to commit time and resources to quality control may see some economic advantage in mixing their own, although the price of commercial media goes down with increasing order size.

The ingredients for peat-lite media are usually available clean and free of disease organisms, weed seeds, and pests. Components can become contaminated once on site. Mixing equipment, tools, and even the blending site should be steam sterilized or washed with a disinfectant. An effective disinfectant can be prepared with 1 part household chlorine bleach to 9 parts water. All pots, flats, and trays should be clean and sterile. New containers should remain in their packing cartons until use. Remove all unclean media and plant debris from the mixing area. Store clean media in covered areas that can be protected from outside contamination.

Mixing is done with a variety of equipment, from a shovel to sophisticated blending systems. All can do a good job, but each must be approached with different precautions. High capacity laminar-flow systems are used by media manufacturers and growers with very large media needs. They provide the best combination of speed, accuracy, and minimum blending time for components. Generally such systems are expensive and somewhat complicated to set up. The best option for most growers is 1 or 2 cubic yard (0.75 to 1.5 m^3) batch mixers that will mix ingredients with minimal degradation. Batch mixers with continuous ribbon turners are especially gentle in mixing, giving little degradation. Rotary cement mixers can also be used effectively. These machines work well for small batches (1 to 5 cubic feet [30 to 150 l]).

Many growers have traditionally used front-end loaders and a concrete pad to make media. While this technique works, it has the potential of producing the least uniform media with the most degradation since it allows the wheels of the equipment to come in contact with the components during blending. Because of the small size of the cells in flats and trays, media for bedding plants and plugs should be extremely uniform and consistent. Inconsistent media can cause difficulty in managing water and fertility. Remember, the key to producing successful media is the grower's attitude and the people who handle, mix, and fill the containers, so put good staff in charge of media mixing and pot filling.

Formulations

Growers who choose soil-based media must mix their own. Soil-based formulations are listed in table 5.4. Test these formulations on a small portion of the crops to be grown to determine proper fertility and watering practices. All field soil must be decontaminated before blending. Pasteurization (preferably with aerated steam) gives the best results. Chemical cleaning with methyl bromide will work but should not be used with sensitive crops, such as carnation, snapdragon, and salvia.

Most soilless media used in the United States are derivatives of two groups established by university research. The first group was developed by Dr. Baker at the University of California and is known as the UC System. The UC System consists of five different mixes of peat and sand, or entirely of peat or sand, with six base fertilizers for a total of 30 combinations. Two of the most popular UC mixes used today are Mix D (75% peat, 25% sand) with added nutrients (table 5.5) and Mix E, an all-peat media (table 5.6).

The second group of media is by far the most popular, serving as the basis for most commercial media used in the greenhouse industry. This group was developed at Cornell University by Drs. Boodley and Sheldrake. The Cornell peat-lite media are based on combinations of peat and vermiculite or peat and perlite. Nutritional additives vary depending on the crop.

For general crop production, Peat-lite Mix A (table 5.7) combines equal volumes of peat and vermiculite along with a nutrient package. For more drainage, or for situations where poor water quality demands higher leaching rates, Peat-lite Mix B replaces vermiculite with perlite (table 5.8). The nutrient package is altered slightly to compensate for the reduced nutrient content of perlite. Perhaps the most widely used formulation today was designated as the Peat-lite Foliage Plant mix (table 5.9). It combines 50% peat, 25% vermiculite, and 25% perlite. This mix has high porosity and high water retention properties while providing adequate aeration.

Along with the nutrient additives in most media, a nonionic wetting agent is usually added to peat- and bark-based media to improve initial wetting. Sphagnum peat and pine bark can become hydrophobic when moisture content drops below 40%. Baled peat moss is

Table 5.4   Suggested mixures using field soil in media for plant production (by volume)

Mix 1
1 part field soil
1 part sphagnum peat moss
1 part coarse vermiculite or perlite

Mix 2
2 parts silty clay soil
1 part sphagnum peat

Mix 3
1 part sandy soil
2 parts muck peat

Mix 4
1 part sandy soil
1 part sphagnum peat moss
1 part muck peat

Mix 5
1 part sand soil
2 parts sphagnum peat moss

Mix 6
2 parts muck peat
1 part perlite, calcined clay, or expanded polystyrene

Table 5.5   University of California Mix D

Components	Ratio (by volume)	
Peat moss	75%	
Fine sand	25%	
Additives[a]	**kg/m³**	**per yd³**
potassium nitrate	0.15	4 oz.
potassium sulfate	0.15	4 oz.
superphosphate	1.2	2 lbs.
dolomitic limestone	3.0	5 lbs.
calcium carbonate	2.4	4 lbs.

[a]Added nutrient content = 20 ppm N, 95 ppm P, 123 ppm K.

Table 5.6 University of California Mix E

Components	Ratio (by volume)	
Peat moss	100%	

Additives[a]	kg/m³	per yd³
potassium nitrate	0.2	6 oz.
superphosphate	0.6	1 lbs.
Dolomitic limestone	1.5	2 lbs. 8 oz.
calcium carbonate	3	5 lbs.

[a]Added nutrient content = 26 ppm N, 48 ppm P, 76 ppm K.

Table 5.7 Cornell Peat-lite Mix A

Components	Ratio (by volume)	
Peat moss	50%	
Vermiculite	50%	

Additives[a]	kg/m³	per yd³
calcium or potassium nitrate	0.9	1 lb. 8 oz.
superphosphate	0.6	1 lbs.
ground limestone	3.0	5 lbs.
fritted trace element (FTE 503)[b]	0.07	2 oz.

[a]Added nutrient content = 117 ppm N, 48 ppm P, 340 ppm K.
[b]FTE 503 nutrient content = 3% B, 3% Cu, 18% Fe, 7.5% Mn, 17% Zn, 0.2% Mo.

extremely dry, and moisture content in pine bark piles can vary with location and rainfall. Wetting agents can be in granular or liquid forms. Granular forms are convenient and precise for batch mixing systems, whereas liquid agents can be easily applied to continuous line mixing systems or as a drench to media in containers. High concentrations of wetting agents should not be used because they can be toxic to plants, especially seedlings. Horticultural supply distributors carry wetting agents that are safe and effective. Most commercial media contain wetting agents, although blends without wetting agents are also available.

Table 5.8   Cornell Peat-lite Mix B

Components	Ratio (by volume)	
Peat moss	50%	
Perlite	50%	

Additives[a]	kg/m³	per yd³
potassium nitrate	0.9	1 lb. 8 oz.
superphosphate	1.2	2 lbs.
ground limestone	3.0	5 lbs.
fritted trace element (FTE 503)[b]	0.07	2 oz.

[a]Added nutrient content = 117 ppm N, 48 ppm P, 340 ppm K.

[b]FTE 503 nutrient content = 3% B, 3% Cu, 18% Fe, 7.5% Mn, 17% Zn, 0.2% Mo.

Table 5.9   Cornell Foliage Plant Mix

Components	Ratio (by volume)	
Peat moss	50%	
Vermiculite	25%	
Perlite	25%	

Additives[a]	kg/m³	per yd³
potassium nitrate	0.6	1 lb.
superphosphate	1.2	2 lbs.
10-10-10 granular fertilizer	1.6	2 lbs. 12 oz.
dolomitic limestone	4.9	8 lbs. 4 oz.
iron sulfate	0.4	12 oz.
fritted trace element (FTE 503)[b]	0.07	2 oz.

[a]Added nutrient content = 238 ppm N, 165 ppm P, 360 ppm K.

[b]FTE 503 nutrient content = 3% B, 3% Cu, 18% Fe, 7.5% Mn, 17% Zn, 0.2% Mo.

References

Baker, K.F., ed. 1957. *The UC system for producing healthy container-grown plants.* Univ. of California Agri. Exp. Sta. and Ext. ser. Manual 23. Berkeley, Calif.

Bilderback, T.E., and W.C. Fonteno. 1987. Container Modeling. *J. Environ. Hort.* 5(4): 180–182.

Boodley, J.W., and R. Sheldrake, Jr. 1982. *Cornell peat-lite mixes for commercial plant growing.* N.Y. State College of Agri. and Life Sci., Ext. Info. Bul. 43.

Bunt, A.C. 1988. *Media and mixes for container-grown plants.* London: Unwin Hyman.

Fonteno, W.C. 1991. A common misconception about media. *N.C. Comm. Flower Growers' Bull.* 36(3):1–4.

———. 1991. Media considerations for plug production. In *Proceedings,* Plug Symposium, International Floriculture Industry Short Course, July 13, 1991.

———. 1994a. Growing media. In *Tips on growing bedding plants.* 3rd ed. H.K. Tayama, T.J. Roll, and M.L. Gaston, eds. Ohio Florists' Assoc.

———. 1994b. Growing media. In *Bedding Plants* IV. E.J. Holcomb, ed. Batavia, Ill.: Ball Publishing.

Fonteno, W.C., and P.V. Nelson. 1990. Physical properties of and plant response to rockwool amended media. *J. Amer. Soc,. Hort. Sci.* 115: 375–381.

Kute, A., ed. 1986. Methods of soil analysis, Part 1. *Physical and mineralogical methods.* 2nd ed. Amer. Soc. Agronomy and Soil Sci. Soc. Amer.

Milks, R.R., W.C. Fonteno, and R.A. Larson. 1989. Hydrology of horticultural media: III. Predicting air and water content in limited-volume plug cells. *J. Amer. Soc. Hort. Sci.* 114: 57–61.

Nelson, P.V. 1991. *Greenhouse operation and management.* 4th ed. Englewood Cliffs, N.J. Prentice Hall.

Spomer, L.A. 1979. Three simple demonstrations of physical effects of soil amendments. *HortScience* 14(1):75–77.

Chapter 6

Growing Media Testing and Interpretation

Harvey J. Lang

Soilless potting media are commonly used in the greenhouse industry because of their light weight, availability, and consistency. Compared to soils, soilless media are well drained and provide relatively low nutrient-holding capacity. Because of this, greenhouse crops require more frequent fertilization and nutritional management.

Analyzing media

Analyzing greenhouse potting media for pH, electrical conductivity (EC), and specific nutrients is an important management tool to monitor plant nutrient status and control fertilizer use. For growers who are blending their own media, a preplant analysis provides information on the amount of preplant amendment to add to media to bring it into the proper pH and soluble salt range. Analyzing media after planting will allow the grower to observe trends in pH and nutrient accumulation over time and to make fertilization adjustments.

Four test methods

The four media testing methods that are most commonly used by growers and analytical labs are 1:2 dilution, 1:5 dilution, saturated media extract (SME), and the pour-through procedure. Each method has its particular merits and drawbacks, but all are based on extracting a suitable amount of solution from the media that can be tested for pH, EC, or specific nutrients. Since the water in growing media is the primary source of nutrients for plant growth, a water extract of potting media gives a good indication of the current and available nutrient status.

Unfortunately, determining pH, EC, and nutrients in greenhouse potting media can be complex and interpreting the results confusing. For each of the four methods, you must decide when and how samples will be taken, the equilibration time for samples, if readings will be taken in the slurry or extract, and method of filtration. Reliable and consistent media analysis readings come from consistent procedures developed at both the sampling stage and analysis stage. Each of these is discussed here in more detail.

Sampling and sample handling

Consider the following factors when sampling media for analysis: 1) the number of samples to take, 2) when to take the sample relative to fertilization, and 3) the sampling location within the pot or bed.

Before beginning the sampling process, first decide what the sampling unit or area is. For greenhouses and nurseries, the unit may be a particular crop planted at a given time and grown under the same media and fertilization regime. For some operations, this could be a block of plants occupying a one- or two-bench area or a larger block of plants occupying an entire house.

Sampling units

Once the sampling unit is determined, obtain a pooled sample from the unit. Pooling (mixing small random samples together to form a larger collective sample) is the fastest and most economical way to estimate the crop's nutrient status. It also sacrifices fewer plants (if any) and allows for a smaller number of analyses (versus several individual analyses).

Cut flower beds. For cut flower beds, take several 6- to 8-inch (15 to 20 cm) core samples through growing media and combine these for the pooled

Fig. 6.1 When sampling 4-inch (10 cm) and larger-sized potted plants, it is common to slide the root ball out of the pot and remove a small sample from the root zone vicinity. To avoid depleting all of the media, try to limit samples to one per pot. Sampling about 10 pots should be enough to make up a sufficient pooled sample. Avoid collecting any sample from the top third of the container.

sample. Sampling tools are available through most greenhouse supply catalogs and generally have one side of the coring tube removed to permit easy removal of the soil core.

Potted plants. For 4-inch (10 cm) and larger-sized pot plants, take a narrow core sample through media, or knock the plant out of the pot and take a small sample around the root zone (fig. 6.1). Take a minimum of 10 samples throughout the unit area to make the collective pooled sample for analysis. Take samples from both the middle and edges of the bench since differences in drying along the bench can affect salt accumulation. In the case of potted plants, growers might want to limit themselves to one sample per pot, and sample from different pots for subsequent sampling periods. This will prevent media from being depleted from a particular pot due to repeated sampling.

Plugs, small cell packs. For plugs and small cell packs, growers should have several (five to 10) representative flats that are to be used for sampling placed randomly throughout the unit area; coring or taking a small sample from each individual plug or pack cell is difficult and does not provide a sufficient sample. Consequently, the plant should be sacrificed and its associated growing media collected for the pooled sample. If a grower wishes, the remaining harvested shoots can be combined and sent off to a commercial lab for tissue analysis. For smaller plug sizes (greater than 200 cells per flat), harvest several plants from the representative flat. Having specific flats designated strictly for sampling surmounts the cost and labor in replacing missing plants taken for analysis from flats that are to be sold.

Maintain consistency in the sampling procedure. Weekly or biweekly sampling is normally sufficient for most greenhouse crops while plugs and other short-term crops might require more frequent sampling. To maintain comparative values from one sampling period to another, take samples from pots, beds, or flats at about the same time relative to the last fertigation. For example, a grower may wish to collect his samples weekly and about two to four hours after irrigating. Drier samples are slightly easier to work with than those collected shortly after an irrigation; however, research has shown that there is increased variability in the bed or between pots the longer you wait to harvest growing media after irrigation. The key is to be consistent as to when samples are taken, since there can be significant differences in pH and EC readings between different sampling times.

Depth of sampling. In the case of potted plants, take samples from the same volume within the pot. Figure 6.2 illustrates the difference in EC readings from samples that were taken from the upper one-third or lower two-thirds of the pot. You can expect significant differences in EC between potting media layers at higher fertilizer application rates, as the cropping period increases, and where there is rapid drying of the potting medium. Greater differences should be expected with subirrigation or where pots are not well leached. To minimize variations within the pot, remove the very top layer of media (about 0.5 inch [1 cm]) before analysis. The very top layer is removed because of the high accumulation of salts from water evaporation and because few roots grow in this area. In addition, for coarser media such as those containing rock wool or coarse bark, growers might want to take a larger sample or core as compared to finer media, where sample uniformity is less of a problem.

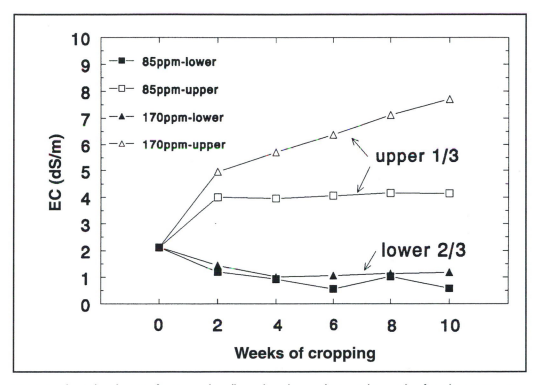

Fig. 6.2 Electrical conductivity of potting media will vary depending on where samples are taken from the container. New Guinea impatiens fertilized regularly with either 85 ppm (6 mM) N or 170 ppm (12 mM) N had potting media that varied in EC depending on whether samples were taken from the upper one-third or lower two-thirds of the pot. The differences were greater at the higher fertilization rate.

Pooled samples. At this point, the samples should be uniformly mixed to make up the pooled sample for analysis. Remove large roots, slow release fertilizer, and other debris as best possible. Growers who wish to mail their samples to a testing laboratory should put about 1 pint (~500 cc) in a durable plastic bag and mail it immediately. For in-house testing using the 1:2 and 1:5 dilution methods, it is imperative that the sample be air-dried to assure similar moisture levels for all samples. Since the 1:2 and 1:5 dilution methods are based on potting media to water dilution ratios, varying media moisture content between samples or between sampling periods will significantly affect analysis results. Drying can be done using an oven set at 100F to 120F (40C to 50C) or by spreading the sample on a clean tray and placing it in a warm, dry area. For the SME method, the sample does not need to be dried.

Determining pH and soluble salt

Determining pH and soluble salts in potting media is a useful crop management tool that can be performed by the grower or commercial lab. Potting media pH is a measure of the acidity or basicity of the media and can ultimately affect the availability of nutrients to the plant. Soluble salts are quantified by measuring the electrical conductivity (EC) of the growing medium solution and give an indication of the fertility level in media. Consistent analysis of both of these parameters depends on selecting a suitable extraction method, properly measuring media solution, and correctly interpreting results using published tables or in-house scales.

Extraction methods

Once the pooled sample is collected, decide on the extraction method. The four methods currently in use are the 1:2 dilution, the 1:5 dilution, SME, and the pour-through. Each is discussed below.

1:2 or 1:5 dilution. When preparing samples for the 1:2 or 1:5 dilution, potting media should be air-dried. If samples cannot be dried within a reasonable period of time, it is important that the moisture content of media be consistent between samples and over time, although moisture level is less critical for higher dilution volumes (i.e. 1:5). A volume of media between one-quarter to one-half cup (50 to 100 cc) is normally sufficient and should be firmly filled into a small beaker or cup. The grower or technician doing the extractions needs to be consistent from sample to sample in their method of packing. For the 1:2 or 1:5 dilution methods, one part dry potting media is placed into the container and mixed with either 2 parts (1:2) or 5 parts (1:5) distilled or deionized water. Some laboratories make just a 1:1 ratio initially, read the pH in that slurry, then dilute to the full volume to read the EC.

If tap water is to be used for the extraction, the water should be of high quality with an EC below 0.5 dS/m (mmhos/cm), otherwise abnormally high readings can occur in the slurry and extract. The EC of the tap water also has to be subtracted from the EC reading of the final extract measured.

Mix the sample by stirring gently with a spatula, swirling the mixture, or capping and shaking the container. Leave it to equilibrate for 15 to 30 minutes. After equilibration, gravity filter the sample by pouring the slurry through a small filter funnel lined with a fluted coarse filter paper. (Some growers have found that coffee filters placed over a small beaker work just as well.) Once a sufficient quantity of extract has been collected, the solution can then be tested for pH, EC, and other nutrients.

Saturated media extract (SME). The SME method was originally developed at Michigan State University and is used by most commercial media analysis labs. It differs significantly from the 1:2 or 1:5 dilution method and requires a different set of interpretive guidelines. In the SME method, the starting moisture content of potting media and the total amount of media used do not influence the results. About 1 pint (~480 cc) of potting media is added to a beaker or plastic cup and brought just to the saturation level with distilled or deionized water. Saturation occurs when the media paste glistens, and there is little or no free water standing on top. For very dry media, facilitate saturation by stirring with a spatula or knife. After saturation, let the sample equilibrate. Recent studies have shown that 30 minutes is an adequate time period for equilibration of the extracting solution and the potting media (fig. 6.3). The samples can be equilibrated for longer time periods; however, they should be tightly covered to prevent evaporation. After equilibration, vacuum filter the saturated media through a Büchner funnel using medium to coarse filter paper. Many commercial and in-house labs will read pH directly in the saturated slurry before filtering for EC analysis. Whatever decision is made in regard to protocol, the method should be consistently followed from one sampling period to the next.

Pour-through. The pour-through technique is a simple, practical procedure for extracting nutrient solution from a container of growing media. It has advantages over the above mentioned methods in that no potting media is actually sampled or handled, and there is no specialized extraction equipment needed. Its major drawback, however, is that it is not widely used and interpreting the results can be tricky. Collect the container with media (and plant) from the production area shortly after irrigating and place in a small tray or collection vessel large enough to

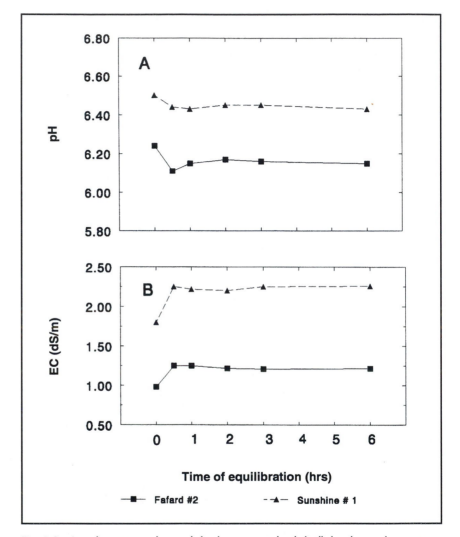

Fig. 6.3 Once the potting media sample has been extracted with distilled or deionized water, it should equilibrate for about 30 minutes. Samples can equilibrate for longer periods, however, without any significant change in pH (A) or EC (B).

collect leachate from both the side and bottom holes of the container. The potting media's moisture level should be at or near saturation. Varying the media's moisture level from one sampling period to the next will influence the level of nutrients extracted and produce inconsistent results. For 6-inch (15 cm) containers, approximately 75 to 100 ml (2.5 to

3 oz.) of distilled or deionized water should be evenly applied to the media surface to extract 50 to 75 ml (1.5 to 2 oz.) of solution for analysis. For smaller or larger containers, such as cell packs or baskets, growers will have to experiment with the volumes needed for extraction. The basic principle of the pour-through procedure is to provide enough leachate for analysis without completely diluting the sample. After collecting the leachate, it should be poured (and filtered if necessary) into a suitable container for analysis of pH, EC, and nutrients.

Measuring pH and EC

Once the potting media has been extracted with water, the slurry or extract can be measured for pH and EC. If possible, take the measurement in a clean, dry area away from soil, dust, or water. Many growers have separate labs away from the production area for analysis of potting media. There are different pH and EC meters on the market ranging in price from $40 to over $500. These include the relatively inexpensive pocket pens, the moderately priced card-type meters, and the more expensive bench-top models. Many of the instruments have the pH and EC electrodes combined into one meter.

pH. Before measuring the slurry or extract, calibrate the pH meter using buffer standards. Companies that sell pH meters generally supply pH buffer solutions. Calibrate using a pH 7.0 and pH 4.0 buffer on a daily basis or before reading a large number of samples. Once the meter is calibrated, the analyst must decide whether to read the pH in the slurry or the filtered extract. Reading in the slurry generally produces numbers 0.1 to 0.5 units lower than if read in the filtered extract (fig. 6.4A). If the readings are taken in the slurry or saturated media, gently place the pH electrode in the media to avoid scratching or abrading the electrode tip. This is especially important in analyzing very coarse media containing bark or sand. If the reading is taken in the filtered extract or pour-through leachate, the electrode should be submersed about 1 inch (2.5 cm) into the solution, completely covering the tip. For some instruments, pour the filtered solution into a small reservoir that contains the built-in pH electrode. Take measurements using either method when the readings on the meter have stabilized. Generally this occurs after about 15 to 20 seconds. Many of the more sophisticated meters have a microprocessor that automatically locks in the reading when it appears

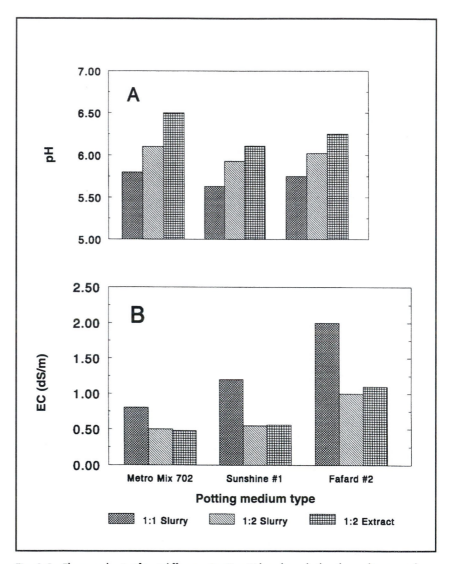

Fig. 6.4   There can be significant differences in pH or EC based on whether the readings are taken in the slurry or filtered extract.

(A) Measuring pH in a 1:1 slurry generally produces readings considerably lower than readings in the filtered extract. Reading directly in the solution phase of a 1:2 slurry produces numbers intermediate between the two.

(B) EC is normally read in the filtered extract, however, readings can be taken in the solution phase of a 1:2 slurry with similar results. Taking readings in a 1:1 slurry or saturated media is not recommended.

stable. After reading, rinse off the electrode with distilled or deionized water and gently blot it dry with a soft tissue.

EC. Measurements of EC have traditionally been expressed in millimhos per centimeter (mmhos/cm), but that has recently been changed to deciSiemens per meter (dS/m). Some meters read in milliSiemens per centimeter (mS/cm). One mmhos/cm is equal to one dS/m which is equal to one mS/cm, hence, the units are interchangeable. To estimate the total parts per million (ppm) salts in solution, multiply the EC reading (in dS/m, mS/cm or mmhos/cm) by 700. Estimating ppm from EC in this manner can be in error by 10 to 20%, so take the ppm conversion as an approximation.

As with pH, before measuring EC on the sample, calibrate the EC meter using known conductivity standards. These can normally be purchased from the same companies that supply pH buffer solutions. Calibrating EC meters should be done periodically, but usually not as often as pH meters. EC readings are generally taken in the filtered extract, but they can also be taken in the solution phase of a 1:2 or 1:5 slurry (fig. 6.4B). It is not recommended to take EC readings directly in the 1:1 slurry or saturated media paste, since errors can occur in trying to maintain a current between the two electrode plates. When reading the solution, submerge the electrode deep enough to completely cover the electrode plates (usually 1 inch [2.5 cm] is sufficient). Readings from EC meters should stabilize very quickly and can be taken within a few seconds. If a reading does not register on the meter or is zero, the electrode probably has not been submerged deep enough into the sample solution. After the reading is taken, rinse off the electrode with distilled or deionized water and gently blot it dry.

Interpretation and analysis ─────────

Interpreting test results

Correctly interpreting potting media pH and soluble salts is important to provide the crop's optimum fertilization regime. Tables 6.1 and 6.2 list the optimum ranges for established crops using the various methods described above. For seedlings or for crops requiring very high nutrients, shift the range slightly downward or upward, respectively. Also be

Table 6.1 Interpretive scales for pH in greenhouse potting media prepared by various methods

	SME		1:2 or 1:5 Dilution		
	Extract[a]	Slurry[b]	Extract[a]	Slurry[b]	Pour-through
Optimum range	5.5–6.5	5.4–6.2	5.5–6.5	5.4–6.2	5.5–6.5

[a]Extract is the filtered solution phase of the potting medium-water mixture.
[b]Slurry is the mixture of potting medium-water prior to filtering.

Table 6.2 Interpretive scales for electrical conductivity (EC) in greenhouse growing media

	Electrical conductivity—dS/m[a]			
Optimum range	Saturated media extract (SME)	1:2 Dilution	1:5 Dilution	Pour-through[b]
Established plants	2.0 to 3.0	0.8 to 1.2	0.3 to 0.6	3.0 to 5.0
Seedlings, plugs	1.0 to 2.0	0.5 to 0.9	[c]	[c]

[a] For conversion between different units of expressing electrical conductivity:
   $1\ dS/m = 1\ mS/cm = 1\ mmhos/cm$

[b] The pour-through method has not been thoroughly tested, and the 3.0–5.0 dS/m optimum level given is based primarily on grower observations.

[c] Optimum level not available.

aware of the sampling and analysis procedures used for each scale. It could lead to disaster if 1:2 dilution results were interpreted on an SME scale. Some of the scales, such as the SME, have been developed from the results of thousands of greenhouse media samples and have proven to be reliable over a range of greenhouse crops. Others, such as the 1:5 and pour-through methods, are currently being used but have not been documented for the majority of greenhouse crops. For these scales, pay close attention to the crop, and modify the scales based on your own observations of crop growth and health.

Once pH and EC measurements have been taken and interpreted, plot them on a graph to observe trends. Figure 6.5 shows a set of sample graphical sheets for tracking both pH and EC that can be photocopied for growers' use. These charts can be useful to monitor a crop's nutritional progress and tracking the movement of acidity or basicity within the container. It will also give the grower long-term information on how changes in the fertility program (i.e., fertilizer boost or water leaching) affect the soluble salt and pH levels in media.

Specific nutrient analysis

Checking the nutrient level and balance can be an important part of analyzing potting media. Specific nutrients can be determined in the filtered extract of the 1:2 or 1:5 dilution, saturated media, or pour-through leachate. There is, however, limited documentation on specific nutrient analysis for the 1:2, 1:5, or pour-through procedures as described earlier. Most nutrient analysis results for greenhouse potting media have been based on the vacuum-filtered extract of saturated media (SME). Table 6.3 lists the recommended values for greenhouse media analyzed by the SME method. The results are normally reported in ppm or milligrams per liter (mg/liter). Most commercial laboratories do a complete analysis of N (both nitrate and ammonium), P, K, Ca, and Mg, along with pH and EC. Some labs may also do a complete micronutrient analysis, although this may involve extraction with specific metal chelating agents, such as DTPA.

For growers wanting to do their own nutrient analysis, there are nitrate and potassium meters available that are reliable and easy to use. Some are sold as separate electrodes or as small card-type meters. Since nitrogen and potassium are two of the most important nutrients to track and can vary significantly based on fertilizer practices, the investment in these meters may be justified for high dollar crops. There are also colorimetric testing kits available through greenhouse supply companies that allow growers to easily estimate the concentration of several macro- and micronutrients in the filtered extract. The Simplex Soil Testing Outfit is an example of such a kit. It is reasonably priced and includes everything for the colorimetric determination of up to 13 elements and related compounds. For commercial analysis, consult the *Soil and plant analysis registry* which lists the commercial labs available throughout the country.

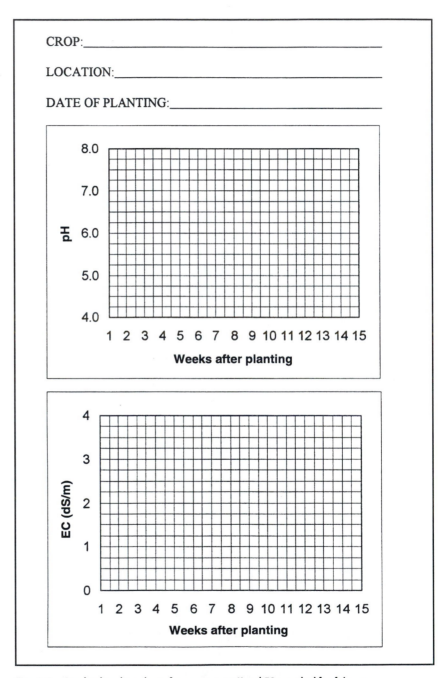

CROP:_____

LOCATION:_____

DATE OF PLANTING:_____

Fig. 6.5 Graphical tracking sheets for monitoring pH and EC over the life of the crop.

Table 6.3   Interpretive scales for various nutrients in greenhouse potting media using the SME method[a]

	ppm nutrient content				
	Nitrate	**Phosphorus**	**Potassium**	**Calcium**	**Magnesium**
Optimum range	100–200	6–9	100–200	150–250	40–80

[a]Modified from Warncke and Krauskopf.

Media testing is a powerful tool for tracking the growth and nutritional status of crops. Although guidelines have been laid out in this chapter, growers and analysts need to be aware of the procedures and details used in both the sampling and analysis of potting media samples. With routine analyses, growers can gradually develop their own interpretive scales based on crop observations and in-house testing. This will lead to fewer disasters, better quality crops, and the reduction of excess fertilizer use.

Summary of guidelines

1. Determine the sampling unit or area within the greenhouse to be sampled.
2. Collect a minimum of 10 samples from pots or flats placed randomly throughout the sampling unit or area.
3. Collect samples from the same volume within the pot and shortly after irrigating.
4. Avoid sampling the top third of the pot or bed.
5. Pool the samples and mix thoroughly.
6. For the 1:2 and 1:5 dilution methods, dry the pooled sample before diluting with water.
7. Determine the method of extraction and moisten accordingly.
8. Equilibrate the sample for about 30 minutes before taking pH and EC readings.
9. Calibrate pH and EC meters using standard solutions.

10. Read directly in the slurry or filter the slurry and read the extract.
11. Use published tables or in-house scales to interpret results.
12. Plot readings over time to determine trends in pH and salt accumulation.

References

Berghage, R.D., D.M. Krauskopf, K.D. Warncke, and I. Widders. 1987. Micronutrient testing of plant growth media: extractant identification and evaluation. *Comm. Soil Sci. Plant Anal.* 18(10):1089–1110.

Biernbaum, J. 1992. Water and media testing essential to managing root zone environment. *PPGA News*. Vol. 23.

Council on Soil Testing and Plant Analysis. 1992. *Soil and plant analysis registry for the United States and Canada.* Athens, Ga.: Council on Soil Testing and Plant Analysis.

Kirven, D.M. 1986. An industry viewpoint: horticultural testing—is our language confusing? *HortScience* 21(2):215–217.

Holcomb, E.J., J.W. White, and S.A. Tooze. 1982. A vacuum extraction procedure for N, K, and conductivity evaluation of potted crop media. *Comm. Soil Sci. Plant Anal.* 13(10):879–889.

Lang, H.J. 1994. Variation associated with testing procedures for pH and electrical conductivity of soilless potting media. *HortScience* 29(5):502.

Lang, H.J., and G.C. Elliott. 1993. How to read your media. *GrowerTalks* 57(7):57–65.

Nelson, P.V. 1991. Greenhouse operation and management. 4th ed. Englewood Cliffs, N.J.: Prentice-Hall, Inc.

Pannkuk, T., and H.J. Lang. 1994. Growth of New Guinea impatiens at three fertilizer concentrations and two irrigation regimes using solid-state microtensiometers. *HortScience* 29(5):503.

Prasad, M., T.M. Spiers, and I.C. Ravenwood. 1981. Soil testing of horticultural substrates (i) evaluation of 1:1.5 water extract for nitrogen. *Comm. Soil Sci. Plant Anal.* 12(9):811–823.

Sonneveld, C. 1990. Estimating quantities of water-soluble nutrients in soils using a specific 1:2 by volume extract. *Comm. Soil Sci. Plant Anal.* 21(13–16):1257–1265.

Sonneveld, C., J. Van Den Ende, and S.S. De Bes. 1990. Estimating the chemical composition of soil solutions by obtaining saturation extracts or specific 1:2 by volume extracts. *Plant and Soil.* 122:169–175.

Warncke, D.D. 1986. Analyzing greenhouse growth media by the saturation extraction method. *HortScience* 21(2):223–225.

Warncke, D.D., and D.M. Krauskopf. 1983. *Greenhouse growth media: testing and nutrition guidelines.* MSU Ext. Bul. E-1736.

Wright, R.D. 1986. The pour-through nutrient extraction procedure. *HortScience* 21(2):227–229.

Wright, R.D., K.L. Grueber, and C. Leda. 1990. Medium nutrient extraction with the pour-through and saturated medium extract procedures for poinsettia. *HortScience* 25(6):658–660.

Yeager, T.H., R.D. Wright, and S.J. Donohue. 1983. Comparison of pour-through and saturated pine bark extract N, P, K, and pH levels. *J. Amer. Soc. Hort. Sci.* 108(1):112–114.

Chapter 7

Macronutrient Fertilizer Programs

Paul V. Nelson

Essential elements

There are 17 commonly accepted essential elements required by plants (table 7.1). Three are obtained naturally, exclusive of fertilizer application, and are called nonfertilizer nutrients. They are: oxygen (O), from oxygen gas in the atmosphere and water; hydrogen (H), from water; and carbon (C), from carbon dioxide gas. Of the three, only C is intentionally supplied at times by the grower through releasing carbon dioxide gas into the greenhouse atmosphere to increase the rate of photosynthesis.

Macronutrients

Six essential elements are termed macronutrients because they are incorporated in large quantities into plant tissue. Three of the macronutrients, nitrogen (N), phosphorus (P), and potassium (K), are known as primary macronutrients because they are included in most complete fertilizers. The three numbers in the analysis of a fertilizer consecutively indicate the weight percentages of N, P (reported as the oxide P_2O_5), and K (reported as the oxide K_2O). The other three macronutrients are called secondary macronutrients and include calcium (Ca), magnesium (Mg), and sulfur (S). These may or may not be included in greenhouse fertilizers. At times a grower may need to

Table 7.1 Essential elements required by plants along with their chemical symbol, classification, and typical content in greenhouse plants

Element	Chemical symbol	Classification	Typical plant content (% of dry wt.)
Carbon	C	Nonfertilizer	collectively
Hydrogen	H	Nonfertilizer	89.0
Oxygen	O	Nonfertilizer	
Nitrogen	N	Macronutrient	4.0
Phosphorus	P	Macronutrient	0.5
Potassium	K	Macronutrient	4.0
Calcium	Ca	Macronutrient	1.0
Magnesium	Mg	Macronutrient	0.5
Sulfur	S	Macronutrient	0.5
Iron	Fe	Micronutrient	0.02
Manganese	Mn	Micronutrient	0.02
Chlorine	Cl	Micronutrient	0.01
Boron	B	Micronutrient	0.006
Zinc	Zn	Micronutrient	0.003
Copper	Cu	Micronutrient	0.001
Nickel	Ni	Micronutrient	0.0005
Molybdenum	Mo	Micronutrient	0.0002

apply one or more of these elements, so it is important to read fertilizer labels to know if secondary macronutrients are included.

Micronutrients

The remaining eight essential elements are micronutrients because they are required in small quantities in plants. Six micronutrients are considered fertilizer nutrients and include iron (Fe), manganese (Mn), zinc (Zn), copper (Cu), boron (B), and molybdenum (Mo). These are supplied in most commercial growing media, most complete greenhouse fertilizers, and irrigation water. Often, those three sources provide sufficient micronutrients, however, there are situations that require an additional application. Commercial mixtures of micronutrients are available that can be applied in a single application or as an additive in a constant liquid feed program. The remaining micronutrients are chlorine (Cl) and nickel (Ni). They are not intentionally included in fertilizer programs because both exist in sufficient quantities to meet plant requirements in many materials, such as media and fertilizers.

Thus, out of a total of 17 essential nutrients there are 12 that must be considered in a fertilizer program for greenhouse crops. We will refer to these as the 12 essential fertilizer nutrients. These include the six macronutrients and the six micronutrients, exclusive of chlorine and nickel. This chapter will be concerned with systems for delivering the macronutrients. (See Chapter 8, Micronutrient Nutrition for a detailed discussion of micronutrients.)

Fertilizer programs

Preplant fertilization

Preplant fertilizers are incorporated into media prior to planting (table 7.2). These additions serve two purposes. First, they establish a sufficient media level of the nutrients to meet plant requirements at the beginning of the crop. Second, all or a significant amount of the total crop requirement for some of these nutrients can be supplied before planting. This simplifies subsequent postplant fertilization by eliminating or reducing the amount required during crop production.

Preplant fertilizers can include all of the 12 essential fertilizer nutrients. Virtually all media contain the two macronutrients Ca and Mg. These are supplied when calcitic limestone (supplies Ca) and/or dolomitic limestone (supplies Ca and Mg) are incorporated into media to adjust it to the proper pH level. Generally, as long as media pH level remains in the desired range, the supply of Ca and Mg will remain adequate for plant growth. There are some exceptional cases involving low transpiration rate and an imbalance between Ca and Mg where availability is not sufficient in spite of a proper pH level. These issues will be discussed later in the section on secondary nutrients.

Some media contain S, always as sulfate. Sulfate leaches at a moderate rate from media. Thus, preplant S additions might not last for the entire crop period. The loss of S increases with increasing leaching percentage,

Table 7.2 Preplant fertilizer sources and rates of application

Nutrient source[a]	Rate per cubic yard (per m³)[b]	
	Soil-based media	Soilless media
To provide calcium and magnesium		
Dolomitic limestone	0–10 lbs. (0–6 kg)	10 lbs. (6 kg)
To provide phosphorus and sulfur[c]		
Single Superphosphate (0-20-0), or	3.0 lbs. (1.8 kg)	4.5 lbs. (2.7 kg)
Treble Superphosphate (0-45-0),	1.5 lbs. (0.9 kg)	2.25 lbs. (1.3 kg)
plus gypsum (calcium sulfate)	1.5 lbs. (0.9 kg)	1.5 lbs. (0.9 kg)
To provide micronutrients: iron, manganese, zinc, copper, boron, molybdenum		
F-555HF, or	3 oz. (112 g)	3 oz. (112 g)
F-111HF, or	1 lb. (0.6 kg)	1 lb. (0.6 kg)
Esmigram, or	5 lb. (3 kg)	5 lb. (3 kg)
Micromax	1–1.5 lb. (0.6–0.9 kg)	1–1.5 lb. (0.6–0.9 kg)
To provide nitrogen and potassium (optional)		
Calcium nitrate, or	1 lb. (0.6 kg)	1 lb. (0.6 kg)
Potassium nitrate	1 lb. (0.6 kg)	1 lb. (0.6 kg)

Source: P.V. Nelson. 1991. *Greenhouse Operation and Management.* 4th ed.

[a] Choose only one source from each category.

[b] Rates of all fertilizer materials except limestone should be reduced to half for plug seedlings.

[c] These superphosphate rates are designed to supply phosphorus for the entire crop. They may be reduced to 50% or lower when phosphorus is included in the postplant fertilization program.

which is the percentage of the total volume of water or fertilizer solution applied to media that passes through the bottom of the container. The most common source of S for preplant application is gypsum, i.e., calcium sulfate. In the past, almost all greenhouse media contained gypsum because single superphosphate (0-20-0), about half gypsum by weight, was a staple ingredient. Today triple superphosphate or soluble phosphate salts that do not contain S are frequently used in media. While S deficiency occurs infrequently, it is important to monitor its availability through soil and/or tissue tests. When making media, include gypsum at 1.5 pounds per cubic yard (0.9 kg/m³) (see table 7.2) to safeguard against a S deficiency. If irrigation water analysis contains at least 48 ppm supply then it may supply all the sulfate needed by the crop (see p. 36, Chapter 2).

A preplant application of P will last for the entire crop in soil-based media because the clay in soil retains P. However, soilless media do not retain P very well. Preplant applications of P will probably run out before the end of the crop in soilless media. Longevity of P decreases with increased leaching and with declining pH. If you want to depend entirely on preplant P, you must rely on media and tissue tests to determine if and when it becomes necessary to supply P in a postplant liquid fertilizer program. The rates for preplant P additions to media presented in table 7.2 are designed to last for the entire cropping time. These rates can be reduced to 50% or lower when P is included in the postplant fertilization program.

Nitrogen and K are generally included in commercial media when P and micronutrients are added. Many growers who formulate their own media leave N and K out because they are difficult to incorporate uniformly. These nutrients are optional as a preplant incorporation. The typical quantity added is designed to last about two weeks. Higher rates would adversely raise the salt level of media. Some common nutrient sources and rates are given in table 7.2.

Micronutrients are usually added as a micronutrient mix incorporated into media. The use of preplant nutrients, other than Ca and Mg which are supplied by lime, is subject to personal preference. While most commercial media for finishing crops include preplant nutrients, some companies offer mixes with only Ca and Mg as preplant nutrients. Some plug and seedling growers omit all preplant nutrients except Ca and Mg, while others use a low rate of nutrients, about half the rate used for general media to finish a crop.

Growers who omit preplant nutrients from media should begin their liquid, postplant fertilization program at planting. Those who incorporate preplant nutrients may postpone fertilization up to seven days for low-nutrient-requiring crops or begin with the first watering after planting. For high nutrient crops, begin the postplant fertilization program at planting.

Postplant fertilization

To develop a postplant fertilization program, decide what concentration of fertilizer to use and what the analysis of the fertilizer will be, i.e., what nutrients it contains and in what ratio. It is easiest to focus on N when setting the fertilizer concentration, but fertilizer analysis is more involved. The myriad of fertilizer analyses available in the greenhouse industry can be bewildering. However, selecting the appropriate analysis doesn't have to be complex if you take the following requirements into consideration. They are: the proportion of K_2O to N that is needed to meet the K requirement; the proportion of P_2O_5 to N that is needed to meet the P requirement; the appropriate source of N (ammonium/urea or nitrate); the acidity or basicity needed for media and whether any of the secondary nutrients Ca, Mg, or S are needed.

Nitrogen

Developing a fertilization program should begin with the concentration of N to apply. Decide first on the frequency of fertilizer application. Many smaller growers may choose to apply fertilizer weekly at high concentrations because they use portable injection equipment that is carried from bench to bench throughout the greenhouse. Larger growers will more likely apply fertilizer with each irrigation, called fertigation, at relatively low concentrations because their injector is permanently plumbed into the water system. For them, it is easier to leave the injector system engaged than to activate it once a week.

The concentration of N to apply is also dependent upon the crop. Many greenhouse crops have published fertilizer recommendations. Collectively, these recommendations give the impression that it is difficult to determine the concentration and analysis needed for any given crop. This isn't necessarily true. By assigning a crop to one of four nutrient requirement categories and to a given frequency of application, it is easy to determine what concentration of N to apply.

Recommended N concentrations are given in table 7.3 for several crops. When dealing with a crop not included in the table, simply categorize its nutrient requirement as very light, light, moderate, or heavy, and then use comparable values in the table. Note that the range of N rates is not very broad. For most crops fertilized weekly, the rate of N ranges from 1 to 3 pounds of a 20% N fertilizer per 100 gallons (0.6 to 1.8 kg/500 l), which yields 240 to 720 ppm N.

Leaching effects on nitrogen rate. A single rate of N rarely works for all growers of a given crop. Because nitrogen is not bound by media, the leach-

Table 7.3 Nitrogen rates for various crops and frequency of application

Crop	Concentration category	Rates and concentrations[a]			
		Weekly fertilization		**Constant fertilization**	
		oz. N/100 gal.	ppm N (or mg/l)	oz. N/100 gal.	ppm N (or mg/l)
Daffodil	None	—	—	—	—
Iris	None	—	—	—	—
Hyacinth	None	—	—	—	—
Tulip[b]	Very light	—	—	—	—
Snapdragon	Very light	3.1	240	1.3	100
Bedding plants	Very light	3.1	240	2.6	200
Elatior begonia	Very light	3.3	260	1.5	120
Azalea	Light	3.8	300	—	—
Gloxinia	Light	4.6	360	2.6	200
Rose	Moderate	6.1	480	2.0	160
Carnation	Moderate	6.1	480	2.6	200
Geranium	Moderate	6.1	480	2.6	200
Easter lily	Moderate	6.1	480	2.6	200
Chrysanthemum	Heavy	7.7	600	2.6	200
Poinsettia	Heavy	9.2	720	3.3	260

[a] Recommended rates and concentrations are based on elemental N. To determine how much actual fertilizer to use, divide the oz. N/100 gal. (or mg/l) from table 7.3 by the fraction of N in the fertilizer you choose to use. A 20% N fertilizer (ex. 20-10-20) contains 0.2 fraction (20%/100) of N. For example, for snapdragon 3.1 oz. N/100 gal. is recommended, and with a 20-10-20 fertilizer, you would add 15.5 oz. (3.1 divided by 0.2) of 20-10-20 fertilizer per 100 gal.

[b] As insurance against nitrogen and calcium deficiencies, apply calcium nitrate at the rate of 32 oz. (2 lbs.) calcium nitrate/100 gal. (2.4 g/l) at the start and at the midpoint of the growth room stages and at the start of greenhouse forcing.

ing percentage has a strong impact. Three poinsettia growers who water heavily, moderately, or lightly with leaching percentages of 40%, 20%, or 0%, respectively, will probably need to apply fertilizer at a N concentration of 300 ppm or higher, 200 ppm, or 100 ppm, respectively. The rates in table 7.3 are based on moderate to heavy leaching percentages (20% leaching or higher).

Table 7.4 Recommended ratios of nitrogen : potassium for greenhouse crops

Ratio of nitrogen:potassium (N:K$_2$O)					
3:1 azalea	2:1 begonia	1.5:1 foliage plants	1:1 general	1:1.5 carnation	1:2 cyclamen

Potassium

With the decision of N concentration out of the way, focus your attention on the rate of K required. It is easiest to deal with this decision by providing K as a proportion of N. Fortunately, most greenhouse crops perform best when N and K$_2$O are in a 1:1 ratio in the fertilizer. There are a few exceptions as indicated in table 7.4. To summarize the exceptions, the N:K$_2$O ratio is best when it is a 1:2 for cyclamen, 1:1.5 for carnation, 1.5:1 for tropical foliage plants, 2:1 for begonia, and 3:1 for azalea.

Phosphorus

The next component in the process of selecting a fertilizer analysis is the requirement for P. None is needed if media contain soil and a preplant application of superphosphate was used. However, most crops are grown in soilless media where a postplant application of P is necessary. For most plants, P (expressed as P$_2$O$_5$) supplied at 50% the rate of N is sufficient. The fertilizer analyses 20-10-20 and 20-9-20 have become the backbone for greenhouse fertilization. Only rarely do these fertilizers fail to provide sufficient P for crops. Lower proportions of P$_2$O$_5$ are probably possible and will undoubtedly be recommended as attempts to reduce nutrient runoff from greenhouses continue. Many crops obtain sufficient P from fertilizers containing P$_2$O$_5$ at 10% of the N concentration. However, some sensitive plug crops become P deficient when P$_2$O$_5$ in the fertilizer is at 15% of the level of N. Since the first symptoms of P stress are compact, deeper green plants, P deficiency is sometimes used by plug and bedding plant producers to grow compact plants.

In summary, a good universal fertilizer for greenhouse crops has a ratio of N : P$_2$O$_5$: K$_2$O of 2:1:2. For tropical foliage plants, a commonly recommended ratio is 3:1:2.

Selecting form of N

The next component in establishing a fertilizer analysis for a crop is selecting the form of N. Most fertilizers contain N in one or more of three forms, nitrate, ammonium, or urea. The form of N raises three points for consideration: ammonium toxicity, plant growth, and shift in media pH.

Ammonium toxicity. Plants safely store large quantities of N in the nitrate form, but they cannot store much N in the ammonium form. Application of the urea form of N leads to ammonium buildup in the plant. Urea is either converted in media by microorganisms to ammonium plus carbon dioxide or is taken up intact by the roots and then converted inside the plant to ammonium. When super-adequate levels of N are available, which is often the case in greenhouse production, plants will store N. Under storage conditions, the higher the proportion of N in the ammonium and/or urea form, the greater the chances of ammonium toxicity. Fortunately, there are nitrifying bacteria in media that convert ammoniacal-N to nitrate-N and decrease the chance of ammonium toxicity. However, these organisms are suppressed at low temperatures, in wet, low oxygen soils, and at low media pH levels.

The best conditions for ammonium conversion occur in the summer. During the summer, a fertilizer program that supplies 40 to 50% of total N in the ammonium and/or urea form is acceptable. During the winter in warmer climates, it is acceptable to use 40% ammoniacal-N. During the winter in colder climates, such as Canada and the northern United States, lower amounts of ammonium and/or urea are desirable. It is the average ammonium content of all fertilizers in a program that is important. For example, in the winter a fertilizer containing 50% of total N in the ammonium plus urea form could be alternated in successive fertilizations with one containing 10% for an average level of 30%. Symptoms of ammonium toxicity are described later in the text.

Plant growth. Rose growers traditionally switch to urea and ammonium fertilizers for lush growth and to nitrate sources for hardening plants. This strategy also works for greenhouse crops in general. Urea and ammoniacal-N generally lead to greater leaf expansion and stem internode elongation. Nitrate-N has the opposite effect, resulting in compact plants. This

Table 7.5 Commercially available fertilizers with percentage of total nitrogen that is in ammonium plus urea form, the potential acidity or basicity, and percentage of calcium (Ca), magnesium (Mg), and sulfur (S) wherever these are greater than 0.2%

Fertilizer	NH_4[a] (%)	Potential acidity[b]	Potential basicity[c]	Ca (%)	Mg (%)	S (%)
21-7-7 acid	90	1700				
21-7-7 acid	100	1560				10.0
24-9-9	50	822			1.0	2.2
20-2-20	69	800				
20-18-18	73	710				1.4
24-7-15	58	612			1.0	1.3
20-18-20	69	610				1.0
20-20-20	69	583				
20-9-20	42	510				1.4
20-20-20	69	474				
16-17-17	44	440			0.9	1.3
20-10-20	40	422				
21-5-20	40	418				
20-10-20	38	393				
20-8-70	39	379			0.9	1.2
21-7-7 neutral	100	369				
15-15-15	52	261				
17-17-17	51	218				
15-16-17	47	215				
15-16-17	30	165				

[a]NH_4 (%) is the percentage total N in the ammonium plus urea forms; the remaining N is nitrate.

[b]Pounds of calcium carbonate limestone required to neutralize the acidity of 1 ton of fertilizer.

[c]Application of 1 ton of fertilizer has the effect of this many pounds of calcium carbonate limestone.

lush growth response occurs when 25% or more of the N is in the ammonium/urea form. Several of the commercial fertilizers listed in table 7.5 (20-10-20, 20-9-20, 20-5-30, 20-0-20, 16-4-12, 15-15-15, and 15-16-17) have 25% or more of their N in the ammonium/urea form and will produce lush growth, while others (13-2-13, 14-0-14, 15-0-15, and 17-0-17) are higher in nitrate-N and will give compact growth. Rose, plug, and bed-

Table 7.5   continued

Fertilizer	NH$_4$[a] (%)	Potential acidity[b]	Potential basicity[c]	Ca (%)	Mg (%)	S (%)
20-5-30	56	153				
17-5-24	31	125			2.0	2.6
20-5-30	54	118			0.5	
17-4-28	31	105			1.0	2.2
20-5-30	54	100				
15-11-29	43	91				
15-5-25	28	76			1.3	
15-10-30	39	76				
20-0-20	25	40		5.0		
21-0-20	48	15		6.0		
20-0-20	69	0	0	6.7	0.2	
16-4-12	38		73			
17-0-17	20		75	4.0	2.0	
15-5-15	28		135	5.0	2.0	
13-2-13	11		200	6.0	3.0	
14-0-14	8		220	6.0	3.0	
15-0-15	13		319	10.5	0.3	
15.5-0-0 cal. nitrate	6		400	22.0		
15-0-15	13		420	11.0		
13-0-44 pot. nitrate	0		460			

ding plant growers probably use the form of N more than other growers to control growth. Many growers use high nitrate finisher fertilizers at the end of their crops. The commercial fertilizer 15-0-15 or a combination of 2 weights of calcium nitrate to 1 weight of potassium nitrate (also 15-0-15) serves well as a finish fertilizer. These fertilizers keep foliage green, but depress lush growth that would discourage flowering.

Media pH. Ammonium and urea usually lower media pH, while nitrate generally increases media pH. The shift in pH is partially the result of plant uptake. In table 7.5, the 37 fertilizers listed are arranged in decreasing order of acidity. Note that the proportion of N in the urea plus ammonium forms tends to decline from top to bottom of the table. The relationship between the form of N and acidity or basicity of fertilizers has several discrepancies, because N is not the only nutrient impacting pH. Whenever a positively charged nutrient ion such as ammonium, potassium, calcium, or magnesium is taken up by plant media, pH usually declines. Conversely, when negatively charged nutrient ions such as nitrate, phosphate, sulfate, or chloride are taken up by plant media, pH usually increases. But, because plants take up more N ions than any other nutrient ion, it is N that has the predominant effect on media pH. Also, the nitrification reaction (conversion of ammonium to nitrate by soil bacteria) has an acidifying effect on media.

In summary, it is not enough to know how much N is needed in a fertilizer. You must also decide whether the N will be supplied as ammonium/urea or nitrate. When either acidification of media or lush growth is desired, the choice is ammonium or urea. If a rise in media pH, compact growth during production, or toning of the plant at the end of production is desired, nitrate is the choice. When ammonium or urea N is applied, monitor media to ensure that excessive levels of ammoniacal N do not accumulate. Excessive ammonia levels would be greater than 20 ppm for plugs and 40 ppm for crops in general using a saturated paste extract.

Secondary macronutrients

Under unusual circumstances the three secondary macronutrients—S, Ca, and Mg—can become deficient. Analyze media and tissue periodically to monitor these and all other essential nutrients (see Chapter 9).

Sulfur. As mentioned earlier, incorporating S into media prior to planting is good insurance. Since sulfate is subject to leaching, it is important to monitor S in media and in the plant tissue. Some fertilizers contain S as sulfate (table 7.5) and if these are used, S deficiency will not occur. Alternatively, if S deficiency should occur, it can be corrected by switching to a commercial fertilizer containing sulfur. A good, single application remedy for S deficiency is to apply a drench of 2 pounds (1 kg) Epsom salt (magnesium sulfate) in 100 gallons (500 l) water to media. Irrigation waters may supply sufficient sulfate if water analysis reveals 48 ppm or greater sulfate (see p. 36, Chapter 2). Symptoms of S deficiency are presented in the nutritional disorders section in this chapter.

Calcium and magnesium. Under most conditions these two nutrients should not be a problem because they are incorporated into media as limestone, which slowly releases Ca and/or Mg over several months. On occasion these nutrients dissolve and leach prematurely from media. Another problem occurs when either Ca or Mg builds up to a high concentration in media and blocks uptake of the other one. Although precise research is lacking, a good ratio for these two nutrients in media and irrigation water appears to be 3 to 5 ppm Ca and 1 ppm Mg. Conduct routine media and tissue tests to monitor the levels and balance of Ca and Mg.

There are five common reasons for Ca and Mg deficiencies. The first is low pH in media. At low pH, limestone dissolves faster, releasing soluble Ca and Mg into the media solution from which it can be leached. The second cause of deficiencies comes from an imbalance. Ca and Mg are reciprocally antagonistic. A high level of either nutrient in media will reduce uptake of the other member of the pair. Calcium deficiency can occur in media that have ordinarily adequate levels of Ca if the concentration of Mg in media is super-optimum. The reciprocal is also true. The third reason for deficiency affects Ca only. A low rate of transpiration can lead to Ca deficiency. Ca is carried passively into the plant in the transpirational water stream. Deficiency can occur during humid periods when lower evaporation from plant foliage reduces the transpiration rate. The fourth reason applies to Mg only. If only calcitic lime, which contains only calcium, is used, a Mg deficiency can occur if Mg is not supplied by the irrigation water or other fertilizers. Dolomitic lime contains both Ca and Mg. The fifth reason is use of irrigation water that is low in Ca and/or magnesium.

Understanding the sources of Ca and Mg is important in order to maintain the correct levels and balance of the two in the plant growing system. There are three sources—the liming materials in media, the irrigation water, and fertilizers. The liming materials should rarely be the cause of imbalances. Calcitic limestone can be used to supply Ca or dolomitic limestone to supply Ca and Mg. Dolomitic limestone is the common type used in greenhouse media. Make shifts in the form of limestone to accommodate the Ca and Mg balance in the irrigation water.

When irrigation water contains high quantities of Mg relative to Ca, calcitic limestone is used in media to bring the total Ca and Mg in the plant growing system into balance. When irrigation water contains very high levels of Ca and almost no Mg, dolomitic limestone plus Epsom salt (magnesium sulfate) at a rate of up to 3 pounds per cubic yard (2 kg/m^3) are incorporated into media to provide a balancing level of Mg. When Ca and Mg are in balance in water (3 to 5 ppm Ca to 1 ppm Mg), use dolomitic limestone to maintain the balance. If the concentrations of Ca and Mg are low in water, then the issue of balance of these two nutrients in irrigation water is not important and dolomitic limestone can be used.

It is very important to read fertilizer labels. Many Ca and Mg problems come about because only one of these nutrients was contained in the fertilizer used. Many growers will switch to 15-0-15 when they need to raise media pH. Most, but not all, 15-0-15 fertilizers on the market contain about 11% Ca, but little or no Mg. Unless Mg was unusually high in media before using the 15-0-15 fertilizer, it will elevate Ca out of balance to Mg and eventually cause a Mg deficiency. The 15-0-15 fertilizer can be used, but it will be necessary to make occasional applications of Epsom salts to keep the Ca and Mg ratio in balance.

An alternative would be to use a fertilizer such as 13-2-13 that contains 6% Ca and 3% Mg, rather than 15-0-15. Poinsettia growers apply Epsom salts periodically to meet the high Mg demands of this crop. Some growers have shifted to poinsettia special 15-5-25 without noticing on the label that it contains 1.3% Mg. When they continue to apply Epsom salts along with this fertilizer, they run the risk of elevating the Mg level to a point where it could cause Ca deficiency. Had they realized that the fertilizer contained the necessary Mg, they could have dropped Epsom salts. There are several fertilizers listed in table 7.5 that provide only Mg or only Ca, or a combination of the two. Media, water, and tissue tests will indicate which is best for a given situation.

Fertilizing at finish

Plants will last longer in the consumer environment if nutrient availability is reduced during the last two weeks of greenhouse production. To make an appropriate shift in fertilization, know the nutrient status of media two weeks before market date. Constant-feed fertigation usually results in much higher nutrient levels in media at the end of the crop than weekly fertilizer applications do. When media analysis indicates that the available levels of nutrients, particularly N, are at or above the high end of the optimum range, discontinue fertilization for the last two weeks of production.

If media nutrient levels are in the middle of the optimum range, cut fertilization in half for the last two weeks. This may be done by reducing the fertilizer concentration to one half or by applying the full strength fertilizer at half of the frequency. If nutrient levels in media are at the low end of the optimum range, it may be sufficient to stop fertilization for the last week only. In the unlikely event that the crop is receiving insufficient nutrition when the last two weeks start, fertilize up to market date.

Slow-release fertilizer programs

The technology for using synthetic slow-release fertilizers as the sole source of N, P, and K for greenhouse crops has been available since 1960. But slow-release fertilizers have not been widely adopted. Once a slow-release fertilizer has been applied, there is no effective means to reduce or stop nutrient release and many growers are reluctant to use a fertilizer they cannot control. There are times crop growth needs to be held back. Bedding plant crops, for example, are customarily held back when inclement weather delays the anticipated market date. Furthermore, during periods of inclement weather, crop growth is generally slower and the demand for water and nutrients is reduced.

Most slow-release fertilizers fit two applications in the greenhouse industry. First, they may be mixed into media prior to planting in order to supply about half to two-thirds of a crop's nutrient requirements. The remaining nutrient requirements are met through periodic, postplant application of liquid fertilizer. The number and timing of liquid fertilizer applications is gauged by plant appearance. The advantage here is that most liquid fertilizer applications are eliminated. This saves labor where a central fertilizer system is not available. It also reduces nutrient waste where overhead sprinkler systems are used that place much of the irrigation solution outside of the plant containers.

The second application for slow-release fertilizer is really an insurance program: A small quantity is applied to the surface of a pot during or shortly after planting. A standard liquid fertilization program is then used, which essentially ignores the presence of the slow-release fertilizer. The slow-release fertilizer provides insurance against deficiency between liquid fertilizer applications. This combination system has given superior plant performance, particularly with poinsettia, that cannot be duplicated by simply altering a liquid fertilization program.

Forms of slow-release fertilizer. Slow-release fertilizers differ in their method of manufacture, mechanism of nutrient release, and form of N supplied. Selecting the proper type is more important in the greenhouse industry than in most other industries. This is true because of greenhouse crops' low tolerance to ammoniacal and urea nitrogen. The ammonium- and urea-supplying types of slow-release fertilizers include urea aldehydes, such as urea formaldehyde, sulfur-coated fertilizers, and MagAmp. With the exception of MagAmp, these fertilizers are rarely used in greenhouses.

Slow-release fertilizers that supply safe mixtures of ammonium and nitrate for greenhouse crops include Nutricote and Osmocote. Each is available in several formulas and various periods of release. Osmocote is available as 14-14-14 and 19-6-12 formulas with a release period of three to four months, 13-13-13 and 18-6-12 with a release period of eight to nine months, and 17-7-12 with a release period of 12 to 14 months. Note that the ratios in these formulas are basically 1:1:1 and 3:1:2. The former suits crops with general 1:1 $N:K_2O$ needs, while the latter is desirable for crops with a heavier N than K_2O requirement, such as begonia and foliage plants. Nutricote is also available as 14-14-14 or in other formulas favoring N. Each formula is available in several release periods ranging from 40 days to one year.

Rates of application. Osmocote is frequently used for some crops, most notably bedding plants, to provide up to about two thirds of the primary macronutrient requirement. Rates of 3 to 7.5 pounds per cubic yard (1.8 to 4.4 kg/m³) are used for bedding plants. The lower rate is used in winter in colder climates, while the high rate is used for crops later in the spring season in warmer climates. Supplemental liquid fertilizer applications are made only as required to maintain foliar color and desired growth rate. MagAmp is also used for bedding plants for the same purpose. Rates of 6 to 10 pounds per cubic yard (3.5 to 5.9 kg/m³) are used.

Since MagAmp supplies all N in the ammoniacal form, use supplemental liquid fertilizers that are high in nitrate-N. Nitrate will balance ammonium, thereby averting ammonium toxicity. This would not be a problem with Osmocote and Nutricote. If media is to be steam pasteurized, MagAmp may be added prior to steaming. Do not incorporate Osmocote and Nutricote into media prior to steaming because their coatings are adversely affected by steaming and will release nutrients too fast.

A top-dress application of slow-release fertilizers can be used at planting time. Many poinsettia and pot chrysanthemum growers apply one rounded teaspoon of 14-14-14 Osmocote (6 g) to the media surface of a filled 6- or 6.5-inch pot (15 or 16.5 cm), then they insert the transplant. Others apply this quantity to the top of the pot after planting. Since azaleas respond well to ammoniacal-N, growers often apply one rounded teaspoon (5 g) of urea formaldehyde type slow-release fertilizer to the surface of each 6-inch (15 cm) pot every two months during periods of heavy growth. This keeps foliage deep green.

Fertilizer injectors

Fertilizer injectors allow use of fertilizer concentrates, often 100 to 200 times more concentrated than the single-strength fertilizer solution applied to the plant. Because this concentrate can be injected into the water line, it is not necessary to have a prohibitively large tank of single strength fertilizer solution. The savings on tanks and space justifies the injector system.

Plumbing

Ideally, the fertilizer injector should be plumbed into the main water line in the service building. It should be located on a bypass to the main water line A shown in fig. 7.1. This allows for the application of fertilizer or water. Moving a portable injector around the greenhouse is too time consuming. Using the service building as a location is desirable because of accessibility, availability of space for dry fertilizer storage, and for location of a hot water heater to facilitate dissolving fertilizers into the concentrate.

Use a dual delivery line so that water or fertilizer is available at each irrigation station (B in fig. 7.1). Most older firms have a single water delivery line to the greenhouse. The difficulty with a single water main system lies in the residual fluid between the injector and the plants. This residual volume may be sufficiently large to meet the needs of the first or second irrigation station. But consider a situation where the crop

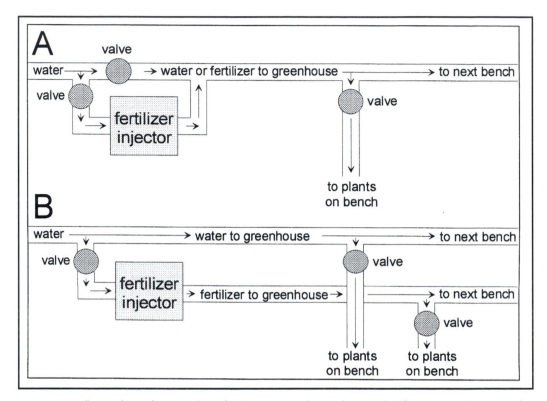

Fig. 7.1 Installation schemes for a greenhouse fertilizer injector. Valves can be manual or the system can be automated using solenoid valves.
(A) Injector on bypass loop of a single water main system. This scheme has a problem of residual solution in the lines when switching between water and fertilizer solution.
(B) Injector installed in a more ideal dual main system. Water or fertilizer solution is available at each plant station.

only needs to be watered. Yet because fertilizer solution was applied the day before, the water mains are still filled with fertilizer solution. The first irrigation station may unintentionally receive fertilizer, the second station may receive some fertilizer followed by water, and at the third station the plants receive only water.

This scenario repeats itself every time the grower switches from fertilizer to water or back to fertilizer. The result is a highly variable response across the crop. To solve this problem, install a valve at the end of the water main beyond the last irrigation station. That way, when a switch is made, the line can be purged. The problem then becomes one of releasing residual fertilizer solution into the environment.

Fig. 7.2   Timing device used to regulate liquid fertilizer application.

If fertigation is automated with timing devices (fig. 7.2), considerable time is saved, and the quantity of fluid applied and the leaching percentage is more uniform. The grower with manual valves must wait at each set of irrigation stations for the three to five minutes that irrigation generally requires. Hours are wasted each day, usually by a highly paid employee. With an automated system, the manager passes through the greenhouse recording the decision at each station for no irrigation, irrigation, or fertilization. These decisions are then entered into the timing device, and the manager is free to go about other tasks. The timer sequentially moves through the irrigation stations activating appropriated solenoid valves for the prescribed period of time.

Selecting an injector

A variety of fertilizer injectors are available. Use four criteria to select the appropriate injector for a given situation. The first is the injector's flow rate. A mature crop may need to be watered two times on a hot summer day. Thus, only four hours may be available for each watering. Typical water consumption rates are 2 quarts per square foot ($20\,l/m^2$) of bed for cut flowers and vegetables. Potted crops consume about one quarter this amount of water per unit area. One acre (0.4 ha) of greenhouse with beds covering 67% of the floor would require application of 14,500 gallons (55 kl) of water in four hours. This requires a flow rate of 60 gallons per minute (565 l/minute/ha of greenhouse).

The second criteria is fertilizer proportion. The proportion is the dilution rate at which the injector injects the fertilizer concentrate into the water line. For example, a 1:100 proportion injects one part of fertilizer concentrate for every 100 parts of irrigation water. Some injectors have a fixed proportion. Others can be varied. The variable injector is particularly useful for greenhouses with a mixture of crops having a wide range of fertilizer requirements. With a single proportion injector, several different fertilizer concentrates are needed to meet these differences in final fertilizer concentration. It is expensive to purchase tanks, provide space for them, and maintain solutions.

The third criteria is multiple head injection ability. Some injectors can draw from two or more concentrates simultaneously. A single head injector draws from only one fertilizer concentrate. The problem with a single head injector is that all nutrients in the concentrate must be compatible at high concentration. This is not the case when either calcium or magnesium are mixed with sulfate or phosphate. With a dual head injector, calcium and/or magnesium can be dissolved in one concentrate tank and sulfate and/or phosphate in the other. When these nutrients come together in the injector they are at the compatible single strength concentration. Vegetable growers often use triple head injectors in order to supply magnesium sulfate in the first concentrate, calcium nitrate in the second, and the remaining nutrients, including phosphate, in the third.

The final criteria is ability to inject acid. Growers with alkaline water may need to inject sulfuric, nitric, or phosphoric acid into the water to lower alkalinity. The injector head through which the acid passes must be acid resistant.

Monitoring the injector

Never trust the proportion at which injectors inject fertilizers. It can change with time. If the proportion changes slowly, one can simply change the concentration in the fertilizer concentrate tank or the proportion adjustment on the injector to compensate for the change. If the proportion changes erratically, then the injector must be repaired. In either event, it is necessary to monitor the proportion. This can be done in two ways. One method calls for measuring the output volume of single strength fertilizer solution coming out of the injector and at the same time measuring the volume of concentrate going into the injector. Find the correct proportion by dividing the concentrate volume used into the output volume recovered.

When the injector is plumbed into the central water main it might not be possible to measure output volume, so a second method can be used. Most of the nutrients in fertilizers are derived from salts. For each fertilizer solution there is a relationship between the concentration of that solution and its electrical conductivity (EC). On the fertilizer bag or in the technical literature, most greenhouse fertilizer formulators publish a table relating fertilizer concentration to electrical conductivity. For instance, when 21-0-20 fertilizer is dissolved to yield a concentration of 100 ppm N, the electrical conductivity should be 0.5 dS/m. Simply collect some of the injector output, and check its EC with a conductivity meter. If the wrong reading is obtained, either the fertilizer concentrate was made up wrong, or the injector is not proportioning the fertilizer at the proper dilution rate.

Formulating fertilizers

Following are procedures to formulate any fertilizer. The example outlines preparation of a fertilizer solution containing 200 ppm nitrogen (N), 100 ppm phosphorus (P_2O_5), and 200 ppm potassium (K_2O) formulated from ammonium nitrate, potassium nitrate, and monoammonium phosphate.

Steps to follow

1. List the fertilizer sources to be used and their percentages (analyses) of N-P_2O_5-K_2O (see table 7.6 for a list of commonly used fertilizer carriers and their analyses).

Fertilizer sources	N-P_2O_5-K_2O
potassium nitrate (PN)	13-0-44
monoammonium phosphate (MAP)	12-62-0
ammonium nitrate (AN)	33-0-0

Table 7.6 Common fertilizer sources of nutrients for formulating liquid fertilizers

Fertilizer sources	N-P_2O_5-K_2O
ammonium nitrate	33-0-0
ammonium sulfate	21-0-0
calcium nitrate	15.5-0-0-20Ca
diammonium phosphate	21-53-0
magnesium nitrate	11-0-0
monoammonium phosphate	12-62-0
monopotassium phosphate	0-53-35
potassium chloride	0-0-60
potassium nitrate	13-0-44
potassium sulfate	0-0-51
sodium nitrate	16-0-0
urea	45-0-0

2. Prepare a balance sheet as follows.

	oz./100 gal.	N	P_2O_5	K_2O
Desired levels (ppm)		200	100	200
potassium nitrate				
monoammonium phosphate				
ammonium nitrate				
Total (ppm)				

3. Select one of the above fertilizer sources that contains two desired nutrients. In this case, select potassium nitrate (PN). Begin with the nutrient that is contained in this fertilizer source at the highest concentration. Since nitrogen is 13% and potassium is 44%, we will start with potassium. In table 7.7 go to the column that is headed by 44. Read down the table until you come to 200 ppm. The value 198 is close enough. Stop at that point and read across that row to the extreme left entry which is "6". This is the number of ounces of PN to dissolve in 100 gallons (500 l) of water to achieve a fertilizer solution that contains 198 ppm potassium as K_2O. Now determine how much nitrogen you will receive from

Table 7.7 Converting ppm of desired nutrient to ounces of fertilizer carrier to add to 100 gallons of water (or grams in 1 liter), or vice versa[a]

	Percentage (analysis) of desired nutrient in fertilizer carrier													
	12	13	14	15.5	16	20	20.5	21	33	44	45	53	60	62
Ounces of fertilizer carrier per 100 gallons					ppm of resultant solution									
1	9	10	11	12	12	15	15	16	25	33	34	40	45	46
2	18	20	21	23	24	30	31	31	49	66	67	79	90	92
3	27	29	31	35	36	45	46	47	74	99	101	117	135	139
4	36	39	42	46	48	60	61	63	99	132	135	159	180	186
6	54	58	63	70	72	90	92	94	148	198	202	238	269	278
8	72	78	84	93	96	120	123	126	198	263	269	317	359	371
16	144	156	168	186	192	240	246	252	395	527	539	635	719	742
24	216	234	252	278	288	359	368	377	593	790	808	952	1078	1114
32	288	311	335	371	383	479	491	503	790	1054	1078	1269	1437	1485
40	359	389	419	464	479	599	614	629	988	1317	1347	1587	1796	1856
48	431	467	503	557	575	719	736	754	1186	1581	1617	1904	2155	2227
56	503	545	587	650	671	838	859	880	1383	1844	1886	2221	2515	2598
64	575	623	671	742	767	958	982	1006	1581	2108	2155	2539	2874	2970
Grams of fertilizer carrier per liter					ppm of resultant solution									
0.1	12	13	14	16	16	20	21	21	33	44	45	53	60	62
0.2	24	26	28	31	32	40	41	42	66	88	90	106	120	124
0.3	36	39	42	47	48	60	62	63	99	132	135	159	180	186
0.4	48	52	56	62	64	80	82	84	132	176	180	212	240	248
0.6	72	78	84	93	96	120	123	126	198	264	270	318	360	372
0.8	96	104	112	124	128	160	164	168	264	352	360	424	480	496
1.0	120	130	140	155	160	200	205	210	330	440	450	530	600	620
1.5	180	195	210	233	240	300	308	315	495	660	675	795	900	930
2.0	240	260	280	310	320	400	410	420	660	880	900	1060	1200	1240
2.5	300	325	350	388	400	500	513	525	825	1100	1125	1325	1500	1550
3.0	360	390	420	465	480	600	615	630	990	1320	1350	1590	1800	1860
3.5	420	455	490	543	560	700	718	735	1155	1540	1575	1855	2100	2170
4.0	480	520	560	620	640	800	820	840	1320	1760	1800	2120	2400	2480

[a]Adapted from J.W. Love. Unpublished.

using this rate of PN. Start in the left column with the value 6 oz./100 gal. (28 g/378.5 l) and read across to the right until you reach the column under 13 (the percent nitrogen in PN). The value you find is 58, which is the ppm concentration of nitrogen provided by this rate of PN. Enter the two concentration values, 58 ppm N and 198 ppm K_2O, and the quantity value, 6 oz./100 gal., into the balance sheet as follows. To develop a fertilizer formula in metric units, use the lower half of table 7.7.

	oz./100 gal.	N	P_2O_5	K_2O
Desired levels (ppm)		200	100	200
potassium nitrate	6	58		198
monoammonium phosphate				
ammonium nitrate				
Total (ppm)				

4. Select the next fertilizer source that contains two desired nutrients and the nutrient in it that is in the highest quantity. The source is monoammonium phosphate (MAP), and the nutrient in the highest concentration is phosphorus (P_2O_5). Read down the column in table 7.7 headed by 62 (the percentage of P_2O_5 in MAP) until you come to the closest value to 100 ppm. The value is 92 ppm. Now read across that row to the extreme left entry which is 2 oz./100 gal. Two ounces of MAP in 100 gallons will yield 92 ppm P_2O_5. However, we need 8 ppm more which is roughly 10% more—thus we need 2.2 ounces MAP per 100 gallons. This will give us 101 ppm P_2O_5. Determine the amount of nitrogen that is supplied by this concentration of MAP by starting in the left column at the value 2 and reading across the row to the column headed by 12 (the percentage of nitrogen in MAP). The value you find is 18 ppm (nitrogen). Since you are actually dissolving 2.2 ounces of MAP you need to increase this nitrogen concentration value by about 10% to 20 ppm. Enter these numbers into the balance sheet as follows.

	oz./100 gal.	N	P₂O₅	K₂O
Desired levels (ppm)		200	100	200
potassium nitrate	6	58		198
monoammonium phosphate	2.2	20	101	
ammonium nitrate				
Total (ppm)				

5. We have already supplied 78 ppm nitrogen (58 from PN + 20 from MAP); thus, 122 ppm of N is still needed to achieve the goal of 200 ppm. This will be supplied by ammonium nitrate (AN) (33-0-0). Go to the column in table 7.7 headed by 33 (the percentage of nitrogen in AN). The closest value to our desired 122 is 99. The reading at the left of that row tells us 4 oz. of AN/100 gal. will yield a nitrogen concentration of 99 ppm. Note that the first entry in the column headed by 33 is 25 ppm and that this concentration is achieved by dissolving 1 ounce AN in 100 gallons. Therefore, we can use 5 ounces of AN per 100 gallons to achieve a concentration of 124 ppm nitrogen (99 ppm from 4 ounces AN plus 25 ppm from 1 ounce AN). This value is close enough to 200 ppm and should be added into the balance sheet. At this time the concentrations in the balance sheet are summed. The resulting fertilizer solution contains nutrient concentrations close enough to the desired levels and was achieved by dissolving 6 ounces of PN, 2.2 ounces of MAP and 5 ounces of AN in 100 gallons of water.

	oz./100 gal.	N	P₂O₅	K₂O
Desired levels (ppm)		200	100	200
potassium nitrate	6	58		198
monoammonium phosphate	2.2	20	101	
ammonium nitrate	5	124		
Total (ppm)		202	101	198

Correcting nutritional disorders ————

Recognizing nutritional disorders is an important part of managing a fertility program. There are three ways to diagnose nutritional disorders: tissue analysis, soil testing, and recognizing visual symptoms. Recognizing visual symptoms is necessary as a routine production practice and can save the time delay of tissue and soil analyses. Typical visual symptoms of nutrient disorders are shown in fig. 7.3. The following descriptions are of the most common symptoms of macronutrient disorders. Table 8.1 in Chapter 8 contains a key to diagnose deficiencies from visual symptoms. Table 7.8 gives corrective procedures you can use once you have identified the nutrient disorder.

Nitrogen deficiency. Older leaves become uniformly chlorotic. After considerable time, older leaves become necrotic and drop off if abscission is possible for the species in question.

Ammonium toxicity. The margins of older leaves curl upward or downward depending on the plant species. Older leaves develop chlorosis. The form of chlorosis is highly variable and depends on the plant species. Necrosis follows chlorosis on older leaves. Root tips are burned.

Phosphorus deficiency. The plant becomes severely stunted; at the same time, foliage becomes deeper green than normal. In some species, older leaves develop purple coloration. Older leaves then develop chlorosis followed by necrosis. See fig. 7.3(A).

Potassium deficiency. The margins of older leaves become chlorotic followed by immediate necrosis. Similar necrotic spots may form across the blades of older leaves, but more so toward the margin. Soon the older leaves become totally necrotic. See fig. 7.3(B).

Calcium deficiency. Symptoms are expressed at the top of the plant on new growth. Young leaves may develop variable patterns of chlorosis and distortion such as dwarfing, straplike shape, or crinkling. The edges of poinsettia bracts may burn. Shoots stop growing. Petals or flower stems may collapse. Roots are short, thickened, and branched. See fig. 7.3(C).

Magnesium deficiency. Older leaves develop interveinal chlorosis. See fig. 7.3(D).

(A) Early stages of phosphorus deficiency in chrysanthemum; stunting of the shoot and deeper green color than normal (note normal plant on the left).

(B) Potassium deficiency in poinsettia: necrosis of the margins of older leaves.

Fig. 7.3   Visual symptoms of nutrient disorders.

(C) Calcium deficiency in poinsettia: chlorosis and distortion of young leaves followed by necrosis of leaf margins.

(D) Magnesium deficiency in rose: interveinal chlorosis of lower leaves.

Figure 7.3   continued

Table 7.8   Corrective procedures for various macronutrient deficiencies

Deficient nutrient	Corrective procedure	Rate[a] oz./100 gal.	g/l
N	Switch to a fertilizer formulation high in N such as 24-7-15, or to calcium nitrate (15-0-0), or ammonium nitrate (34-0-0) until the N to K_2O balance is restored		
P	switch to a fertilizer formula with P equal to half or more of the N level such as 20-10-20, or one application of diammonium phosphate or monoammonium phosphate	32	2.4
K	switch to a fertilizer formulation high in K_2O such as 20-5-30, 17-5-24, 15-11-29, 15-10-30, or switch to potassium nitrate (13-0-44) until the N to K_2O balance is restored		
Ca	switch the N source to calcium nitrate (15-0-0) or switch to a high calcium content fertilizer formula such as 20-0-20, 21-0-20, 15-0-15, 15-5-15, or 13-2-13		
Mg	apply magnesium sulfate (Epsom salt) once, or switch to a Mg-containing complete fertilizer such as 13-2-13, 14-0-14, 15-5-15, or 17-0-17	32	2.4
S	apply magnesium sulfate (Epsom salt) once, or switch to a S-containing complete fertilizer such as 20-18-18, 20-18-20, or 20-9-20	32	2.4

[a]Rates apply to general crops in the greenhouses. Lower rates may be required for lightly fertilized crops. Rates should be reduced to half for plug seedling crops.

Sulfur deficiency. Foliage over the entire plant becomes uniformly chlorotic. Sometimes symptoms tend to be more pronounced toward the top of the plant. While symptoms on the individual leaf look like those of nitrogen deficiency, it is easy to distinguish sulfur deficiency from nitrogen deficiency because nitrogen deficiency begins in the lowest leaves first. Sulfur deficient leaves may sometimes take on a beige coloration, which is different from nitrogen deficiency.

References

Love, J.W. Department of Horticultural Sciences, North Carolina State University, Raleigh, N.C. Unpublished.

Nelson, P.V. 1991. *Greenhouse operation and management*. 4th. ed. Englewood Cliffs, N.J.: Prentice Hall.

Chapter 8

Micronutrient Nutrition

David Wm. Reed

Essential elements

Plants require 17 essential elements for normal growth and development. Three of these are supplied by air and water: Carbon (C) is supplied by CO_2, hydrogen (H) is supplied by water and oxygen (O) is supplied by oxygen gas and water. Since these three are supplied naturally, they are not regarded as nutrients or fertilizers. However, adding CO_2 to an enclosed greenhouse during the winter really is carbon fertilization. The remaining 14 essential elements are termed nutrients (also called essential nutrients or mineral nutrients), and the compounds that supply them are fertilizers. The 14 nutrients are divided into two groups, macronutrients and micronutrients.

Macronutrients

Macronutrients (also called major elements, major nutrients, or macroelements) get their name from the fact that they are required by plants in greater quantities. The concentration of macronutrients in dry plant tissue ranges from 0.2% to 7% (2,000 ppm to 70,000 ppm). The six macronutrients are nitrogen (N), phosphorus (P), potassium (K), magnesium (Mg), calcium (Ca), and sulfur (S). Some references refer to N, P, and K as primary nutrients and Mg, Ca, and S as secondary nutrients.

Micronutrients

This chapter addresses micronutrients (also called minor elements, minor nutrients, or trace elements), which get their name from the fact that they are required by plants in lesser quantities. The eight micronutrients are iron (Fe), manganese (Mn), zinc (Zn), copper (Cu), boron (B), molybdenum (Mo), chlorine (Cl), and nickel (Ni). Some nutritional physiologists consider silicon (Si), cobalt (Co), sodium (Na), iodine (I), vanadium (V), and selenium (Se) as micronutrients, or at least beneficial, for some crops. This chapter will not address this last group. In addition, chlorine is ubiquitous in nature and nickel is required in such small quantities that they both always appear to be present in sufficient quantities, therefore neither Cl nor Ni will be discussed.

The concentration of micronutrients in dry plant tissue ranges from 1 ppm (0.0001%) to 600 ppm (0.06%). These are very small concentrations. For example, molybdenum (Mo) is only required by plants at about 1 ppm of dry weight. If you had 1 million pounds of dry poinsettia leaves, they would contain only 1 pound of Mo. Keep in mind you would need about 10 million pounds of fresh poinsettia leaves to get 1 million pounds of dry leaves. Now that's a little bit of Mo in a lot of poinsettia leaves! But even this minute amount of Mo is required for normal growth, and 0.5 ppm can cause a deficiency and severe growth abnormalities.

Are micronutrients less important than macronutrients? Absolutely not. They are just as necessary but in much smaller quantities. A micronutrient deficiency can cause devastating effects, so you can say that they are somewhat analogous to the importance of vitamins in human nutrition.

Nutrient mobility and deficiency symptoms

The mobility of nutrients is a very important concept to grasp. All micronutrients are immobile. An immobile nutrient can be absorbed by roots and move up the plant through the transpirational stream of the xylem and thereby be distributed to all plant parts. However, immobile nutrients cannot be "loaded" into the phloem, thus they cannot move out of organs through phloem translocation. So micronutrients have a one-way transport into organs and cannot get out to be redistributed to other plant parts when needed. This is an extremely important diagnostic tool in identifying micronutrient deficiencies.

Deficiencies of micronutrients usually appear on new leaves. This happens when the soil is deficient, and because old leaves cannot sacrifice their micronutrient content, the new leaves are deprived. Conversely, all macronutrients, except calcium, are mobile. A mobile nutrient can move in both the xylem and the phloem and will always be translocated to where it is needed most, such as new growth, flowers, fruits, etc. Thus, macronutrient deficiencies (except for calcium) usually occur on the old leaves first. This topic is addressed in more detail in Chapter 9 on tissue analysis. Table 8.1 is a generalized key to nutrient deficiency symptoms for use in identifying possible deficiencies of micronutrients as well as macronutrients.

Effect of media and media pH on micronutrients

The solubility of nutrients is dramatically affected by the growing media pH. At low pH (below pH 5.5 to 6), the micronutrients iron, manganese, copper, zinc, and boron become more soluble and available for absorption by plants. If the pH gets too low (below 5), these micronutrients can become so soluble and available that they may become toxic. This has been reported to be one of the causes of leaf bronzing and chlorosis in some bedding plants such as marigold and geranium. Low growing media pH appears to result in iron and/or manganese toxicity. At low pH, the micronutrient molybdenum becomes less soluble, thus less available for absorption by plants, and deficiencies might occur.

At higher pH (above 6.5 to 7.0), the reverse is true. Molybdenum becomes more soluble and available for absorption by plants. Iron, manganese, copper, zinc, and boron become less soluble, are less available for absorption by plants, and deficiencies occur, even though there may be ample micronutrient levels in the growing media.

Maintaining the proper pH balance of growing media is the most important factor in maintaining optimum micronutrient nutrition. The recommended pH for soil or soil-containing growing media is 6.2 to 6.9,

Table 8.1 General key to nutrient deficiency symptons

Part of plant affected	Plant deficient in:
Older, lower leaves affected first, may spread to younger leaves when severe.	
Leaves overall pale, chlorotic or dark green; leaves dry and die.	
Plants light green; lower leaves overall yellow; stalks short and slender; usually no necrosis	**Nitrogen (N)**
Plants dark green to red or purplish; lower leaves yellowish, necrosis and leaf drop if severe; stalks short and slender	**Phosphorus (P)**
Leaves with localized mottling, chlorosis or necrosis; leaf margins cupped.	
Lower leaves with large and general chlorosis to necrotic spots, which evenually involve veins; leaves thick; new growth rosetted and stunted	**Zinc (Zn)**
Lower leaves with mottling or chlorosis mainly between veins or leaf margins.	
Lower leaves mottled or chlorotic between veins; sometimes coloration; necrotic spots if severe; stalks slender, bushy growth	**Magnesium (Mg)**
Lower leaves mottled or chlorotic between veins and at margins with leaf tips or margins scorched; stalks slender, bushy growth.	**Potassium (K)**
Young or upper leaves affected first; may spread to older leaves when severe.	
Terminal buds die; young leaves distorted and necrotic.	
Young leaves hooked, die back at tips and margins; distorted apex; stunted, darkened root tips	**Calcium (C)**
Young leaves darkened or light green at base; leaves thick and brittle and die back from base or twisted; lateral branches grow, then die; flowers and fruits abort	**Boron (B)**
Terminal buds remain alive but become chlorotic or wilted.	
Young leaves without chlorosis, also wilted or rolled, leaves drop; tips die back or tips weak	**Copper (Cu)**
Young leaves with chlorosis or necrotic spots; not wilted.	
Leaves with chlorotic or necrotic spots.	
Necrotic spots large or irregular; new growth rosetted and stunted	**Zinc (Zn)**
Necrotic or chlorotic spots small and interveinal; veins remain green, also possibly on older leaves	**Manganese (Mn)**
Leaves only chlorotic with no necrotic spots	
Veins remain green; overall yellowing to interveinal chlorosis	**Iron (Fe)**
Veins and blades chlorotic, overall yellowing on older leaves when severe	**Sulfur (S)**

Chlorotic = yellowing; necrotic = brown, dead areas; interveinal = between the veins.

Source: D.W. Reed. 1993. *General Horticulture Laboratory Manual.*

and for soilless growing media high in sphagnum peat moss or composted bark, 5.6 to 6.2. These intermediate pH ranges allow sufficient levels of all the micronutrients to be sufficiently soluble and available for absorption, without causing deficiencies or toxicities. Maintaining the optimum growing media pH is addressed in Chapter 4 on alkalinity, pH, and acidification.

Micronutrient fertilizers

Inadvertent micronutrient sources and problems

In the old days, micronutrient deficiencies were a lot less common. Very small quantities of micronutrients are required by plants and the amount needed was often satisfied by contamination from other sources. Potential sources of micronutrients are low grade insoluble fertilizers, growing media components (especially soil and composted materials), water (especially surface water), and fungicides. In fact, a common recommendation to alleviate a deficiency of heavy metals is to use one of the heavy metal containing fungicides. Zineb contains zinc, maneb contains manganese, ferbam contains iron, and Bordeaux mixture contains copper.

In modern production systems, everything is becoming much more refined. We use highly soluble pure fertilizers for liquid and slow release fertilizer programs. Growing media are almost entirely soilless; many lack even composted components. Growers put more emphasis on improved water quality, and even purified water is sometimes used. When some of the tropical foliage plant producers in the Rio Grande Valley switched from surface water to reverse osmosis water on selected salt sensitive crops, a multitude of disorders appeared that we had never observed before. Most turned out to be micronutrient deficiencies or imbalances that hadn't occurred before because plants had obtained micronutrients from surface water.

Current production methods are more similar to hydroponics than to soil culture. As such, the plant's entire nutritional requirements must be met with proper timing, quantities and proportions of nutrients. This is especially critical for micronutrients, where the difference between deficient, optimum, and toxic levels is often a fine line. The situation becomes very tricky in intense culture systems, such as plug culture.

This makes the case seem hopeless. Not at all. There are excellent micronutrient fertilizers available, which, when coupled with proper control of growing media pH, allow excellent micronutrient fertility programs.

Inorganic sources

The traditional form of micronutrients for iron, manganese, copper, and zinc are the sulfates. The trend in some of the more recently released micronutrient mixes is to use the oxide form of iron, manganese, copper, and zinc. Boron is usually applied as borate, and molybdenum is usually applied as molybdate. Borate and molybdate perform very well under a wide variety of production situations and are still the primary forms used. However, problems often arise with the use of sulfate and oxide forms of iron, manganese, copper, and zinc.

Iron, manganese, copper, and zinc are heavy metals and are very reactive. They can exist in many forms (multiple valences and as various hydroxides and oxides), only some of which are soluble. All tend to be oxidized by air to rather insoluble forms. One of the main factors that affects their solubility is pH. At acid pH, they tend to exist in forms that are more soluble, and at high or alkaline pH they tend to exist in very insoluble forms. Thus, they are excellent fertilizer sources if the pH of growing media is kept on the acid side. Since the recommended pH for soilless growing media high in sphagnum peat moss or composed bark is 5.6 to 6.2, they perform adequately if the recommended pH is maintained. A problem arises if the pH of growing media increases over time due either to use of basic fertilizers (mainly nitrates) or irrigation water with low alkalinity. When the pH of growing media approaches neutrality or above, the sulfates become less soluble and available for plant absorption, and deficiencies occur. There are two solutions to this problem. Correct the pH imbalance (see Chapter 4 on alkalinity, pH, and acidification) or use chelated forms of iron, manganese, copper, and zinc which are less sensitive to pH.

Fritted trace elements

Fritted trace elements are slow release forms of micronutrients that are impregnated into glass. The micronutrients are added to molten glass, which is then cooled, fractured, and ground to a fine powder. When the

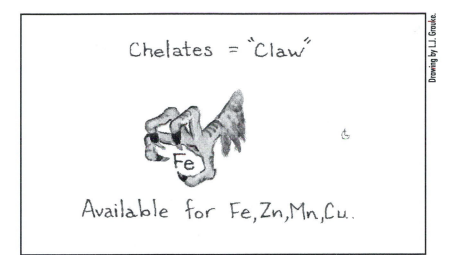

Fig. 8.1   The term chelate is derived from the Greek word meaning "claw." The large organic chelate molecule holds the heavy metal in the center by bonds called ligands. This keeps the micronutrient soluble and protected from precipitation by adverse conditions in growing media. (Drawing by L.J. Grauke)

frit is added to growing media, the micronutrients slowly leach out and become available to the plant. They can be formulated to release nutrients for up to a year. They are plagued with some of the same problems that occur with the use of sulfates. If a pH imbalance is present, then the micronutrients may become fixed as they are released from the frit and therefore are not as readily available to the plant. Frits are excellent slow release micronutrient sources if the proper pH is maintained. Frits are also available for macronutrients, mainly potassium.

Chelates

A chelate is a large organic molecule that contains heavy metals such as iron, copper, zinc, or manganese, or divalent cations such as calcium or magnesium. The word chelate comes from the Greek word "chele" meaning claw, because the micronutrient is protected inside a molecular claw (fig. 8.1). The large organic molecule portion of the chelate is called a chelating agent. The chelating agent holds the nutrient by ligand bonds and keeps the nutrient protected from factors that would cause its precipitation or oxidation. Since the chelates used are very soluble, the

Table 8.2 Stability of the various chelating agents used for iron, copper, zinc, and manganese[a]

Chelating agent	Stability of chelates and their formation constant			
	Iron	**Copper**	**Zinc**	**Manganese**
EDDHA[b]	35	25	18	—[g]
methyl-EDDHA[c]	—[h]	—[h]	—[h]	—[h]
DTPA[d]	29	23	20	17
EDTA[e]	27	20	17	15
HEDTA[f]	21	18	15	12
citrate	13	7	6	5
lignosulfonate	variable, low	variable, low	variable, low	variable, low

[a] The data are expressed as the formation constant of each chelate-micronutrient complex (M+L→ML); the higher the number the more stable the chelated micronutrient.

[b] ferric ethylenediaminedi-o-hydroxyphenylacetic acid.

[c] ferric methyl-ethylenediaminedi-o-hydroxyphenylacetic acid.

[d] ferric diethylenetriaminepentaacetic acid.

[e] ferric ethylenediaminetetraacetic acid.

[f] ferric hydroxyethylethylenediaminetriacetic acid.

[g] does not form a stable chelate with Mn.

[h] unknown, but probably close to EDDHA.

micronutrient remains soluble. The micronutrients boron and molybdenum cannot form chelates.

Table 8.2 lists commercially available chelating agents. The various micronutrient chelating agent combinations differ greatly in their stability. In general, the stability of the chelates is: EDDHA ≅ methyl-EDDHA > DTPA > EDTA > HEDTA >> citrate. The stability of the lignosulfonate chelates is variable and probably lower than the ranking above. The micronutrients also vary in how strongly they are chelated. They are generally in the order of: iron > copper > zinc > manganese.

Another factor to consider in choosing a chelate is its stability at various pH levels. Figure 8.2 demonstrates how pH affects the stability of the various chelates of iron in mineral soil. EDDHA is stable over the entire range of pH values that would be encountered in growing media

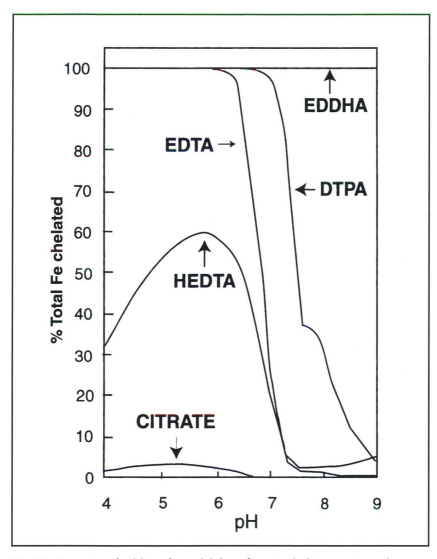

Fig. 8.2 Comparison of stabilities of several chelates of iron in soil solution at various soil pH levels. (*Source*: W.W. Norvel. 1971. *Micronutrients in Agriculture.*)

or soil. The chelating ability decreases sharply for DTPA above 7.0 to 7.5 and for EDTA above 6.0 to 6.5. HEDTA only develops about 50% chelating ability under slightly acid pH and looses its chelating ability above pH 6.0 to 6.5. Only about 5% of the citrate forms a chelate complex, and it is only stable at pH values below 6. Thus, at high or alkaline soil pH, the stability of the iron chelates is: EDDHA >> DTPA > EDTA >> HEDTA >> citrate.

Based on stability of the chelate and resistance to pH, EDDHA is by far the most effective chelate available. It can be used in any growing media or soil, regardless of pH, and field trials have shown it to be effective for up to a year. However, there is one problem. EDDHA also happens to be the most expensive fertilizer on the market, currently costing about $9 to $10 per pound ($20 to $22/kg). Because of this, it is only used when all else fails and even then only if the potential damage to the crop exceeds the fertilizer costs. Probably the only EDDHA application in greenhouse crops would be in ground beds that have a very high pH or content of calcareous soil (a soil high in carbonates and pH).

Most commercial products with chelates use either DTPA, EDTA, or HEDTA. They are more economical and just as effective if growing media or soil pH is near the recommended range. But even these chelates are expensive by fertilizer standards. DTPA costs about $4 per pound ($9/kg). Lignosulfonates are more economical and are used as chelating agents. They are effective if the pH is not out of balance. At pH values above 7, the lignosulfonate itself tends to precipitate even though it may still be chelating the micronutrient. The expense of chelates can be avoided if proper pH balance of growing media or soil is maintained, allowing the use of inorganic micronutrient sources.

For liquid fertilizer programs in areas where water has high pH and alkalinity, the use of chelated micronutrients is recommended. I visited a grower who was using inorganic micronutrients in his liquid feed program, and everything appeared fine because the inorganic micronutrients readily dissolved in the stock solution. However, over time the alkaline water caused the micronutrients to precipitate in the tank and water lines.

Micronutrient fertilizer mixes

There are numerous very effective and high quality micronutrient fertilizer mixes commercially available. Table 8.3 lists common micronutrient mixes and the fertilizer sources used in each. They are all very similar in their boron and molybdenum source. However, they vary greatly in their source for iron, copper, zinc, and manganese. Some only contain inorganic sources (Micromax, Esmigran), some contain a combination of inorganic and chelated sources (Woodace Perk, Clean Crop), and some contain only chelated sources (Complete Micro Blend, Compound 111).

The nutrient analysis (table 8.4) and recommended rates of application (table 8.5) vary greatly among commercial micronutrient mixes. Because of this, the amount of each micronutrient delivered to the plant also varies greatly. Table 8.6 gives the application rates of each micronutrient on an elemental basis for those mixes that are recommended for incorporation into growing media, and table 8.7 gives the micronutrients supplied on an elemental basis for those mixes that are recommended for incorporation into a liquid fertilizer program. Some of the differences between the mixes can be accounted for because chelated micronutrient sources are applied at a lower rate since they are more effective. Due to the variation between mixes, as shown in table 8.6, some products are excellent sources of one micronutrient but not another.

A grower should study the analysis, source of micronutrients, and ratio of micronutrients in the various products and match it to his crop needs and past problems. For example, if a grower has a problem with growing media pH increasing over time, then a chelated source might be advisable. If a crop has a past history of iron deficiency, then a formulation higher in iron might be advisable.

We conducted a trial one growing season where we tested about six different commercial micronutrient mixes at three different rates of application (0.5x, 1x, 1.5x label rate) on six tropical foliage plant species. In general, most of the treatments were better than the control, but no one commercial mix was superior, and the differences between rates were not consistent. No toxicities were observed. The take-home lesson is that plants grown under standard cultural practices are much more tolerant of differences in micronutrient nutrition than macronutrient nutrition (i.e., N, P, and K). Incorporating a micronutrient mix into a fertility program offers a relatively cheap insurance policy against possible micronutrient deficiencies

Micronutrient fertilizer rates

Micronutrient mix rates. The most common way to apply micronutrients is to incorporate micronutrient mixes in growing media. Table 8.5 gives the label rates of some of the commercial mixes; however, always follow the manufacturer's rate on the label. The rates for incorporation into growing

Table 8.3 Fertilizer sources used in commercial micronutrient mixes

Sources	Micromax[a]	ParEx Perk-SR[b]	Soluble Trace Element Mix[a]	Complete Micro Blend[c]	Esmigran[a]	Micromax Plus[d]
Iron						
ferrous sulfate	X	X	X			X
ferrous chloride					X	
iron oxide		X				
iron humate		X				
iron citrate						
iron lignosulfonate				X		
ferric EDTA						
ferric HEDTA						
ferric DTPA						
Manganese						
manganese sulfate	X		X		X	X
manganese oxide		X				
manganese ammonium phosphate		X				
manganese citrate						
manganese lignosulfonate				X		
manganese EDTA						
Zinc						
zinc sulfate	X		X		X	X
zinc oxide		X				
zinc ammonium phosphate		X				
zinc citrate						
zinc lignosulfonate				X		
zinc EDTA						

[a]The O.M. Scott & Sons Company, 14111 Scottslawn Rd., Marysville, OH 43041

[b]Vigoro Industries, P.O. 1272, 2121 SW Third St., Winter Haven, FL 33882-1272

[c]Ruffin, Inc., 500 East Trail, P.O. Box 940, Dodge City, KS 67801

[d]Platte Chemical Company, 150 South Main St., Fremont, NB 68025-5697

[e]W.A. Cleary Chemical Corporation, Southview Industrial Park, 178 Ridge Rd., Ste. A, Dayton, NJ 08810

Compound 111[a]	Scott Trace Element Package[a]	Clean Crop M-4 Mix[d]	Woodace Perk[b]	Soluble Trace Element Mix-HiMag[a]	Micro Booster Complex[c]	Extra Iron[e]
	X	X	X	X	X	X
	X		X	X		
					X	X
		X				
			X			
			X			
X						
		X	X	X	X	X
	X		X	X		
		X			X	X
X		X				
		X	X	X	X	X
	X		X			
		X			X	X
X		X				

Table 8.3   Continued

Sources	Micromax[a]	ParEx Perk-SR[b]	Soluble Trace Element Mix[a]	Complete Micro Blend[c]	Esmigran[a]	Micromax Plus[d]
Copper						
copper sulfate	X		X		X	X
copper oxide		X				
copper ammonium phosphate		X				
copper citrate						
copper lignosulfonate				X		
copper EDTA						
Boron						
sodium borate	X	X				X
boric acid			X	X	X	
Molybdenum						
sodium molybdate	X	X	X			X
ammonium molybdate					X	
molybdic acid						
ammonium dimolybdate						
molybdenum hydrozide				X		

media on a volume of growing media basis (per cubic yard) and surface area or bed basis (per 100 square feet [9.2 m^2]) are given. The surface area rate can also be used as a postplanting drench. The solution rate (per 100 gallons/500 l) is used as a postplanting container drench. Two of the micronutrient mixes (Soluble Trace Element Mix, Compound 111) are designed to be added to a constant liquid fertilizer program. The rates are based on adding a certain amount of micronutrient mix per 100 ppm of N used in the fertilizer program. This supplies a constant micronutrient feed at a very reduced rate to satisfy the plant's micronutrient requirement (table 8.7). For comparison, the concentration of micronutrients in Hoagland's hydroponic solution is also given in the table.

Individual micronutrient rates. Table 8.8 gives recommended rates for each of the micronutrients for greenhouse floriculture crops, and table 8.9 gives

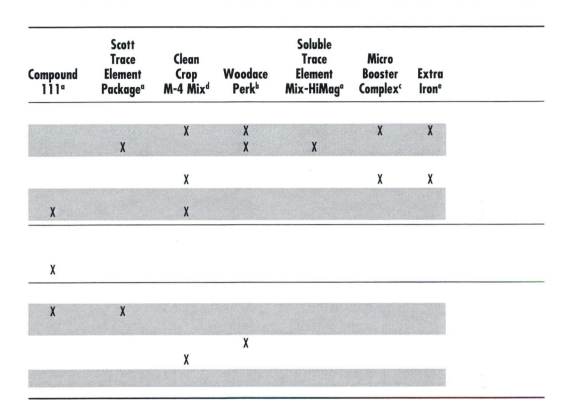

Compound 111[a]	Scott Trace Element Package[a]	Clean Crop M-4 Mix[d]	Woodace Perk[b]	Soluble Trace Element Mix-HiMag[a]	Micro Booster Complex[c]	Extra Iron[e]
		X	X		X	X
	X		X	X		
		X			X	X
X		X				
X						
X	X					
			X			
		X				

rates for tropical foliage plants. What if a grower wants to use a fertilizer source that is not listed in the tables, or if a grower wants to use a rate similar to a micronutrient mix he has had success with? No problem. Rates can be calculated from the information in tables 8.3, 8.6, and 8.7. Tables 8.6 and 8.7 give the elemental rates supplied by the various micronutrient mixes. From this elemental basis and from knowing the fertilizer sources contained in the product (table 8.3), you can calculate a rate of application for the fertilizer source used. *However, this can only be done for those micronutrient mixes that supply each micronutrient as a single source.* All you need to know is the percent analysis of the fertilizer source you plan to use. For example, if the elemental rate of iron desired is 1.9 ounce/cubic yard (conversion formula 1.9×37.1 g/m³) (table 8.6), the fertilizer source to be used is ferrous sulfate (table 8.3), and the percent analysis of elemental iron in ferrous sulfate is 20% (obtained from

Table 8.4 Nutrient analysis of commercial micronutrient mixes

Commercial micronutrient mixes	Micronutrient analysis						Macronutrient analysis					
	% Fe	% Mn	% Zn	% Cu	% B	% Mo	% N	% P₂O₅	% K₂O	% S	% Ca	% Mg
Micromax[a]	12.0%	2.5%	1.0%	0.50%	0.100%	0.0500%				15%		
ParEx Perk-SR[b]	10.0%	4.0%	2.0%	0.50%	0.100%	0.0080%	4%	25%				4.0%
Soluble Trace Element Mix[a]	7.5%	8.0%	4.5%	3.20%	1.350%	0.0400%				14%		
Complete Micro Blend[c]	5.0%	1.0%	1.0%	0.05%	0.020%	0.0050%	4%			10%		0.5%
Esmigran[a]	2.0%	0.5%	1.0%	0.30%	0.020%	0.0006%				1%		
Micromax Plus[d]	1.8%	0.3%	0.1%	0.07%	0.015%	0.0070%		4%		2%	16%	8.0%
Compound 111[a]	1.5%	0.7%	0.1%	0.11%	0.232%	0.0242%						0.7%
Scott Trace Element Package[a]	9.0%	2.6%	1.3%	0.50%	—	0.0260%				11%	6%	
Clean Crop M-4 Mix[d]	2.0%	2.0%	3.0%	1.00%	—	0.1000%				4%		
Woodace Perk[b]	15.0%	3.2%	2.7%	0.68%	—	0.0020%				15%		2.5%
Soluble Trace Element Mix-Hi Mag[a]	8.0%	3.0%	1.0%	0.50%	—	—				9%		12.0%
Micro Booster Complex[c]	6.0%	0.5%	1.0%	0.50%	—	—				6%		
Extra Iron[e]	4.0%	1.0%	1.0%	0.25%	—	—				5%		

[a]The O.M. Scott & Sons Company, 14111 Scottslawn Rd., Marysville, OH 43041

[b]Vigoro Industries, P.O. 1272, 2121 SW Third St., Winter Haven, FL 33882-1272

[c]Ruffin, Inc., 500 East Trail, P.O. Box 940, Dodge City, KS 67801

[d]Platte Chemical Company, 150 South Main St., Fremont, NB 68025-5697

[e]W.A. Cleary Chemical Corporation, Southview Industrial Park, 178 Ridge Rd., Ste. A, Dayton, NJ 08810

Table 8.5 Recommended label rates of commercial micronutrient mixes[a]

Commercial micronutrient mixes	Rates		
	lbs. per cu. yd.	lbs. per 100 sq. ft.	per 100 gal.
Micromax	1–1.5	2–3	
Micromax Plus	10	18.5	
Esmigran	3–6	0.3–0.4	
Soluble Trace Element Mix		0.125	0.5 lbs.
Complete Micro Blend	1–2	2–3	
Woodace Perk	2	3	
Scott Trace Element Package	1.25	2.7	
Clean Crop M-4 Mix		1–3 oz.	
Extra Iron		0.15–0.3 oz.	2 qt.
Soluble Trace Element Mix - HiMag	1.5–3	0.15	
Micro Booster Complex			1 gal.

[a]Always read the label and use the rate published by the manufacturer.

the label of the product you have chosen to use), then the generalized equation is:

$$\text{fertilizer rate} = \frac{\text{elemental rate}}{\%\text{ analysis}/100}$$

and for this specific example:

$$\text{ferrous sulfate} = \frac{1.9 \text{ oz. iron (Fe)/cu. yd.}}{0.2}$$

$$\text{ferrous sulfate} = 9.5 \text{ oz./cu. yd.} => 9.5 \times 37.1 \text{ g/m}^3 \cong 350 \text{ g/m}^3$$

You could use this method if you have been using a particular micronutrient mix and have been satisfied with its results, but need to add a supplement of one or more individual micronutrients.

As you can see from tables 8.6, 8.7, 8.8 and 8.9, there is no standard application rate for each individual micronutrient. This is because micronutrient fertilizers vary in their elemental concentrations and the

Table 8.6 Conversion of label rates of commercial micronutrient mixes to an elemental basis for each micronutrient[a]

| | Rates of application on an elemental basis at the high and low label rate | | | | | | | | | | | |
| | Fe | | Mn | | Zn | | Cu | | B | | Mo | |
	low	high	low	high	low	high	low	high	low	high	low	high
Micronutrient mix					Ounces of each micronutrient supplied per cubic yard							
Micromax	1.9	2.9	0.4	0.6	0.16	0.24	0.08	0.12	0.016	0.024	0.008	0.012
Micromax Plus		2.9		0.5		0.16		0.112		0.024		0.0112
Esmigran	1.0	1.9	0.2	0.5	0.48	0.96	0.144	0.288	0.0096	0.0192	0.0003	0.0006
Complete Micro Blend	0.8	1.6	0.2	0.3	0.16	0.32	0.008	0.016	0.003	0.006	0.0008	0.0016
Woodace Perk		4.8		1.0		0.90		0.20				0.0006
Scott Trace Element Package		1.8		0.5		0.26		0.10				0.0052
Soluble Trace Element												
Mix-HiMag	1.9	3.8	0.7	1.4	0.24	0.48	0.12	0.24				
					Grams of each micronutrient supplied per cubic yard							
Micromax	53	82	11.3	17.0	4.5	6.8	2.3	3.4	0.45	0.68	0.227	0.340
Micromax Plus		82		14.2		4.5		3.2		0.68		0.318
Esmigran	28	54	5.7	14.2	13.6	27.2	4.1	8.2	0.27	0.54	0.009	0.017
Complete Micro Blend	23	45	5.7	8.5	4.5	9.1	0.2	0.45	0.09	0.17	0.023	0.045
Woodace Perk		136		28.9		25.5		5.7				0.017
Scott Trace Element Package		51		14.2		7.37		0.28				0.147
Soluble Trace Element												
Mix-HiMag	54	107	19.8	39.7	6.8	13.6	3.4	6.8				

[a]This information can be used to compare the various mixes for their nutrient delivery capacity or as a guide for the rate to apply individual micronutrients.

Table 8.7 Final concentration of micronutrients in fertilizer solutions with soluble micronutrient mixes incorporated[a]

Fertilizer	Micronutrient ppm at 100 ppm N liquid feed					
	Fe	Mn	Zn	Cu	B	Mo
Soluble Trace Element Mix	0.25	0.27	0.15	0.11	0.05	0.001
Compound 111	0.25	0.13	0.012	0.019	0.04	0.004
Hoagland's solution	up to 2.79	0.494	0.046	0.019	0.497	0.008

[a]Soluble micronutrient mixes are incorporated at recommended label rates with a liquid feed program. Hoagland's solution, which was developed for hydroponics, is given for comparison.

rate of application, i.e., some products are two- or three-fold higher or lower compared to other products when comparing the actual amount of each micronutrient added. Yet most of the mixes and recommended rates for individual micronutrients function quite adequately in avoiding deficiency and toxicity.

Special considerations for individual micronutrients

Iron. Iron is probably the most frequently applied micronutrient. There are two major reasons for this. First, iron is required in the greatest quantity of the micronutrients. Second, iron's unique chemistry makes it easily fixed and unavailable in growing media or soil. Iron is one of the most abundant elements on earth, and it is seldom lacking in any soil. Soilless growing media may have a true deficiency, but even in soilless growing media there is often ample iron present from inadvertent sources. The problem is that at pH values of above approximately 4.5 there is barely enough soluble iron in soil to satisfy plant needs, regardless of the amount of total iron present. The situation is not as critical in soilless growing media because of the high organic matter content. High organic matter increases iron solubility because it forms more soluble complexes.

Following are several factors that can upset this delicate equilibrium of iron in the soil or growing media and induce an iron deficiency (many of these factors can also cause a deficiency of the other heavy metals manganese, copper, and zinc).

Table 8.8 Application rates for individual micronutrients for greenhouse floriculture crops

Micronutrient and source[a]	% Analysis	Bench drench		Container drench		yields ppm
		oz./100 ft²	g/100 ft²	oz./100 gal	g/100 gal	
Iron ferrous sulfate	20%	16	454	50	1418	750
Boron sodium tetraborate (borax)	11%	0.5	14.2	1	28.4	8.3
boric acid	17.5%	0.6	17.0	0.65	18.4	8.5
Manganese manganese sulfate	33%	0.25–0.5	7.1–14.2	0.1	2.8	2.4
Zinc zinc sulfate	23%	0.25–0.5	7.1–14.2	0.1	2.8	1.7
Copper copper sulfate	25%	0.25–0.5	7.1–14.2	0.1	2.8	1.9
Molybdenum ammonium molybdate	54%			0.025	0.7	1.0
sodium molybdate	46.6%			0.029	0.8	1.0

[a]Iron, manganese, zinc, and copper are commercially available from most companies that sell micronutrient mixes (see table 8.3) as chelates of EDDHA, DTPA, HEDTA, or EDTA. Apply according to the recommended rate on the label.

Source: Adapted from *1981 Cornell Recommendations for Commercial Floriculture Crops Part I. Cultural Practices and Production Programs.*

1. **High pH:** High pH causes the formation of insoluble iron oxides and hydroxides.
2. **High bicarbonate and carbonate:** High bicarbonate and carbonate in the soil solution interfere with the absorption of iron by plants. Calcareous soils are naturally high in carbonates. This is in addition to the adverse impact of high pH, which accompanies high carbonates.
3. **Excessive lime application:** Lime is made from carbonates, hydroxides, and oxides of calcium and magnesium. Thus, excessive lime application can cause the pH to increase as well as

Table 8.9 Application rates for individual micronutrients for tropical foliage plants

Micronutrient and source[a]	Soil drench oz./100 sq. ft.	Soil incorporation oz./cu. yd.	Foliar spray oz./100 gal.
Iron ferrous sulfate	0.3	1.0	16
Boron sodium tetraborate (borax)	0.003	0.01	0.16
Manganese manganese sulfate	0.15	0.5	8
Zinc zinc sulfate	0.1	0.3	4.8
Copper copper sulfate	0.03	0.1	1.6
Molybdenum sodium molybdate	0.001	0.001	0.16
	g/100 sq. ft.	g/cu. yd.	g/100 gal.
Iron ferrous sulfate	8.51	28.4	454
Boron sodium tetraborate (borax)	0.09	0.28	4.5
Manganese manganese sulfate	4.25	14.18	227
Zinc zinc sulfate	2.84	8.51	136
Copper copper sulfate	0.85	2.84	45
Molybdenum sodium molybdate	0.03	0.03	4.5

[a] Iron, manganese, zinc, and copper are commercially available from most companies that sell micronutrient mixes (see table 8.3) as chelates of EDDHA, DTPA, HEDTA, or EDTA. Apply according to the recommended rate on the label.

Source: Joiner, 1981, *Foliage Plant Production*.

increase the carbonate content of growing media, both of which can induce an iron deficiency.

4. **Gradual increase in growing media pH:** Factors that cause growing media pH to increase over time can induce a progression towards iron deficiency. This is mainly due to the use of basic fertilizers, which are fertilizers that contain nitrate as the nitrogen source, or the use of alkaline irrigation water.

5. **Excessive phosphate fertilization:** Phosphate precipitates iron, thus overfertilization with phosphorus can induce an iron deficiency, even under acid pH. This occurs in field-grown palms.

6. **Excessive manganese, copper, or zinc fertilization:** The heavy metals compete with iron for absorption by plants. Usually this is only prevalent with manganese, where overfertilization with manganese can induce an iron deficiency.

7. **Root damage:** Anything that causes root damage can exaggerate an iron deficiency.

8. **Excessive watering:** Persistent waterlogged conditions in a ground bed or container interferes with the roots' ability to absorb iron and can exaggerate an iron deficiency. Complete waterlogging, however, can cause an iron toxicity (see toxicity below).

9. **Plant species:** Some species are iron efficient, which means they can absorb iron from the soil even if the pH is high and the iron is mostly insoluble. These plants actually secrete their own chelates, reducing compounds and/or hydrogen for soil acidification from their roots. These species almost never exhibit an iron deficiency. Other plants are iron inefficient, which means they can only absorb iron when the pH is in balance and there is adequate soluble iron in the soil. An example would be acid-loving plants, such as azaleas.

Even though there is usually plenty of iron in the soil and some soil-less growing media, iron toxicity can result if the pH gets too low. Overuse of chelated iron can cause a buildup of soluble iron in the soil and cause an iron toxicity. Iron toxicity appears in some bedding plants under these conditions. The symptoms are a bronze coloration, brown speckling, or small necrotic spots on leaves of bedding plants such as marigold and geranium.

Waterlogged conditions can also cause iron toxicity because under anaerobic conditions the more soluble ferrous form of iron predominates. This is a major problem in rice, but I have not seen reports of it being a problem in horticultural plants such as water lilies, rushes or reeds, which are grown under waterlogged conditions.

There are many iron fertilizers on the market. The sulfates and oxides work well if the proper pH balance is maintained. The chelates are excellent if the pH is high or in liquid feed programs with alkaline irrigation water. There are many other iron fertilizers on the market of variable origin (such as acidified mining residue, extracted or liquefied plant extracts, humates of unknown composition, etc.) and they should be tested in your production situation before wide use.

Manganese. Next to iron, manganese is the micronutrient required by plants in the largest quantity. The deficiency symptoms of manganese are very similar to those of iron. They both cause interveinal chlorosis (yellowing between the veins) of the young leaves. The major difference is that an iron deficiency causes interveinal chlorosis, which may progress to an almost white appearance, whereas manganese causes interveinal chlorosis, which usually progresses to a necrosis (brown, dead areas) on the young leaves. Many manganese deficiencies are likely diagnosed as iron deficiencies, and vice versa. If one misdiagnoses a manganese deficiency as a iron deficiency and adds iron fertilizers, it will make the problem worse, because the added iron competes with manganese in absorption by the roots. Conversely, excessive manganese fertilization can induce iron deficiency. Manganese deficiency can be induced by many of the same factors mentioned in the section on iron.

Boron. Boron is present in many irrigation water sources (see Chapter 2 on water analysis). If a water analysis reveals less than 0.3 ppm boron, then boron fertilizer should be used. If a water analysis reports between 0.3 to 1.5 ppm boron, then supplemental boron in the fertilizer program may not be needed. In such a case, choose a micronutrient mix that lacks boron (table 8.3). If the water analysis reports more than 1.5 ppm boron, then toxicities might occur. On tropical foliage plants it is recommended that irrigation water contain less than 0.5 ppm boron. Boron toxicity causes a variety of symptoms, but it often appears as a marginal chlorosis or necrosis of older leaves. Boric acid is used as a roach poison, and boron toxicity cases have been reported when boric acid was put out as a pesticide around container crops grown on a solid-bottomed bench.

Zinc. Zinc is required by plants in rather small quantities. Zinc deficiencies are uncommon on greenhouse crops. Deficiencies are more common on fruit trees grown in alkaline soil. It is a major problem on pecans in west Texas. When a zinc deficiency does occur on an ornamental crop, it can often be corrected by using a zinc-containing fungicide, such a Zineb.

Copper. Copper is a micronutrient where too little causes a deficiency and a little bit too much can cause a toxicity. Copper is required by plants in small amounts, so a deficiency seldom is encountered. When a deficiency does occur, it can often be corrected by using a fungicidal spray containing copper, such as Bordeaux mixture.

Molybdenum. Molybdenum is required by plants in the smallest quantities of all the nutrients, therefore a molybdenum deficiency is rare in most crops. A deficiency is usually associated with a pH below about 6.0. Molybdenum is less soluble at low pH or in peat-lite type growing media that are completely soilless and lack composted amendments. Poinsettias are particularly susceptible to molybdenum deficiency.

Fluoride. Fluoride is not a micronutrient, but it does cause toxicity in some foliage plants and greenhouse crops such as Easter lily. Fluoride toxicity can be avoided by: 1) maintaining growing media pH between 6.0 to 6.5; 2) avoiding superphosphate, which contains high fluoride; 3) leaching perlite, which contains high levels of leachable fluoride; and 4) avoiding water high in fluoride. Fluoride levels of 1 ppm or less usually are not damaging (see Chapter 2 on water testing and analysis), but some particularly sensitive plants may be damaged by levels as low as 0.25 ppm. The level of fluoride added to municipal water supplies usually is not damaging.

References

Biernbaum, J., W. Carlson, C. Shoemaker, and R. Heins. 1988. Low pH causes iron and manganese toxicity. *Greenhouse Grower*. March, 92–97.

Broschat, T., and H. Donselman. 1985. Causes of palm nutritional disorders. In *Proceedings*, Florida State Hort. Soc. 98:101–102.

Chase, A.A., R.T. Poole and C.A. Conover. 1980. Fungus or fluoride—A constant dilemma. *Foliage Digest* 3(5):5–7.

Cornell recommendations for commercial floriculture crops, Part 1. Cultural Practices and Production Programs. 1981. Cooperative Extension, New York State College of Agriculture and Life Sciences, Ithaca, N.Y.

Joiner, J.N., ed. 1981. *Foliage plant production.* Englewood Cliffs, N.J.: Prentice-Hall, Inc.

Lang, H.J., C.L. Rosenfield, and D.W. Reed. 1990. Response of *Ficus benjamina* and *Dracaena marginata* to iron stress. J. Amer. Soc. Hort. Sci. 115(4):589–592.

Ludwick, A.E., ed. 1990. *Western fertilizer handbook—horticultural edition.* California Fertilizer Assoc. Danville, Ill.: Interstate Publ., Inc.

Marschner, H. 1986. *Mineral nutrition of higher plants.* Orlando, Fla.: Academic Press.

Mengel, K., and E.A. Kirkby. 1978. *Principles of plant nutrition.* Bern, Switzerland: International Potash Institute.

Norvell, W.W. 1971. Equilibria of metal chelates in soil solution. In *Micronutrients in Agriculture.* J.J. Mortvedt, P.M. Giordano, and W.L. Lindsay, eds. Madison, Wisc.: Soil Science Soc. of Amer., Inc.

Poole, R.T., and C.A. Conover. 1986. Boron and fluoride toxicity of foliage plants. *Foliage Digest* 9(3):3–5.

Reed, D.W. 1993. *General horticulture laboratory manual.* Edina, Minn.: Burgess International Group, Inc.

Rosenfield, C.L., D.W. Reed, and M.W. Kent. 1991. Dependency of iron reduction on development of a unique root morphology in *Ficus benjamina. Plant Physiol.* 95:1120–1124.

Chapter 9

Tissue Analysis and Interpretation

Richard P. Vetanovetz

Tissue analysis, or foliar analysis, is an analytical technique that measures the nutrient content of plant tissue. It is useful in assessing the nutrient status of a crop by helping the grower determine if proper uptake of essential plant nutrients has occurred. Tissue analysis measures the nutrient content of the tissue analyzed at that particular time, like a snapshot. But tissue analysis will not predict what *will* occur. To determine if the plant has received proper nutrition, the grower compares nutrient levels found in the plant tissue to published sufficiency ranges for the specific plant type being analyzed. Tissue analysis is an effective tool for monitoring nutritional programs. Tissue analysis combined with routine growing media analysis allows the grower to judge the effectiveness and efficiency of a fertilization program. Using analysis results, the grower can anticipate the potential for problems and rectify the situation. Tissue analysis is useful for diagnosing plant abnormalities caused by deficiencies or excesses of essential or nonessential elements, or contaminants. Although tissue analysis is widely available through analytical labs, it is not used routinely, and when it is, tissue analysis is typically used when there is a problem. At times it is used incorrectly, resulting in wasted time and money.

This chapter will provide the basic concepts behind tissue analysis and offer guidelines about proper sampling and interpretation of results. It is not intended as a set of hard rules. Since plants are a dynamic system, thinking of the concepts and guidelines that follow as absolutes will only lead to frustration. This chapter is not intended to be a comprehensive treatment of how to use tissue analysis to diagnose nutritional disorders. Refer to other texts for information on nutritional disorders.

A list of texts providing information on diagnostics can be found at the end of this chapter. Most commercial or university labs offer technical assistance that can help answer questions regarding tissue analysis. The information that follows is written with the assumption that most growers will have plant tissue analyzed by an analytical laboratory specializing in this service.

Nutrient uptake, movement, and retention in the plant

To understand how to interpret tissue analysis data or to determine the proper tissue sampling strategy, it is important to know and understand how plant nutrients and other elements move and accumulate in the plant. This understanding is especially important when diagnosing suspected nutritional disorders of a crop. Nutrients and contaminants commonly found in plants are listed in table 9.1.

Nutrient uptake and leaf content

Nutrients are taken up by plant roots and translocated to the rest of the plant (leaves, stems, flowers, fruit, etc.) for use as part of the plant's structure or biochemical systems.

Generally, there is a direct relationship between the amount of nutrients taken up and the growth of a plant. Figure 9.1 shows this concept. When tissue content of a nutrient is very low, plant growth usually is low and the nutrient is considered to be deficient. With severe deficiency, growth may be curtailed or the plant may die. As the uptake and tissue content of a nutrient increases, the plant's growth also increases, often with mild deficiency symptoms. As the tissue level of the nutrient further increases, deficiency symptoms disappear and growth may continue to improve until the maximum growth rate is

Table 9.1 Plant nutrients and contaminants commonly found in plants[a]

Elements	Symbol	Mobility	Tissue concentration %[b]	Tissue concentration ppm[b]	Relative number of atoms in the plant[b]
Macronutrients					
Nitrogen	N	mobile	1.5		1,000,000
Phosphorus	P	mobile	0.2		60,000
Potassium	K	mobile	1.0		250,000
Calcium	Ca	immobile	0.5		125,000
Magnesium	Mg	mobile	0.2		80,000
Sulfur	S	mobile	0.1		30,000
Micronutrients					
Iron	Fe	immobile		100	2,000
Manganese	Mn	immobile		50	1,000
Zinc	Zn	immobile		20	300
Copper	Cu	immobile		6	100
Boron	B	immobile		20	2,000
Molybdenum	Mo	immobile		0.1	1
Contaminants					
Sodium[c]	Na	mobile			
Chlorine[c]	Cl	mobile			
Aluminum	Al	immobile?			

[a]These values are considered adequate for plant growth.

[b]Adapted from E. Epstein. 1972. *Mineral Nutrition of Plants: Principles and Perspectives.*

[c]Considered plant nutrients for some plants in very small amounts but considered contaminants here.

attained. Thereafter, there is an ample supply of the particular nutrient. This is called the luxury range. If tissue levels of a nutrient continue to increase, however, the nutrient can reach a level that may become toxic, causing growth disorders.

This is the basis for sufficiency ranges (fig. 9.1). The "acceptable range" or "normal range" is when a nutrient concentration in the plant is adequate for plant growth. Below the normal range, the nutrient is

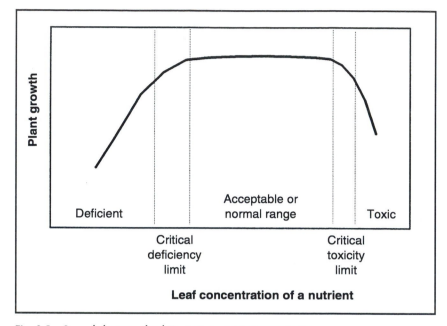

Fig. 9.1   General plant growth relative to tissue nutrient concentration.

inadequate for acceptable growth. The lowest boundary below the acceptable range is called the critical limit or more precisely the "critical deficiency limit." At levels above the acceptable range, the nutrient is thought to be more than adequate. The upper boundary of the acceptable range is usually called the "critical toxicity limit." The degree to which a nutrient is above or below the acceptable range determines the severity of the deficiency or toxicity symptoms.

Different plant types vary in their nutrient requirements and response to plant nutrients or contaminants. This is why recommended acceptable ranges often differ among plant types.

Nutrient movement

Nutrients are categorized by their ability to retranslocate or remobilize throughout the plant. Nutrients or nonessential elements are taken up by plant roots and translocated to areas of growth via the transpirational stream. Some elements can also move downward in the plant or move from slow growing areas to areas of more rapid growth. This is called remobilization. Remobilization of nutrients is especially important in certain circumstances such as seed germination, when there is an insufficient or interrupted supply of nutrients (pulse feeding or errors in fertilization), during reproductive stages (flowering or fruiting) or before leaf drop (deciduous plants in the fall).

Mobile nutrients. Mobile nutrients are capable of remobilization. Mobile nutrients can move out of older leaves (called sources) and into new leaves (called sinks) in areas of growth. They move less often from newer leaves down to older leaves or roots. Basically, mobile nutrients move to the area of the plant with the greatest nutrient demand—the strongest sink. The strongest sinks in the plant are fruit > flowers > new growth and leaves > stems > old leaves > roots.

Mobile nutrients are: nitrogen (N), phosphorous (P), potassium (K), magnesium (Mg), and sulfur (S). Plants will often demonstrate lower levels of mobile nutrients in older or more mature leaves. Deficiency symptoms or abnormalities appear in the older leaves first, since nutrients are moving out of the older, mature leaves (sources) to growing leaves or plant parts (sinks). An exception is sulfur. It is mobile, but it is slow to respond. A sulfur deficiency may appear on the new leaves first and then progress to the old leaves as sulfur is mobilized from the older to younger leaves.

Two classic examples of deficiency of mobile nutrients are magnesium deficiency of poinsettia and nitrogen deficiency of chrysanthemum. Magnesium deficiency of poinsettia is typically evident on older, mature leaves. With chrysanthemum, nitrogen deficiency may become evident on more mature leaves, especially before flowering, which can be a significant sink.

Immobile nutrients. Immobile nutrients do not move out of organs once they arrive at their final destination. While this is an oversimplification, on a whole plant basis this is seemingly the way it works. Therefore, if supply of a particular nutrient from growing media is stopped, lower nutrient levels or deficiency symptoms typically appear on younger growth first. Sometimes they appear on intermediate growth. However, if a particular immobile nutrient is not interrupted and is provided at levels more than necessary for a particular plant type, it can accumulate in older, more mature leaves.

The immobile nutrients are: calcium (Ca), iron (Fe), manganese (Mn), zinc (Zn), copper (Cu), boron (B), and molybdenum (Mo).

Three examples of this phenomena are iron/manganese toxicity of geraniums or marigolds, calcium deficiency of poinsettia, and boron deficiency of pansy. Symptoms of iron/manganese toxicity typically appear on lower older leaves first and are a result of iron accumulating in these plant parts. Manganese can also cause toxicity, and symptoms also show up in the lower leaves first. Calcium deficiency symptoms will typically show up on new growth first, as often seen in the culture of poinsettia stock plants. Boron deficiency is usually evident on new growth when supply of this nutrient is low or uptake is inhibited.

Antagonisms

Following plant uptake and translocation, nutrients interact within the plant. A concept that is important to note is the phenomena of antagonisms. Certain elements, when in high enough tissue concentrations, will suppress the activity of other elements in lesser tissue concentrations. This same phenomena also occurs for the uptake of plant nutrients. Antagonistic effects usually become important when nutrients are near the deficiency range. This is where nutrient "balance" becomes critical in interpretation of analysis data.

Table 9.2 lists some common antagonisms. Notable antagonisms include potassium and magnesium and potassium and nitrogen. An example would be a potassium-induced magnesium deficiency in poinsettia. A tissue analysis may show magnesium levels in the sufficient or normal range (but close to the critical deficiency level), but if potassium levels are very high, then a magnesium deficiency can occur. In this case, potassium is suppressing the utilization of magnesium so that magnesium becomes deficient.

There are no known guidelines for interpreting the effects of antagonisms for specific floral crops. Confer with university or technical laboratory service personnel for guidance in interpreting analytical data if you suspect a nutrient antagonism.

Table 9.2 List of common antagonisms between nutrients

If excessive in media or tissue[a]	May cause deficiency of
Nitrogen	Potassium
Potassium	Nitrogen, calcium, magnesium
Phosphorus	Iron, zinc, copper
Calcium	Magnesium, boron
Magnesium	Calcium, potassium
Sodium	Potassium, calcium, magnesium
Manganese	Iron, molybdenum
Iron	Manganese
Zinc	Manganese, iron
Copper	Manganese, iron, zinc
Molybdenum	Copper

[a] High levels of these elements in root media or tissue may cause deficiencies of the nutrients listed in the right column, especially if their tissue levels are borderline or low.

Sampling strategies ━━━━━━━━━━

Before sampling tissue, develop a strategy. There are two sampling strategies: sampling for routine analysis and sampling for diagnosing nutritional problems.

Sampling for routine analysis

Use this strategy when no problems exist and you plan to employ tissue analysis as an integral part of a sound nutritional management program.

First, determine the crop to be tested. Ideally, every crop is tested. However, in most greenhouses this is impractical, except in greenhouse or nursery establishments that grow only one or two plant types where this would be a relatively easy decision.

Next, determine how many times to sample the crop during the cropping cycle. This will be contingent on the sampling interval (the time between samplings) that you desire. The typical sampling interval is about two to four weeks, with three weeks the most common. Some labs offer specific sampling guidelines that suggest when to sample. The type and age of tissue from each plant to be sampled must be considered. Following are suggestions:

One or two crop scenario. Poinsettias and pot chrysanthemums will be used as examples. Consider a poinsettia crop with several cultivars and finishing times. As first priority, choose the difficult cultivars or the ones that tend to develop a particular abnormality. Next in priority, choose the most widely grown and economically important cultivar. If the most widely grown crop is also the one that typically has the most problems, then the answer is clear where to place your sampling emphasis. The third priority is to sample crops that differ in timing (i.e., mid-November flowering, mid-December flowering), placing emphasis on the main cropping period. Take samples about every three weeks.

For growers who grow on a regular rotation, such as pot chrysanthemums, choose the difficult cultivar(s) and the most important cultivator(s) in each flowering period. Again, sample about every three weeks (two to four weeks). If a weekly rotation is followed and sampling is conducted on every crop rotation, data is generated quickly. Once a sufficient data base is developed, place emphasis on only the difficult-to-grow cultivar(s) while spot checking the easier ones. If less frequent crop rotations are used, sample the appropriate cultivar(s) from each rotation.

Multiple crop scenario. A similar scenario holds for the multicrop grower. For example, consider a bedding plant grower who grows a multitude of varieties in one year. A possible sampling schedule would be to sample from three plant types, including two crops with frequent problems and one major crop. Geraniums, vinca, and impatiens are examples. Be certain to test varieties of each plant type that historically develop nutritional problems since routine tissue analysis may help uncover the causes and lead to corrective action. Since bedding plants are not in production for very long, one or two tests are usually made at about two to four week intervals. Sampling should be repeated for every crop rotation.

Sample the correct plant part. The next step in the sampling strategy is to determine what plant part and age will be sampled. For routine analysis, leaf tissue is sampled. Sampling plant parts other than leaf tissues should be avoided unless the lab recommends the grower do so. For most crops, the leaf age sampled is the most recently matured leaf, which is the first leaf from the apex that has expanded to its matured size.

Sample enough leaf tissue to provide a sufficient sample size for the type of analysis to be performed. Typically, analytical laboratories ask for about 1 ounce (25 to 30 g) fresh weight (not including leaf petioles) for each sample. This is 24 to 75 leaves, depending on leaf size.

Nutrient content varies with leaf age. Unfortunately, the selection of the most recently matured leaf is somewhat subjective, so it is very important to determine what you consider is the most recently matured leaf and then be consistent in sampling.

Select samples from various plants throughout the crop. Avoid taking samples from plants in close proximity to each other. It is best to sample from at least five different plants from various areas, then combine the samples to form a composite sample for analysis. This gives a better average of the crops' nutritional status.

The time of sampling is important: Sample plants at the same time of day and the same length of time following fertilization or watering. When in doubt, always err on the side of consistency.

Sampling for nutritional problems

Use comparative sampling strategies when diagnosing plant problems. Comparing nutritional levels of affected plants to those of healthy plants often leads to a more accurate diagnosis of the problem. The strategy will depend on whether or not there are affected and unaffected plants present and the location on the plant where the abnormality is evident.

Where affected and unaffected plants are present. Take leaf samples from the area on the plant where the abnormality exists. Take a similar sample of leaves from plants that are unaffected or where the abnormality is not as severe. Make certain the plants are the same type (species and cultivar or variety) and same age. Take a minimum of two tissue samples. To improve the data obtained and the chance of a proper diagnosis, two additional samples can be taken from unaffected leaves of the affected plant and a sample from the same location on the unaffected plant. This sampling strategy identifies differences in nutrient levels within the plant as well as between plants to be assessed.

Always take growing media samples from the affected plants as well as the unaffected plants.

For example, assume a pot chrysanthemum grower has a cultivar where the older leaves developed necrotic spots, and affected and unaffected plants are present. The grower should sample the older, affected leaves from affected plants and take another sample of the older leaves from unaffected plants. Additionally, the grower may wish to sample the younger leaves from the affected and unaffected plants. Differences in nutrient levels may be more apparent in the younger leaves, or other causes may become evident.

Where all plants of the crop are affected. There is no alternative but to sample only affected plants in this case. Take samples from both new and old growth. Sample the most recently matured leaves of the new growth. Since there are no unaffected plants to be used for comparison, the results must be compared to values published in sufficiency tables, which are discussed later. Interpreting this information may require experienced individuals.

Investigating the total crop history. The above examples provide guidance when using tissue analysis to identify suspected nutritional disorders. But realize that tissue analysis alone will not lead to the correct answer. Tissue analysis may need to be coupled with companion growing media, water, and fertilizer solution analysis. Also consider all cultural practices and environmental conditions the crops were exposed to during production. Only then may the cause of a problem become apparent. This may seem like a lot of work, but in many cases, it pays off even when time is of the essence.

Plugs. There are no published acceptable ranges for plugs. It's best to use comparative sampling. Depending upon the size of the plug, usually entire shoots are sampled. It is probably most practical to use tissue analysis when initially setting up nutritional programs and for diagnostic purposes.

Sampling part of the same leaf. Many nutritional disorders cause a chlorosis (yellowing) or necrosis (brown, dead) of the margin or tip of the leaf. Separating the affected leaf edges or leaf tips from the rest of the leaf blade for separate tissue analysis is commonly recommended. Usually such a test indicates an accumulation or lack of a suspect element in the affected part of the leaf. This may occur with nutrients such as boron or iron. Again, comparative sampling is important to successfully interpret data when this technique is used.

Cut flower crops

The protocols for sampling certain cut flower crops are different than those outlined above.

Roses. Select a flowering stem with a calyx that is cracking and beginning to show color. Sample the two uppermost five-leaflet leaves.

Carnations. The following scenario assumes a pinched crop. Prior to the first pinch, collect the fourth and fifth leaf pairs from the base of the main stem. Following the first pinch, continue to sample from the fourth and fifth leaf pairs at the base of the main stem until seven new leaf pairs develop on the emerging lateral shoots, then sample from the fifth and sixth leaf pairs at the base of the lateral shoots. Thereafter, continue to sample from the fifth and sixth leaf pairs from the base of the lateral shoots.

Orchids. Sample the second leaf from the tip of young shoots.

Anthurium. Sample the leaf just below the most recently harvested bloom.

Handling the sample

Proper sample handling is critical to obtain data that is representative of the crop. Many labs will provide tissue sampling kits with directions for proper handling. Carefully follow the directions from the lab you intend to use. The keys to success are as follows:

When taking leaf tissue, always remove the petioles. Collect enough tissue for each sample, which usually is about 1 ounce (25–30 g) of material. An ounce is usually about 24 to 75 leaves, depending on leaf size. Use the smaller number for large-leafed plants, such as poinsettia and geranium, and the larger number for small-leafed plants, such as azalea.

Assure that the leaf material is not contaminated with soil, growing media, or fertilizers. If necessary, remove residues with water, preferably distilled water, but tap water will suffice. Blot each leaf dry before packing for shipment. Never ship wet leaves.

Tissue samples must be placed in paper bags or a suitable container to keep the samples from getting moldy. *Do not put samples in plastic bags.* Many times plant material becomes unusable if not packaged properly. Do not send whole plants unless the lab you intend to work with instructs you to do so. Clearly identify the sample bags with your internal labeling system to enable you to trace the crop, time, greenhouse location, etc. Include basic information such as your address and phone number and what nutrients you want measured. Many labs have information sheets to complete for background information needed on the crop and its production history.

It is best to use an overnight courier service to send the samples. This assures your samples will get to the lab promptly and in good condition.

Decontamination practices. Many times leaf tissue is contaminated. You can decontaminate samples yourself if the testing lab does not do so. Soil and potting media are the typical sources, although foliar applications of fertilizers or pesticides containing nutrients may cause contamination. In most cases, rinsing leaves with distilled or deionized water will reduce soil or water soluble fertilizer contamination. Residues from pesticides (especially copper- or manganese- containing fungicides) or foliar feed solutions designed to stick to foliage may not be decontaminated sufficiently by water. In these cases, it is probably best to ignore analysis results of certain nutrients which were applied foliarly.

Some researchers recommend washing tissue in a mild detergent solution before analysis, especially if Fe or Al are to be assayed. Apparently, dust can be a significant contaminant of these elements, which can result in analyses showing elevated levels. It is not clear how necessary it is for growers to utilize this particular technique on a routine basis. However, it would be prudent to use this technique if Fe and Al levels are of primary interest. For decontamination, dip the leaves in a 0.1% detergent solution, gently agitate for about 15 seconds, rinse with distilled or deionized water, then blot the leaves dry. Do not use detergents that contain phosphorus or boron.

Table 9.3   Methods of elements analysis used to quantify plant nutrients or contaminants[a]

Method	Elements	Comments
Combustion then chromatography	N, S	Burns tissue; resultant gas analyzed by gas chromatographic techniques.
Combustion then chemiluminescence	N, S	Burns tissue; resultant gas reacted to cause a chemiluminescent (light) effect that is qualified.
Kjeldahl	N	Utilizes wet digestion and measurement of N via titration or other wet chemical methods.
Flame photometry	K, Na, Ca and Mg	Special procedures necessary to remove effect of interfering ions.
Atomic absorption spectrophotometry	Ca, Cu, Fe, K, Mn, Zn	More precise and sensitive for some elements compared to flame photometry.
Inductively coupled plasma emission spectrophotometry (ICP)	Al, B, Ca, Cu, Fe, K, Mg, Mn, Mo, Na, P, Zn, S	Sensitivity and precision varies compared to atomic absorption spectrophotometry and flame photometry. S can be measured using vacuum attachment, although sensitivity and precision is considered low and requires wet digestion.

[a]Adapted from J.B. Jones, B. Wolf, and H.A. Mills. 1991. *Plant Analysis Handbook*

The risk of any decontamination procedure (other than rinsing with water) is the possibility of adding nutrients to the leaf from the detergent used or of removing nutrients from the leaf by leaching. Nutrients such as potassium or boron are easily leached. Ask the analytical lab or your state extension specialist before you decide to use a specific decontamination procedure.

Analysis

Laboratories use various techniques to analyze tissue and measure the nutrient content (table 9.3). Usually the plant tissue is first dried in a drying oven and then ground and screened through a fine-mesh screen to obtain a uniform particle size. Thereafter, the treatment of the dried tissue will be dictated by what elements are to be measured.

Kjeldahl, combustion/chromatographic techniques

Typically, some of the prepared sample is used to quantify the total nitrogen content using a Kjeldahl, modified Kjeldahl or combustion/chromatographic technique. The remainder of the sample is usually dry ashed and then solubilized using a nitric acid solution. The resulting solution is then analyzed for various elements using flame emission, atomic absorption, or inductively coupled plasma emission (ICP) spectrophotometry. The ICP technique is becoming more widely used because of its sensitivity, precision, and freedom from many interferences. Use of ICP can also quantify many nutrients rapidly and precisely. The advantages that ICP provides are recognized by the many testing labs currently using ICP for analysis of soils, growing media, and plant tissue.

Tissue testing of plant sap

Another testing technique, tissue testing of plant sap, measures nutrients in extracted cellular sap from the plant petioles, leaves, or stems. The tissue is placed in a device similar to a garlic press, and the sap is squeezed out. The technique is usually confined to measuring nitrate (NO_3^-), phosphate (PO_4^{-3}), or potassium (K^+). Usually, colorimetric techniques or test papers are used for measuring these elements. Although more precise hand-held electronic measuring devices are currently being researched for use with this technique, sap testing is reported to be more qualitative than quantitative. This technique has been researched for use in quickly assessing the nutrient status of field crops (grains, vegetables, fruit, and nuts). Little information is available on its use for ornamental crops. Sap testing indicates whether or not the crop requires additional fertilization. This is important for growers of field crops where fertilization adds a considerable expense. It is not clear at this point what place sap testing has for the greenhouse grower, since other nutrients that are quantified by analytical labs are also important (i.e, Ca, Mg, Fe).

Those who wish to learn more about sap testing can refer to the *Plant Analysis Handbook*, by J. Benton Jones Jr., B. Wolf, and H.A. Mills.

Interpreting results

After results of a tissue analysis are received, they must be interpreted. Usually the analytical data are evaluated against sufficiency ranges developed for the particular plant analyzed.

Sufficiency ranges

When evaluating analytical results, the nutrient levels that have been determined must be compared to published sufficiency ranges for that particular nutrient. See tables 9.4 and 9.5 for sufficiency ranges used by the Ohio Agriculture Research and Development Center and Scotts Testing Laboratory as guidelines. Some analytical labs identify categories of ranges (table 9.4: deficient, low, sufficient, high, excess) while others simply identify minimum and maximum levels (table 9.5). Ranges differ somewhat between analytical labs. Regardless, there is always a sufficient, normal, acceptable, or optimum range identified. Ranges are developed through research and especially through experience. Lab-generated data is often compared to crop performance in a client's greenhouse, and from these data, labs can identify which nutrient level results in optimum growth. Sufficiency ranges differ between different plant types and may even differ for different varieties or cultivars within a plant type—so it is often recommended that when you use a specific lab for tissue analysis, you also use the lab's sufficiency ranges for interpretation. These ranges are often included with the tissue analysis report (table 9.6).

Note that when using tissue analysis on a routine basis, it is not absolutely imperative that the crop's nutritional status be within a sufficient or normal range. Many times a particular nutrient may be slightly low or high, but the crop looks great. Nutrient balance is also important, which demonstrates the shortfall in solely using sufficiency levels (see the section on antagonisms, p. 202). Therefore, making dramatic modifications in a nutritional program from one tissue analysis is not advisable. On the other hand, if known nutritional problems have occurred in the past for a particular crop with respect to a particular nutrient, this can signal a need to change the fertility program. Charting your results over time will give better information as to whether a specific nutrient is being over or undersupplied.

Table 9.4 Interpretive ranges including sufficiency or normal ranges (dry weight basis) for selected plant types[a]

	Greenhouse azalea					Carnation				
	Deficient	Low	Sufficient	High	Excess	Deficient	Low	Sufficient	High	Excess
Nitrogen(%N)	<1.8	1.81–1.99	2.00–3.00	3.01–3.20	>3.21	<3.0	3.01–3.19	3.20–5.20	5.21–5.25	>5.26
Phosphorus (%P)	<0.15	0.16–0.19	0.20–0.50	0.51–0.64	>0.65	<0.50	0.06–0.19	0.20–0.30	0.31–0.35	>0.36
Potassium (%K)	<0.75	0.76–0.99	1.00–1.60	1.61–1.70	>1.71	<2.00	2.01–2.49	2.50–6.00	6.01–6.10	>6.11
Calcium (%Ca)	<0.20	0.21–0.44	0.45–1.60	1.61–1.75	>1.76	<0.60	0.61–0.99	1.00–2.00	2.01–2.10	>2.11
Magnesium (%Mg)	<0.17	0.18–0.19	0.20–0.50	0.51–0.55	>0.56	<0.15	0.16–0.24	0.25–0.50	0.51–0.55	>0.56
Manganese (ppm Mn)	<30	31–49	50–300	301–400	>401	<30	31–99	100–300	301–799	>800
Iron (ppm Fe)	<50	51–59	60–150	151–175	>176	<30	31–49	50–150	151–155	>156
Boron (ppm B)	<20	21–30	31–100	101–200	>201	<25	26–29	30–100	101–699	>700
Copper (ppm Cu)	<5	6	7–15	16–20	>21	<5	6–9	10–30	31–35	>36
Zinc (ppm Zn)	<15	16–25	26–60	61–69	>70	<15	16–24	25–75	76–80	>81

	Chrysanthemum					Geranium				
	Deficient	Low	Sufficient	High	Excess	Deficient	Low	Sufficient	High	Excess
Nitrogen(%N)	<3.50	3.51–3.99	4.00–6.50	6.51–6.75	>6.76	<2.40	2.41–3.29	3.30–4.80	4.81–4.85	>4.86
Phosphorus (%P)	<0.20	0.21–0.29	0.30–1.00	1.01–1.20	>1.21	<0.24	0.25–0.39	0.40–0.67	0.68–0.70	>0.71
Potassium (%K)	<3.50	3.51–4.49	4.50–6.50	6.51–6.60	>6.61	<0.70	0.71–2.49	2.50–4.50	4.51–4.60	>4.61
Calcium (%Ca)	<0.50	0.51–0.99	1.00–2.00	2.01–2.10	>2.11	<0.77	0.78–0.80	0.81–1.20	1.21–1.25	>1.26
Magnesium (%Mg)	<0.14	0.15–0.34	0.35–0.65	0.66–0.70	>0.71	<0.14	0.15–0.19	0.20–0.52	0.53–0.55	>0.56
Manganese (ppm Mn)	<20	21–29	30–350	351–800	>801	<9	10–41	42–174	175–800	>801
Iron (ppm Fe)	<50	51–59	60–500	501–525	>526	<60	61–69	70–268	269–280	>281
Boron (ppm B)	<20	21–49	50–100	101–124	>125	<18	19–29	30–280	281–290	>291
Copper (ppm Cu)	<5	6–24	25–75	76–80	>81	<5	6	7–16	17–700	>701
Zinc (ppm Zn)	<15	16–50	15–50	51–55	>56	<6	7	8–40	41–45	>46

Foliage plants (general)

	Deficient	Low	Sufficient	High	Excess
Nitrogen(%N)		<1.49	1.50–3.50	>3.50	
Phosphorus (%P)		<0.19	0.20–0.40	>0.41	
Potassium (%K)		<0.99	1.00–4.00	>4.01	
Calcium (%Ca)		<0.49	0.50–2.00	>2.01	
Magnesium (%Mg)		<0.29	0.30–0.80	>0.81	
Manganese (ppm Mn)		<30	31–300	>300	
Iron (ppm Fe)		<49	50–150	>151	
Boron (ppm B)		<25	26–100	>101	
Copper (ppm Cu)		<5	6–20	>21	
Zinc (ppm Zn)		<15	16–50	>51	

Other crops (general)

	Deficient	Low	Sufficient	High	Excess
Nitrogen(%N)	<2.50	2.50–3.00	3.1–6.00	6.10–6.50	>6.51
Phosphorus (%P)	<0.15	0.16–0.20	0.20–0.50	0.51–0.65	>0.66
Potassium (%K)	<0.90	0.91–0.99	1.00–3.00	3.01–4.50	>4.51
Calcium (%Ca)	<0.50	0.51–0.99	1.00–1.50	1.51–2.00	>2.01
Magnesium (%Mg)	<0.15	0.16–0.29	0.30–0.75	0.76–1.00	>1.01
Manganese (ppm Mn)	<30	31–50	51–300	301–500	>501
Iron (ppm Fe)	<50	50–60	61–150	151–350	>351
Boron (ppm B)	<25	26–30	31–100	101–200	>201
Copper (ppm Cu)	<5	6–10	11–20	20–24	>25
Zinc (ppm Zn)	<14	15–20	21–50	51–75	>76

Rose

	Deficient	Low	Sufficient	High	Excess
Nitrogen(%N)	<3.00	3.01–3.49	3.50–4.50	4.51–5.00	>5.01
Phosphorus (%P)	<0.10	0.11–0.19	0.20–0.30	0.31–0.34	>0.35
Potassium (%K)	<1.80	1.81–1.99	2.00–2.50	2.51–3.00	>3.01
Calcium (%Ca)	<0.90	0.91–0.99	1.00–1.50	1.51–1.60	>1.61
Magnesium (%Mg)	<0.25	0.26–0.27	0.28–0.32	0.33–0.35	>0.36
Manganese (ppm Mn)	<30	31–69	70–120	121–250	>251
Iron (ppm Fe)	<50	51–79	80–120	121–150	>151
Boron (ppm B)	<30	31–39	40–60	61–400	>401
Copper (ppm Cu)	<5	6–7	7–15	15–17	>18
Zinc (ppm Zn)	<15	16–19	20–40	41–50	>51

Poinsettia

	Deficient	Low	Sufficient	High	Excess
Nitrogen(%N)	<3.00	3.01–3.99	4.00–6.00	6.01–7.30	>7.31
Phosphorus (%P)	<0.20	0.21–0.29	0.30–0.65	0.66–0.70	>0.71
Potassium (%K)	<1.00	1.01–1.49	1.50–3.50	3.51–4.00	>4.01
Calcium (%Ca)	<0.50	0.51–0.69	0.70–2.00	2.01–2.20	>2.21
Magnesium (%Mg)	<0.20	0.21–0.39	0.40–1.00	1.01–1.25	>1.26
Manganese (ppm Mn)	<40	41–79	80–300	301–650	>651
Iron (ppm Fe)	<50	51–99	100–300	301–500	>501
Boron (ppm B)	<20	21–29	30–100	101–200	>201
Copper (ppm Cu)	<2	3–5	6–10	11–15	>16
Zinc (ppm Zn)	<15	16–24	25–60	61–70	>71
Molybdenum (ppm Mo)	<0.50	0.51–1.00	1.01–5.00	5.01–9.00	>9.01

[a]Data was generated from the Research Extension and Analytical Laboratory (REAL) at Ohio Agriculture Research and Development Center (OARDC), Wooster, Ohio. Adapted from J.C. Peterson. Monitoring and Managing Nutrition, Part IV–Foliar Analysis. Ohio Florists Association Bulletin No. 632. June 1982.

Table 9.5 Sufficiency or normal ranges (dry weight basis) of tissue concentrations for nutrients of various plants

	Geranium		Lily		Chrysanthemum		Poinsettia		Rose		Foliage plants		Bedding plants	
	min	max	min	max	min	max	min	max	min	max	min	max	min	max
N %	3.3	4.8	2.8	3.44	4.5	6	4.0	6.0	2.5	4.0	2.0	3.5	3.5	4.6
P %	0.4	0.67	0.22	0.5	0.35	1.15	0.2	0.6	0.2	0.35	0.15	0.7	0.4	0.67
K %	2.5	4.5	1.86	3.06	3.5	8	1.5	3.5	1.9	2.7	1.0	4.5	2.0	8.8
Ca %	0.81	1.2	0.65	1.33	1.5	4.0	0.7	2.0	1.3	1.8	0.5	2.0	1.0	2.6
Mg %	0.2	0.52	0.54	1.0	0.5	1.5	0.3	1.0	0.3	0.4	0.3	1.0	0.4	1.9
Fe ppm	70	268	37.7	148	100	300	100	250	70	130	50	300	90	250
Mn ppm	42	174	29.7	92.1	195	260	60	275	80	160	50	300	75	300
B ppm	30	280	27.7	70.4	25	200	30	100	50	60	30	100	50	175
Zn ppm	8	40	20.3	54.6	15	100	25	60	20	50	25	200	25	100
Cu ppm	7	16	4.33	8.3	6	20	5	15	6	9	10	40	5	28
Mo ppm	0.2	5	0.7	10.2	0.2	5	1	5	0.5	5	0.2	5	0.2	5

	Cabbage		Celery		Conifer		Corn		Cucumber		Tomato		General average	
	min	max	min	max	min	max	min	max	min	max	min	max	min	max
N %	3.5	5.5	2.5	4	1.3	3.5	2.7	3.5	2.5	4.5	4.0	5.5	3.5	5.5
P %	0.18	0.38	0.30	6.00	0.20	0.60	0.20	0.5	0.4	0.8	0.3	1.0	0.35	1.0
K %	2.0		4.0	7.0	0.7	2.5	1.5	2.5	6.0	10.0	4.0	7.0	2.0	8.8
Ca %	0.8	3.0	0.4	3.0	0.3	1.0	0.3	1.0	1.5	3.0	0.9	5.0	0.8	3.0
Mg %	0.2	1.5	0.2	0.5	0.1	0.3	0.2	0.5	0.5	1.5	0.4	1.5	0.2	1.5
Fe ppm	60	200	40	200	60	200	30	200	100	420	100	250	60	200
Mn ppm	50	200	200	300	100	250	18	100	100	300	40	300	50	200
B ppm	16	200	30	60	20	100	5	25	40	120	30	100	30	150
Zn ppm	30	150	20	50	30	150	15	50	90	150	30	150	30	150
Cu ppm	5	25	5	10	4	20	2	20	7	10	5	25	5	25
Mo ppm	0.5	5	0.5	5	0.25	5	0.1	2	0.8	3.3	0.15	5	0.5	5

Source: Scotts Testing Laboratory, 6656 Grant Way, Allentown, PA 18106

Table 9.6   Example of tissue analysis test results issued by a commercial laboratory showing measured values and normal ranges[a]

Sample Questionnaire Response: Sample date: 10/20/94   **Crop type:** Poinsettia
Leaves sampled: Recently matured   **Sampled type:** Routine

Element tested	Symbol	Units	Results	Interpretation	Normal range
Total Nitrogen	N	%	4.61		4–6
Phosphorus	P	%	0.354		0.2–0.6
Potassium	K	%	2.89		1.5–3.5
Calcium	Ca	%	2.08	high	0.7–2.0
Magnesium	Mg	%	3.72	high	0.3–1.0
Boron	B	ppm	42.3		30–100
Iron	Fe	ppm	155.0		100–250
Manganese	Mn	ppm	94.8		60–275
Copper	Cu	ppm	6.31		5–15
Zinc	Zn	ppm	49.7		25–60
Molybdenum	Mo	ppm	3.66		1–5
Aluminum	Al	ppm	54.2		—
Sodium	Na	ppm	131.0		—

[a]Scotts Testing Laboratory, 6656 Grant Way, Allentown, PA 18106. All rights reserved.

Nutritional charting

Nutritional charting refers to the technique of graphically representing the nutrient analysis data over time. Simply plotting the data for each nutrient on a graph each time an analysis is completed can help a grower evaluate if nutrients are decreasing or increasing in the plant. Figure 9.2 represents what a nutritional chart would look like for a particular crop. Because trends in nutrient content can then be anticipated with more accuracy, a grower can make better judgments about the fertility program. Nutritional charting is easy using commonly available computer spreadsheet programs.

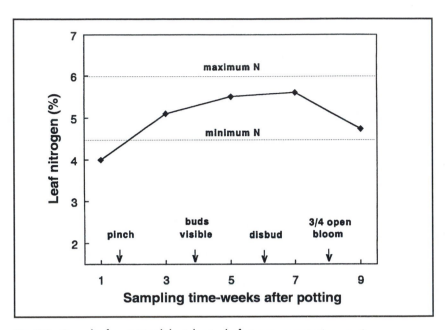

Fig. 9.2 Example of a nutritional chart showing leaf nitrogen concentration over time.

Interpretation when diagnosing nutritional disorders

Interpreting the results from tissue analysis can often be complex. This is where the "art" of interpretation comes in. Many factors are important to properly identify a problem. Plant type, culture, fertilizers used, and nutrient antagonisms affect interpretation. See fig. 9.3 and table 9.7 for a listing of common nutritional problems with interpretive comments.

The key is to first identify the problem. Is it a deficiency or toxicity of a particular nutrient? Interpretive keys (table 9.7) can help suggest the cause. Comparison of visual symptoms with analytical data can help identify the most probable cause of the disorder.

In summary, tissue analysis can be a powerful tool for the grower to use in fine-tuning or troubleshooting a nutritional program. The techniques used to analyze the nutrient content of plant tissue are very accurate, but this is of no value without proper sampling and interpretation of the results. When in doubt, seek advice from qualified experts who have experience in using tissue analysis to assure that you make correct management decisions.

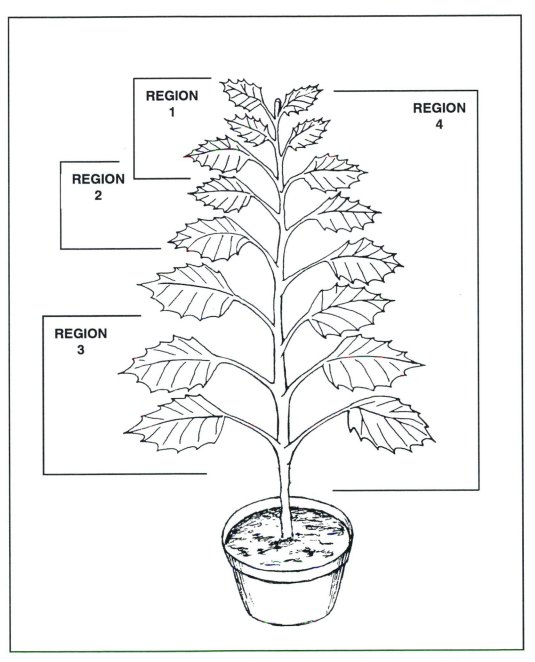

Fig. 9.3   Diagnostic nutritional regions. Refer to table 9.7 for explanation. Adapted from J.F. Knauss. 1988. Managing Crop Nutritional Stress. *Greenhouse Grower*. September.

Table 9.7   Diagnosis of common nutritional problems using symptom development and affected region of the plant[a]

Region on plant[b]	Type of problem	Nutrient	Typical leaf symptoms and other comments
1	deficiency	Fe	Interveinal chlorosis, may turn totally yellow to white with necrosis.
		Mn	Interveinal chlorosis, does not usually turn white and necrotic.
		Cu & Zn	Marginal chlorosis, becomes strap-shaped; leaf deterioration and collapse with shoot and root rot.
		B	New growth impaired, leaves reduced in size; multiple shoot development, pith necrosis, and shoot collapse.
		Ca	New growth with marginal chlorosis, some necrosis, distortion, leaf and shoot collapse, 'wimpy' appearing leaves.
		Mo	New growth showing whiptail appearance; shoot development impaired.
2	deficiency	Mo	Symptoms most common in poinsettias in this region of the plant. Leaves display marginal chlorosis and distortion; may show progressive deterioration with necrosis and collapse.
	toxicity	Fe	Symptoms may show in seedling geraniums in this region instead of expected region 3. Fe excess probably occurred simultaneously in affected tissue during rapid growth phase.
3	deficiency	Mg	Marginal chlorosis, often inverted "V" pattern. Chlorotic area enlarges to encompass total leaf. Unusually limited leaf necrosis, if any.
		K	Similar to Mg deficiency initially, but chlorotic tissue often turns necrotic.
		P	Darker green tissue often turns purple to reddish. Problem rarely occurs in mixes containing vermiculite with nutrient charge containing P.
	toxicity	Fe	Initially chlorotic flecking or spots. Spots and flecks enlarge, coalesce, become reddish-brown to black with eventual leaf collapse.
		Mn	Similar to Fe toxicity. Both Fe and Mn may be implicated in same affected tissue.
		B	Chlorosis precedes ultimate necrosis. Leaf symptoms marginal at the tip or scattered within leaf laminae.
4	deficiency	N	Depending on environmental stress, plants may display chlorosis on older leaves or all over. Reduced leaf and plant size are common.
		S	Pale green to whitish green color. Rarely occurs.
	toxicity	Fe	Appears on cutting geraniums throughout the plant as small necrotic flecks, 0.5 to 3 mm in length. Symptoms most severe in older tissue.

[a]Adapted from J.F. Knauss. 1988. Managing Crop Nutritional Stress. *Greenhouse Grower*. September.

[b]See fig. 9.3 for location of various regions on the plant.

References

Bould. C., E.J. Hewitt, and P. Needham. 1984. *Diagnosis of mineral disorders in plants*. Vol 1. New York: Chemical Publishing.

Chapman, H.D., et al. 1966. *Diagnostic criteria for plants and soils*. Abilene, Tex.: Quality Printing Co.

de Kreij, C., C. Sonneveld, and M.G. Warmenhoven. 1987. Guide values for nutrient element contents of vegetables and flowers under glass. *Voedingsoplossingen glastuinbouw*. No. 15, March 1987.

Epstein, E. 1972. *Mineral nutrition of plants: principles and perspectives*. New York: John Wiley and Sons, Inc.

Jacques, D.J. 1992. *Sampling techniques for correcting nutritional disorders*. Scott's Testing Laboratory Technical Notes. LTN-101. Allentown , Penn.

Jones, J.B., B. Wolf, and H.A. Mills. 1991. *Plant analysis handbook*. Athens, Ga.: Micro-Macro Publishing, Inc.

Knauss, J.F. 1988. Managing crop nutritional stress. *Greenhouse Grower*. Vol 6(10) September.

Marschner, H. 1986. *Mineral nutrition of higher plants*. Orlando, Fla.: Academic Press.

Nelson, P.V. 1985. *Greenhouse operation and management*. 3rd ed. Englewood Cliffs, N.J.: Prentice-Hall.

———. 1985. Fertilization. *Bedding plants III*. J.W. Mastalerz and E.J. Holcomb, eds. Penn. Flower Growers.

Peterson, J.C. 1982. Monitoring and managing nutrition—Part IV—foliar analysis. 1982. *Ohio Florists' Association Bulletin*. No. 632. June.

Reuter, D.J., and J.B. Robinson. 1986. *Plant analysis—an interpretation manual*. Sydney, Australia: Inkata Press.

Scaife, A., and M. Turner. 1984. *Diagnosis of mineral disorders in plants*. Vol 2. J.B.D. Robinson, ed. New York: Chemical Publishing.

Sonneveld, C., and P.J. van Dijk. 1982. The effectiveness of some washing procedures on the removal of contaminants from plant tissue samples of glasshouse crops. *Comm. of Soil Sci. Plant Anal.* 13:487–496.

Winsor, G., and P. Adams. 1987. *Diagnosis of mineral disorders in plants*. Vol 3. J.B.D. Robinson, ed. London: Her Majesty's Stationary Office.

Chapter 10

Closed Production Systems for Containerized Crops:

Recirculating Subirrigation and Zero-Leach Systems

David Wm. Reed

Potential ground and surface water contamination has focused attention on the greenhouse and nursery industry. Regulations are already imposed in a number of states (i.e., California, Florida, Texas) because of the effects of nitrate pollution. Water use in greenhouses and nurseries is of increasing concern because of the amount of water, fertilizers, pesticides and other agricultural chemicals used, and the potential for point-source pollution of surface and ground water.

Nitrate pollution is a particular concern. Flowering potted plants, such as poinsettia and chrysanthemum, have been estimated to require rates as high as 4,000 lb. N/acre/year (724 kg/ha/year). Common fertilizer recommendations for greenhouse foliage plant crops are up to 2,500 lb. N/acre/year (450 kg/ha/year). These rates are many times the recommended rate of nitrogen application for field crops. Even though this represents a significant amount of point-source nitrate pollution, the total pollution potential is not that great due to the relatively small acreage of greenhouse and nursery production.

Water and fertilizer go hand-in-hand in commercial ornamental production. In constant liquid fertilization programs, fertilizer is added to the irrigation water. This is often called fertigation. If the fertilizer is top-dressed or incorporated into growing media, the irrigation water applied is the carrier for dissolved fertilizer within growing media. This water also leaches nutrients out of growing media. Cultural recommendations for producing greenhouse and nursery crops have not changed significantly within the last several decades. However, improved production practices will be necessary to prevent potential contaminants from reaching ground and surface water supplies.

Greenhouse and nursery growers are concerned that federal and state regulations could make it impossible to continue with current irrigation and fertilization practices. It is critical to the greenhouse and nursery industry that alternative irrigation and fertilization technologies be developed, evaluated, and implemented to reduce water and fertilizer consumption and to significantly reduce potential pollution of ground and surface waters.

Conventional production systems will be discussed first, and then we will look at systems designed for minimal to zero runoff.

Conventional production systems

Overhead irrigation

Overhead liquid fertilization by sprinklers or by hand-held hose is a common method of applying fertilizer. Using this practice, growers attempt to maintain an optimum nutrient level within growing media. Leaching heavily with fertilizer solution is sometimes used to prevent salts buildup while maintaining sufficient (usually supra-optimal) nutrient conditions for the crop. In recent years, leaching amounts have increased as relatively poorly drained soil mixes have been replaced with highly drained peat and bark-based soilless mixes. Overhead irrigation is inefficient in delivering water and nutrients to the plant because up to 70 to 80% of the solution applied may fall between the containers, never reaching the plant. Consequently, it is the combination of management practices that causes sprinkler irrigation with fertilizer solutions to be wasteful and to generate excessive runoff.

Drip irrigation

Drip irrigation is an effective method for both water and fertilizer application in greenhouse and nursery production. Advantages include improved water and fertilizer efficiency, better control of nutrient concentrations, better disease control, and greater flexibility in application timing. Drip irrigation can also lead to high leaching rates unless the irrigation system is carefully controlled. It is not uncommon to see leaching rates as high as 40 to 50% of the volume applied using this technique. Thus, if not managed properly, drip irrigation can be wasteful and generate excessive runoff.

Controlled-release fertilizers

Controlled-release fertilizers have shown promise in reducing fertilizer use in container ornamental production. Controlled-release fertilizers have also been used as a supplementary nutrient source in combination with liquid fertilization. A major disadvantage of controlled-release fertilizers is that once the fertilizer is applied, the rate of nutrients supplied is fixed until the nutrient's timed release is completed. Thus, the grower cannot change the nutrients supplied to meet varying environmental conditions and plant nutrient demand. Controlled-release fertilizers are also limited in their nutrient composition and may not contain a full complement of key essential elements needed by plants. As with drip irrigation, the use of controlled-release fertilizers can minimize runoff only if excessive leaching does not occur.

Systems designed for minimal to zero runoff

Production systems have been developed to minimize runoff. Two approaches can be taken. First, continue to use conventional production systems, but capture, retain, and recycle the runoff within the boundaries of the production facility. This is exemplified by whole greenhouse/nursery recycling systems. The second approach is to modify the production system for zero or minimal runoff. This is exemplified by both the zero-leach drip system and recirculating subirrigation systems.

Whole greenhouse/nursery recycling systems

Collecting and recycling irrigation water on the entire property is one management practice that minimizes discharge into the surface water system and to a lesser degree the ground water system. Recycling can be used with conventional irrigation systems or with the zero-leach and recirculating subirrigation technologies. Usually the greenhouse or nursery operation collects runoff in a basin located on the property but away from the production facility. While this method is excellent for catching and conserving surface water, it does not completely prevent percolation of fertilizer and other agricultural chemicals into the ground water before the solution is captured. This system is discussed in detail in Chapter 11 on recycling.

Zero-leach drip system

Modern drip systems that use emitters placed in each container can be modified to generate minimal or zero runoff. A zero-leach system requires that only enough solution is added to each container with each irrigation to saturate growing media and allow no leaching. This is achieved by placing microtensiometers in representative pots to sense the moisture tension in growing media. The tensiometers are connected to a computer. The computer constantly monitors the output from the tensiometer, and when a certain moisture tension is reached, the computer turns the irrigation system on. If the system is allowed to stay on long enough to generate leaching, then it functions as a conventional drip system. This system is discussed in detail as an irrigation technique in Chapter 1 on irrigation systems. If the system is turned off after just enough time has passed to allow saturation of growing media, but before any leaching occurs, then this system can function as a zero-leach or minimal-leach system. To accomplish this, you must know the water holding capacity of the container media and the time that it takes to deliver that volume of water through each emitter. From this you can calculate how long the irrigation system remains on. The computer turns the irrigation system off after this period of time. The tensiometer reading can also be used to turn the system off at a certain moisture tension. The goal is to keep the leaching fraction to a minimum.

Zero-leach systems have the potential for increased soluble salts buildup in growing media. Studies have shown that the greatest salts buildup is in the top layer, with a lesser degree of soluble salts buildup in the lower two-thirds of the container. However, all irrigation systems result in some degree of higher levels of soluble salts in the top layer of the growing media (fig. 10.4), but this is not always damaging because there are very few roots in that region. Few published studies identify the optimum cultural practices (fertility, media, water quality, container size, etc.) to use in a zero-leach system to allow maximum growth while keeping soluble salts buildup below damaging levels. A few studies have demonstrated that plant response in a zero-leach system and subirrigation system is very similar. Therefore, as a "best guess," you could adapt cultural practices given for ebb-and-flow subirrigation systems presented in the next section.

Recirculating subirrigation systems

Production systems using recirculating subirrigation eliminate runoff to surface and ground water. The containerized plants are placed in watertight trays, troughs, or molded concrete floors. Nutrient solution is pumped in to a depth of an inch (2.5 cm) or so and allowed to sit for enough time to saturate the growing media by capillary action. The unabsorbed solution is drained back to a storage tank. The cycle is repeated when another irrigation is needed. The solution is replaced as it is used, thus no runoff occurs. This is the only true closed production system available for containerized crops. In reality, any excess nutrients or salts leave with the crop.

Types of recirculating subirrigation systems

Subirrigation systems are designed to deliver water and fertilizer solutions directly to the root zone or to the bottom of the container where the solution moves up into the container by capillary action.

Costs

All of the recirculating subirrigation systems are rather expensive. The complete system supplies the bench or growing surface, water delivery system, and fertilizer delivery system. In addition, each must have the appropriate plumbing, storage tanks, and manual, electronic or computer control system. Table 10.1 gives a rough cost comparison between

Table 10.1 Cost comparison of various subirrigation systems compared to a conventional drip system on metal benches[a]

Production system	Approximate cost (per sq. ft.)
Conventional drip system on metal benches	$3 to $4.25
Trough system	$2.50 to $4
Ebb-and-flow flooded floor system	$2 to $3.50
Ebb-and-flow tray system	$5 to $7

Source: Ball 1991 and Biernbaum 1993.

[a] Costs are approximate as of the early 1990's, and can vary greatly between suppliers and modifications customized to each greenhouse operation.

the various systems. When compared to a conventional drip system on metal benches, the costs of subirrigation systems fall within the same range. Decreased labor, water and fertilizer costs, increased crop uniformity, and production efficiency may offset the higher costs of subirrigation systems. Current or future regulations relative to runoff also may be deciding factors in choosing a recirculating subirrigation system.

Systems for noncontainerized plants

Nutrient film technique (NFT). In this technique, plants are seeded, rooted, or transplanted into rock wool, oasis or foam cubes, or perforated containers containing growing media. The blocks are set in sloped troughs down which nutrient solution continuously flows at a depth of about one-eighth inch (0.3 cm). The nutrient solution is collected and recirculated. The roots are not confined to the containers and often grow out into the flowing nutrient solution.

Rock wool culture. This is a system where plants are rooted into pots or bags of rock wool which are then irrigated in troughs, similar to NFT, or with drip tubes. Nutrient solution is applied with enough frequency to keep the rock wool moist and the solution may not be recirculated. Neither of these techniques is designed for growing containerized crops, so they will not be discussed here.

Systems for containerized plants

The most common subirrigation systems are the ebb-and-flow, trough, and capillary mat systems.

Ebb-and-flow system. In the ebb-and-flow tray system, watertight trays are placed on top of conventional greenhouse benches and containerized plants are placed in the trays (fig. 10.1).

In the ebb-and-flow flooded floor system, often simply called **flooded floor** system, concrete is poured to form watertight bays (fig. 10.2). In each system either the trays or floors are sloped and grooved to allow drainage and collection of nonabsorbed solution. In both the tray and floor systems, containerized plants are flooded to about an inch (2.5 cm) or so in depth, allowed to absorb the solution by capillarity for a few minutes, then the solution is drained back to storage tanks. The process is repeated when plants require water.

Trough culture. Trough culture has some of the properties of NFT and some of the properties of ebb-and-flow (fig. 10.3). Plants are grown in conventional containers with conventional growing media. The containers are placed in sloped troughs on top of and running the length of the greenhouse benches. Nutrient solution is added at the high end and allowed to flow down the trough. The solution is absorbed into the containers by capillarity, and the remaining solution is collected into storage tanks. The solution is recirculated when plants need water.

Capillary mat system. Containerized plants are placed on flat-topped benches covered with an absorbent mat (similar to the foam mats placed under home carpeting). The mat is watered, and the water moves into the containers by capillary action. Since the capillary mat system usually is not designed for collection and recirculation of nonabsorbed solution, it will not be discussed further.

The ebb-and-flow tray, ebb-and-flow flooded floor, and the trough systems are ideally suited for containerized plants and for recirculation of nutrient solution. They are the systems most commonly used by the industry, so only these three systems will be discussed in greater detail.

(A) Pre-formed trays placed on top of movable metal benches.

(B) Tray being flooded through inlet/outlet valve. When the pump is turned off, water flows back to the storage tank through the same inlet/outlet valve. (Photographs courtesy of Rough Brothers Inc., Cincinnati, Ohio).

Fig. 10.1 Ebb-and-flow tray system.

Fig. 10.2   Ebb-and-flow flooded floor system.

Fig. 10.3   Trough system.

Ebb-and-flow tray system

Advantages and disadvantages. The ebb-and-flow tray system (fig. 10.1), also called ebb-and-flood, is the most common recirculating subirrigation system for growing containerized plants in the U.S. greenhouse industry. It offers many advantages:

- simple engineering and controls
- system can be totally automated
- labor savings
- lower incidence of foliar diseases compared to overhead irrigation
- decreases water use by one-half or one-third
- decreases fertilizer use by one-half or one-third
- system is better suited to plants grown in small containers than drip tubes
- produces more uniform crops
- eliminates runoff if solution is recirculated.

Ebb-and-flow has the following disadvantages:

- more expensive
- best suited to growing one crop and container size per zone
- may cause salinity problems if not managed properly
- may not promote air pruning of roots
- high quality and uniform growing media must be used
- trays and grooves must be kept clean
- larger containers require deeper flooding depths that may cause weight load problems
- best suited for containers with bottom ridges that raise containers slightly above tray.

System design: zones and storage tanks. In general, it takes about 0.5 gallon of solution to flood each square foot (20 1/m^2) of area in the trays to a depth of about three-fourths to 1 inch (2 to 2.5 cm), depending on the container size and the volume they occupy in the tray. It would be impossible to have a storage tank large enough to flood an entire greenhouse range filled with trays, so the growing areas must be subdivided into manageable zones. Zone size is dictated by two factors:

1. What is the largest area of trays that can be flooded in 10 to 15 minutes and drain back into the storage tank in about the same amount of time? Each inlet valve into the tray usually should

not exceed about 7 gallons per minute (25 l/minute), so that the containers are not pushed around by the incoming water. At 7 gallons per minute (25 l/minute), one inlet valve could flood a 6-foot-wide by 30-foot-long bench (2 m × 10 m) or 180 square feet (20 m²) in about 13 minutes. The number of benches that can be flooded simultaneously is determined by the pump size and how many inlet valves the pump can service simultaneously.

2. What is the largest storage tank that is feasible to purchase or construct? For example, a 1,000 gallon (5 kl) tank could irrigate a zone of about 2,000 square feet (240 m²) of tray area. Thus, one zone could be 12 6-foot-wide by 30-foot-long (2 m by 10 m) benches totaling 2,160 square feet (240 m²). The entire zone is not flooded all at once, but usually is subdivided into three sub-zones. In this example, the 12 benches could be divided into three subzones of four benches each with each subzone totaling 720 square feet (80 m²).

   Each of three subzones is flooded in sequence. The first subzone is flooded, then drained. While it is draining, flooding of the second subzone is begun, and while the second subzone is draining, the third subzone is flooded. Sequential flooding and draining of portions of the zone prevents completely pumping the tank dry in any one irrigation cycle and allows a partially full tank to be used if a grower wants to make up the volume periodically rather than after each irrigation. Many operations use large, rigid plastic or fiberglass storage tanks. In-ground cement storage tanks can also be constructed. Storage tanks need to be covered to keep out dust and light, preventing contamination and algae growth. Tanks should be located close to the benches to be irrigated. Many times storage tanks are located under one of the benches in each zone.

Timing, length, and depth of flooding. The timing of irrigation in a subirrigation system is similar to other irrigation systems. Plants should be irrigated after most of the available water has been depleted, but before any water stress begins (discussed in Chapter 1 on irrigation systems). Microtensiometers can be inserted into growing media and used to totally automate the system.

A 5- to 15-minute flood duration is usually sufficient. Studies have shown that a 10-minute flood duration rewets the container to 75% of container capacity. Subirrigation systems usually do not rewet to 100% of container capacity, even with a long flood duration.

Do not let the water sit for extended periods (over 45 minutes), otherwise roots can be damaged from water logging. Do not let growing media become completely dry between irrigations because it is difficult to rehydrate dry growing media by subirrigation. If media does become excessively dry between irrigations, several short flood durations usually are more effective than one long flood duration. The depth of flooding only needs to be three-quarters of an inch to 1 inch (2 to 2.5 cm) in depth for 4- and 6-inch (10 and 15 cm) pots. Flats and plugs can be irrigated at a lesser depth. A good rule of thumb is to flood to about 20 to 25% of the container height.

Solution management. For plants spaced at production density, about 20% of the irrigation solution is retained by the containers with each irrigation. The nutrient solution in the storage tank can be brought up to volume after each irrigation or after several irrigation cycles and before the solution gets too low to pump during irrigation. Any nutrient solution that is lost is replaced with fresh nutrient solution. The nutrient solution can be mixed and added manually or automatically by using float valves and fertilizer injectors. Do not replace the lost solution with water because that would dilute the soluble fertilizer level to too low a level. Do not recirculate clear water because the fertility level in growing media could be reduced to dangerous levels.

When the benches are flooded, the solution is absorbed by capillarity and bulk flow of the solution into the macropores at the container base. Since only the container base is flooded, most of the water is absorbed into capillary pores or remains as a "perched water table" (i.e., a flooded layer present at the bottom of all containers after irrigation and drainage). Very little solution drains out of the container after draining the bench. Relatively clean and unaffected nutrient solution drains back to the storage tank and is recirculated in the system, as long as the bench is kept clean, the containers are not flooded too deep, the flooding time is kept short (10 to 15 minutes), the returning solution is screened and the storage tank is covered to prevent contamination and evaporation. Also, if the storage tanks are sized properly, they are depleted of their nutrient solution every several irrigation cycles, so fresh solution is added frequently.

Most operations completely deplete the solution and clean the tanks periodically. For these reasons, the nutrient level, electrical conductivity

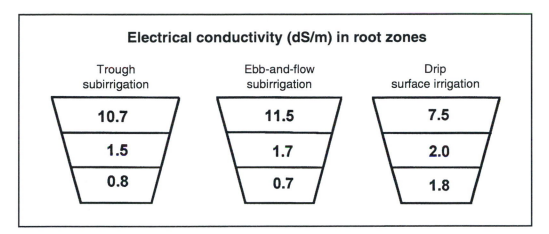

Fig. 10.4 Distribution of soluble salts, as measured by electrical conductivity (dS/m, 1:10 dilution extract), in the top, middle, and bottom root zones of the container from dieffenbachia grown eight weeks by three irrigation methods (modified with permission from H-D Molitor 1990).

(EC), and pH of the recirculated solution usually does not change much over time. If these parameters do change, water, nutrients, acids or base can be added to correct the problem. Again, these corrections can be manual or automatic with in-line sensors (pH, conductivity) and injectors (acid, base, fertilizer). There are several companies that supply systems to monitor and totally automate solution management.

Soluble salts accumulation. Soluble salts accumulation in growing media in ebb-and-flow systems can be a problem. The nutrient solution moves into the container by capillary action and mass flow and very little leaves upon draining. Some of the nutrients not absorbed by the plant migrate to the top of the container along with the water during drying and are left behind when water evaporates. If evaporation is prevented from growing media surface, there is less salt buildup in the top layer. Thus, the salts buildup in the top layer may be more of a problem during the summer and in hotter climates. However, soluble salts accumulation in the top layer is not unique to ebb-and-flow—it occurs with all irrigation systems. Figure 10.4 shows the distribution of salts in growing media with several irrigation systems.

All systems result in a region of high salts, hence, electrical conductivity, in the top one-third or so of the container. Even though the electrical conductivity in the top layer greatly exceeds the recommended EC of growing media, it may not be damaging because there usually are few active roots growing in this zone. However, at higher fertility rates, the EC in the top layer can build up to extremely high levels. In fig. 10.5, notice that the bottom layer remains near or below 1.2 dS/m EC (a commonly used upper salinity level, see Chapter 6) even at the highest N rates, but that the middle layer exceeds 1.2 dS/m EC at 140 ppm N and higher. In this particular study on impatiens, optimum growth was at 112 ppm N, and growth decreased at 140 N and above (fig.10.6).

Soluble salts buildup in the middle layer in the container may determine the upper fertility level and water quality level that can be tolerated without detrimental effects. Oddly, the EC in the middle and bottom layer of the root zone is often lower when plants are grown in a subirrigation system and when the recommended fertility level is used, compared to conventional systems (figs. 10.4, 10.5). This may be due to enhanced migration of salts to the top zone. Because of this, growing media tests may reveal suboptimal nutrient levels when plants are grown in subirrigation, but this should not always be taken as an indication to increase fertility.

Fertility level. Most studies show that the soluble fertility level in a recirculating subirrigation system should be approximately one-half the concentration used in traditional drip or overhead irrigation systems. Figure 10.6 shows the growth response of New Guinea impatiens in an ebb-and-flow tray system. Best growth and quality occurred at about 100 ppm N. The increased fertilizer use efficiency may be because there is no leaching of added fertilizers.

Relatively few studies have identified the optimum soluble fertility level for various greenhouse crops. The few that have been reported are presented in table 10.2. A general rule of thumb would be 50 to 100 ppm nitrogen for most crops. There are virtually no comprehensive studies that have identified the optimum level of the other macronutrients and micronutrients. Also, few studies are published that determine if the ratio of N:P, the ratio of N:K, and the ratio of nitrate N:ammonium N are the same for subirrigation as for traditional drip and overhead irrigation systems. However, there is no reason to believe that these factors would differ significantly.

Use the fertility programs discussed in Chapter 7 and 8 on macronutrients and micronutrients, but try reduced rates. Many growers use

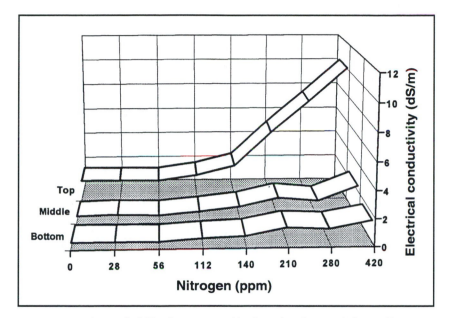

Fig. 10.5 Distribution of soluble salts, as measured by electrical conductivity (dS/m, 1:2 dilution extract), in the top, middle, and bottom root zones in the container from impatiens grown 11 weeks in an ebb-and-flow tray system at various N concentrations. All treatments contained 106 ppm phosphorus (expressed as P_2O_5) and 94 ppm potassium (expressed as K_2O) in the nutrient solution, and micronutrients as Micromax incorporated into growing media at label-recommended rates. (Kent and Reed 1996)

growing media containing the standard rates of incorporated lime, gypsum, superphosphate, and micronutrient mixes and have favorable results. A few studies have indicated that slow-release fertilizers can be used in subirrigation, but refined rates have not been identified.

If you conduct a growing media test, the nutrient content in the lower region of the container may test low. This is a common observation, and adequate growth can be obtained as long as the levels are not too far below acceptable ranges. The low nutrient content is probably a consequence of the salts (and nutrients) migrating a bit more to the top layer of the growing media. Obviously, one wants to avoid sampling the top layer of the growing media. Analytical testing labs are developing adequacy levels for nutrients in the growing media for subirrigation systems.

Water quality. Water quality in an ebb-and-flow system is more critical than in conventional liquid fertilization systems. The lack of leaching

Fig. 10.6 Growth response of New Guinea impatiens Barbados in a ebb-and-flow tray subirrigation system at various levels of nitrogen nutrition. All treatments contained 106 ppm phosphorus (expressed as P_2O_5) and 94 ppm potassium (expressed as K_2O) in the nutrient solution, and micronutrients as Micromax incorporated into growing media at label-recommended rates. (Kent and Reed 1996).

allows soluble salts to build up in the growing media to higher levels. There is very little information on the limits of soluble salts in irrigation water that can be used in an ebb-and-flow system. A study in progress (see Todd 1996) indicates that water containing up to 600 ppm sodium chloride/calcium chloride salts (2:1 $NaCl:CaCl_2$ on a molar basis, with total EC of 1.98 dS/m of salt plus nutrient solution) could be used for New Guinea impatiens in an ebb-and-flow system.

Some greenhouse operations collect rain water from the roofs of their greenhouses to use in the system. If water is collected off roofs with galvanized metal, carefully monitor the possibility of zinc contamination. You could also use water purified by reverse osmosis (see Chapter 3 on water purification systems) blended with raw water to reduce the

Table 10.2 Optimum soluble nitrogen level for selected greenhouse crops grown in a constant-feed recirculating subirrigation system

Crop	Scientific name	Nitrogen (ppm)
English ivy	*Hedera helix*	50
Bedding plants	general	50–75
Peace lily	*Spathiphyllum* sp.	50–100
Asiatic lily	*Lilium* sp.	75
Poinsettia	*Euphorbia pulcherrima*	75–125
Dumbcane	*Dieffenbachia maculata*	80–140
Weeping fig	*Ficus benjamina*	80–140
New Guinea impatiens	*Impatiens hawkeri*	100
Croton	*Codiaeum variegatum*	100
Nephthytis	*Syngonium podophyllum*	140–170

Source: Biernbaum 1993, Holcomb et al. 1992, Poole and Conover 1992, Kent and Reed 1996, Rose and White 1994.

soluble salts level to an acceptable level. Take care to avoid contaminating the recirculating solution with agricultural chemicals. Cases have been reported of growth retardants getting into the recirculating solution and severely stunting an entire zone of poinsettia.

Growing media, containers, and container size. Growing media used in ebb-and-flow systems must readily absorb water by capillary action. The most common growing media used are sphagnum peat moss or composted bark-based mixes. Most good quality commercial mixes appear to work well. Wetting agents can be used to increase the wetting and capillary uptake of water. Plugs, flats, and 4-inch (10 cm) containers are easily wetted. For containers larger than 4-inch (10 cm), growing media may not be fully wetted all the way to the top. This restricts container size to about 6-inch (15 cm) or smaller, or if taller containers are used, the flooding depth may need to be increased.

Containers that have holes only in the bottom of the container and that lie completely flat on the bench should not be used because this interferes with the movement of solution into and out of the container during flooding. This is also a problem with some flats. The containers used should have small ridges on the bottom to slightly raise the container above the bench, or it should have holes or slits that extend up the sides of the container.

Disease and pesticide use. At first you might expect ebb-and-flow systems to offer ideal conditions for soil-borne pathogens to flourish and spread among the containers. However, this has not been the case, and in fact, pathogen problems are no more numerous than in traditional systems. The reason is simple: Most of the nutrient solution that moves into the container upon flooding is absorbed by the growing media or remains in the perched water table and very little flows out upon draining.

Studies have placed plants infected with *Pythium* and *Xanthomonas* in trays with uninfected plants. Very little or no infection spread to the uninfected plants. If the nutrient solution itself becomes infected, the spread of the disease has been shown to range from minimal to high, depending on the disease organism. Apparently, some pathogens cannot survive very well in the nutrient solution. Thus, the key to disease control is to begin with healthy plants, practice good sanitation, and keep the nutrient solution clean. Keep trays clean by keeping growing media, leaves, and other debris from accumulating on the tray top.

Avoid top watering or drenching plants. If you must do so, do not let the runoff flow into the storage tank and wash the tray down before the next irrigation cycle to keep particulate matter and pesticides out of storage tanks. Screen the solution before it reenters the storage tank to keep out debris. Use the smallest storage tank feasible so the solution will be changed as frequently as possible, and clean and disinfect the tank periodically.

High humidity can occur after flooding, which can lead to condensation and increased foliar disease. Minimize this by flooding early in the day, by good ventilation and air circulation, and by use of under-the-bench bottom heat. Currently, there are no pesticides specifically labeled for addition to the subirrigation nutrient solution. So, from a legal standpoint, only conventional drenches and sprays can be used. Some greenhouses use chlorination or bromination of the nutrient solution for disinfection.

Postharvest. Since a high level of soluble salts accumulate in the top layer of the growing media, there is a potential postharvest problem of salts migrating from the top layer down into the active root zone once the plants are top-watered in postproduction use at the retail store or in the consumer's home. We have observed, on occasion, severe wilting of impatiens when top-watered after production, if the plants were grown at the upper limits of acceptable fertility. In such a case, multiple leachings may be required after production and before the plants are shipped. Observations have ranged from none to variable postharvest problems. Actually, the salts in the top layer may serve as a source of fertility in postharvest use situations once top-watering has begun. Postharvest performance of plants should be monitored by growers to prevent problems from developing.

Ebb-and-flow flooded floor system

For all practical purposes, the ebb-and-flow flooded floor system can be managed as described for the ebb-and-flow tray system.

Advantages and disadvantages. The ebb-and-flow flooded floor system (fig. 10.2) has the same advantages and disadvantages as the tray system. Additional advantages are:
- flooded floor systems are less expensive than the tray system (table 10.1) because benches are not needed
- they are ideal for in-floor heating systems
- since they do not contain a fixed size tray or trough, they offer more flexibility in plant spacing and pot sizes.

Ebb-and-flow flooded floors have the disadvantage of requiring workers to stoop to handle the crop. A few Dutch equipment manufacturers produce a fork-lift type of machine that can be used to lay out and pick up pots. There are even robots to automatically set out plug trays or bedding plant trays into ebb-and-flow flooded floor bays. Some growers also consider the requirement for bottom heating from heating pipes embedded in the concrete floor a disadvantage.

Construction and system design. Construction of the concrete floor appears to be the major obstacle to use of flooded floor systems by the U.S. greenhouse industry. Flooded floors are very common in many parts of Europe where there are more firms with the technology to install them. Far fewer firms in the U.S. have the expertise, and especially the experience, to install flooded floors, although they do exist. Figure 10.7 is a schematic diagram of a typical ebb-and-flow flooded floor subirrigation system, and fig. 10.8 is a

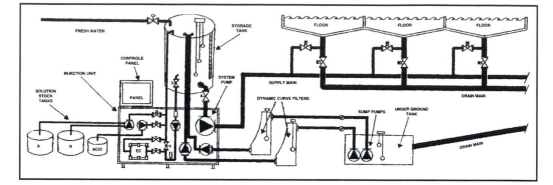

Fig. 10.7 Schematic diagram of a typical flooded floor ebb-and-flow subirrigation system showing the points of injection of fertilizer, acid, and fresh water; the monitoring of electrical conductivity (EC); and layout of supply lines, drain lines, storage tanks, filters and pumps. (Diagram courtesy of PDIC Greenhouse Systems Inc., Hartwood, Virginia)

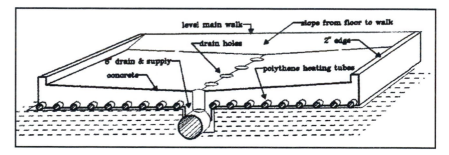

Fig. 10.8 Cross-section of a typical concrete floor in a flooded floor ebb-and-flow subirrigation system showing raised side walls, slope to drain holes, and embedded heating pipes. (Diagram courtesy of PDIC Greenhouse Systems Inc., Hartwood, Virginia)

cross-section showing the construction of a concrete floor. Concrete floors must be engineered and installed with the proper precision to allow uniform flooding depth and proper drainage with no puddling, which is best accomplished by laser leveling. The floor is usually sloped towards the drain one-quarter to three-quarter-inch per 10 linear feet (1 to 3 cm/5 m).

The embedded plumbing, drainage, and heating system must be sized properly. The system must also be "zoned" similar to the tray system so that the area to be flooded, time required to flood and size of storage tank are in a manageable proportion. The size of the zone to be flooded is that which can be flooded to the required depth in 5 to 10 minutes and drained in the same amount of time. In the future, the use of flooded floors should become more common in the U.S. as more firms become available to install or offer consulting advice on the installation of flooded floors. A step-by-step pictorial summary that follows the actual installation of a flooded floor system has been described in a magazine article. (See Chris Beytes in references.)

Bottom heat. Control of moisture on the floor and the resultant high humidity of the surrounding air after flooding is a concern. Most experts recommend embedded heating pipes in the concrete floor to be used to dry the floor after each irrigation cycle, especially during times of the year when the excess moisture does not quickly evaporate. Growers must adapt to managing a bottom heated system. Bottom heat can be used to maintain a warmer root zone and promote early root growth and decrease soil-borne disease problems, but if the temperature is too high it can produce a soft plant with reduced root growth and excessive shoot growth. Some growers use bottom heat only during early stages of production to establish good root growth and switch to conventional air heating for later stages of the crop, especially with plugs.

Trough system

Advantages and disadvantages. Trough systems (fig. 10.3) offer all the advantages of the ebb-and-flow systems relative to labor savings, water, and fertilizer use efficiency, and recirculation of the nutrient solution to minimize runoff. An added advantage is that a trough system is the least expensive recirculating subirrigation system (table 10.1). The troughs become the benches, and they simply need frames for support. Of course, the troughs can also be placed on top of existing benches.

The trough system also offers the advantages of better air circulation and fewer humidity problems than the solid floor or tray system, which some growers feel translates into fewer foliar disease problems. Also, a larger area of greenhouse space can be irrigated with a given size storage tank compared to ebb-and-flow systems.

The major disadvantages are the restrictions on spacing and use of variable container sizes. The width of the trough dictates the maximum container size. Spacing can be variable along the length of the trough, but to space across the width of the bench, the spacing of the troughs must be changed.

System design. Troughs can be stainless steel, aluminum, or plastic. Some growers have adapted rain gutters for troughs, or troughs can be purchased that are formed specifically for that purpose. Trough length is dictated by bench length; some trough systems have been designed that are over 200 feet (60 m) in length. The trough must be sloped at about a 7 degree angle, or about one-half to 1 inch per 10 to 15 linear foot of run (274 cm per 5 to 7.5 m). The nutrient solution is added at the high end and allowed to flow to the lower end, where it is collected and funneled back into the storage tank.

The container size should be large enough in diameter or width to almost fill the width of the trough. The containers then act as multiple dams causing the water to build up slightly on the high side. This allows time for absorption and minimizes the depth of solution and hence the volume of solution that needs to flow down the trough.

The water is kept flowing and recirculating until all plants have absorbed sufficient water by capillarity. The length of time needed is dependent on the length of the trough and depth at which the water is maintained in the trough. The system may have to run for 45 to 120 minutes in very long troughs.

There are no fixed guidelines for sizing the storage tank as with ebb-and-flow systems because the width of troughs and their spacing on benches varies with each operation. Also, long troughs may almost completely fill with water before any solution drains back to the tank for recirculating. Certainly, less than 0.5 gallons of solution is needed per square foot (20 l/m^2) of trough area (not bench area) to be irrigated. For this reason, a given size storage tank can irrigate a larger production area using a trough system than with an ebb-and-flow system.

Cultural practices and management. There is very little published information specifically tailored to trough systems. However, the basic principles are virtually identical to ebb-and-flow systems, so the practices given under the section on ebb-and-flow tray system could be used and modified slightly to fit each specific growing operation.

References

Argo, W.R., and J.A. Biernbaum. 1994. Irrigation requirements, root-medium pH, and nutrient concentrations of Easter lilies grown in five peat-based media with and without an evaporation barrier. *J. Amer. Soc. Hort. Sci.* 119:1151–1156.

————. 1995. Root-medium nutrient levels and irrigation requirement of poinsettias grown in five root media. *HortScience* 30:535–538.

Atmatjidou, V.P., R.P. Fynn, and H.A.J. Hoitink. 1991. Dissemination and transmission of *Xanthomonas campestris* pv. begoniae in an ebb and flow irrigation system. *Plant Disease* 75:1261–1265.

Ball, V. 1991. New irrigation concepts. *The Ball RedBook.* 15th ed. Edited by V. Ball. Batavia, Ill.: Ball Publishing.

Beytes, C. 1995. Flood floor construction in 12 steps. *GrowerTalks* 58:40–44.

Biernbaum, J.A. 1993. Subirrigation could make environmental and economical sense for your greenhouse. *Professional Plant Growers Association News*, April.

Biernbaum, J.A., M.V. Yelanich, W. Carlson, and R.D. Heins. 1989. Irrigation and fertilization go hand in hand to reduce runoff. *GrowerTalks* 53: 26–30.

Blodgett, A.M., D.J. Beattie, J.W. White, and G.C. Elliott. 1993. Hydrophilic polymers and wetting agents affect absorption and evaporative water loss. *HortScience* 28:633–635.

Blom, T., and B. Piott. 1989. Rockwool and peat moss. Reabsorption of growing media by subirrigation. *Greenhouse Canada*, March 1989.

Elliott, G. 1990. Reduce water and fertilizer with ebb and flow. *Greenhouse Grower* 8:70–75.

Fynn, P., H.A.J. Hoitink, and R.W. McMahon. 1994. Controlling irrigation—using a soil tensiometer can help manage the start and stop of irrigation in a ebb-and-flood bench system. *Greenhouse Grower* 12:29–33.

George, R.K., J.A. Biernbaum, and C.T. Stephens. 1990. Potential for transfer of *Pythium ultimum* in production of seedling geraniums with subirrigation and recirculated solutions. *Acta Hort.* 272:203–207.

Hamrick, D. 1989. Subirrigating plugs: Is it the future? *GrowerTalks* 53:54–58.

Holcomb, E.J., S. Gamez, D. Beattie, and G.C. Elliott. 1992. Efficiency of fertigation programs for Baltic ivy and Asiatic lily. *HortTechnology* 2(1):43–46.

Kent, M.W., and D.W. Reed. 1996. Nitrogen nutrition of New Guinea impatiens 'Barbados' and Spathiphyllum 'Petite' in a subirrigation system. *J. American Soc. Hort. Sci.* (in press).

Koch, G.M., and E.J. Holcomb. 1983. Utilization of recycled water on marigolds fertilized with osmocote and constant liquid fertilization. *J. Amer. Soc. Hort.* Sci. 108: 815–819.

Lieth, J.H., and D.W. Burger. 1989. Growth of chrysanthemum using an irrigation system controlled by soil moisture tension. *J. Amer. Soc. Hort. Sci.* 114: 387–392.

Molitor, H.D. 1990. Bedding and pot plants: The European perspective with emphasis on subirrigation and recirculation of water and nutrients. *Acta Hort.* 272:165–171.

Neal, K. 1987. Going with the flow. *Greenhouse Manager* 5:116–128.

———. 1987. Troughs are tough to top. *Greenhouse Manager* 5:137–145.

———. 1989. Subirrigation. *Greenhouse Manager* 7:83–88.

Pannkuk, T. 1995. Growth of New Guinea impatiens under no-leach irrigation. Master's thesis, Texas A&M University.

Payne, R.N., and S.M. Adam. 1980. Influence of rate and placement of slow-release fertilizer on pot plants of African violet grown with capillary mat watering. *HortScience* 15:607–610.

Poole, R.T., and C.A. Conover. 1992. Fertilizer levels and medium affect foliage plant growth in an ebb and flow irrigation system. *J. Environ. Hort.* 10:81–86.

Rose, M.A., and J.W. White. 1994. Nitrogen rate and timing of nitrogen application in poinsettia (*Euphorbia pulcherrima* Willd. Ex Klotz.). *HortScience* 29:1309–1313.

Sanogo, S., and G.W. Moorman. 1993. Transmission and control of *Pythium aphanidermatum* in an ebb-and-flow subirrigation system. *Plant Disease* 77:287–290.

Thomas, D. 1989. Saving money with ebb and flow at Rosedale greenhouses. *GrowerTalks* 53:44–47.

Todd, N. 1996. Response of New Guinea impatiens to various levels of salinity in a subirrigation system. Master's thesis, Texas A&M University.

Yelanich, M.V., and J.A. Biernbaum. 1990. Effect of fertilizer concentration and method of application on media nutrient content, nitrogen runoff and growth of *Euphorbia pulcherrima* 'V-14 Glory.' *Acta Hort.* 272: 185–189.

Chapter 11

Total Nursery Recycling Systems

Conrad A. Skimina

Congress passed its first Water Pollution Control Act back in 1956. Originally, the Environmental Protection Agency considered only point sources of pollution, such as factories that dumped wastewater directly into steams. Agriculture was considered a nonpoint source and as such was not strictly regulated. Since that time, however, water pollution legislation has accelerated at both the national and state levels. Recently, agriculture is being pinpointed as a source of pollution, especially nitrate pollution of ground water. Throughout the country, rural wells have been closed because they exceeded the 10 ppm nitrate nitrogen limit for drinking water.

How should nursery and greenhouse producers deal with the situation? One of the most feasible ways to reduce nitrogen entering ground water supplies is to recycle irrigation water. The amount of nitrogen in recycled water can be substantial, especially if the original irrigation water is nutrient fortified for constant liquid feeding. Not only is recycling good for the environment, but it also makes more efficient use of production inputs such as water and nutrients.

This chapter discusses sophisticated total nursery recycling systems using settling, flocculation, filtration, and disinfection, as well as simple systems using only settling, filtration, and disinfection of irrigation water for container nursery crops. These recycling systems are especially well suited for outdoor and shade nursery/floriculture production. Greenhouse producers who wish to develop recycling systems that handle irrigation and other runoff water (such as rainwater, field water, etc.) in the same system will also find this chapter invaluable.

Economics of water recycling

One of the first considerations a nurseryman or greenhouse operator must make is to determine the costs of recycling water. Costs will vary depending upon: 1) the quantity of water to be recycled, 2) the clarity desired, 3) the kind of construction used, 4) the method of disinfection, and 5) costs of water treatment chemicals and energy. For example, using a sophisticated system of clarification to recycle water for container crops, operational expenses were:

Energy:	48%
Chemicals:	38%
Equipment maintenance:	5%
Labor:	9%
	100%

Initial installation costs

In addition to these costs, there is the initial installation cost. Construction costs vary slightly around the country; however, on the West Coast, costs are approximately $2 per square foot ($21.50/m^2) for installed concrete slabs. For reservoirs or sedimentation pits one must consider grading permits, building fees, excavation, and concrete or plastic linings. Plastic membrane lined reservoirs or pits are difficult to clean with equipment. Concrete structures can be constructed in such a way to facilitate removal of sediments. For example, a ramp with a slope less than 15% will permit access with a front end loader. A 3-inch (7.6 cm) thickness of concrete is sufficient except for the ramp.

For smaller operations, hand cleaning may be the most feasible approach, or you can use plastic tanks instead of concrete. The most expensive concrete structures are vertical walls that require forming. The following are relative costs for concrete work:

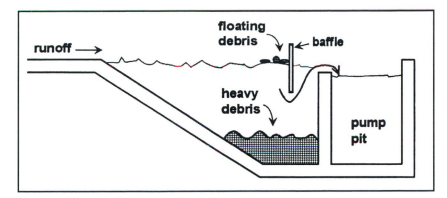

Fig. 11.1 Sedimentation pit. Heavy sediment settles to the bottom and floating debris collects at the top. A baffle system allows clarified water to be collected from the middle layer. On a large system, the ramp must be sloped to allow sediment removal with a front-end loader.

Poured concrete:	1.0
Pumped concrete:	2.0
Gunite:	2.5
Formed walls	4.0

If one makes a sedimentation pit or reservoir with sloping sides, the concrete can be poured and trowelled, or it can be pumped or gunited. The maximum slope one can have with poured or pumped concrete is 1:1, but 1.5:1 is preferable. The cost of this construction will be one-half or less than for formed walls. However, this takes more space than a vertical wall pit. Sedimentation pits should be constructed so that the ramp collects the sediment, and the upper, clarified water can spill into a pump pit to facilitate pumping without disturbing the sediment at the bottom. Floating debris can be baffled and skimmed off the surface with a pool screen (fig. 11.1).

An approximation of costs for sophisticated water clarification can be determined by asking your local sanitation district for their cost of water treatment. The 1994 costs to process sewage water in Los Angeles, California, ranges from $280/million gallons ($74/million liters) for larger operations to $563/million gallons ($149/million liters) for smaller operations. It will cost a grower a little less than this and considerably less if a simplified clarification system is used. (These systems will be explained later.)

Payback formula

When recycling water, you save not only the cost of the water but also the value of the nutrients in the water. A formula to calculate payback time for a processing system is:

$$\frac{\text{Capital costs}}{(N+W-OC)(M)} = \text{Payback time in years}$$

where, N = value of nutrients in 1 million gallons of water,
W = value of 1 million gallons of water
OC = operating cost for 1 million gallons
M = the number of million gallons of water treated per year

If we assume that the cost of N is $0.39/pound ($0.86/kg) and K is $0.46/pound ($1.01/kg) and the concentration in the water is 200 ppm N and 100 ppm K, the value of the nutrients alone in 1 million gallons is $1,034 ($273/million liters).

Treatment methods

Collecting runoff and sedimentation

With container crop production, open ditches (preferably lined) or drain tiles can be used to direct the flow to a sedimentation pit. In quiescent water, sand will settle in less than 20 seconds and silt will settle in two hours. Colloidal clay particles, which are not visible to the naked eye, will partially settle in three to five days. The mass of clay particles can be seen but not the individual particles. Clay is by far the most difficult contaminant to remove.

Flocculation

To remove colloidal matter, decide whether to use a sophisticated system of clarification (fig. 11.2) or a simplified system (fig. 11.3).

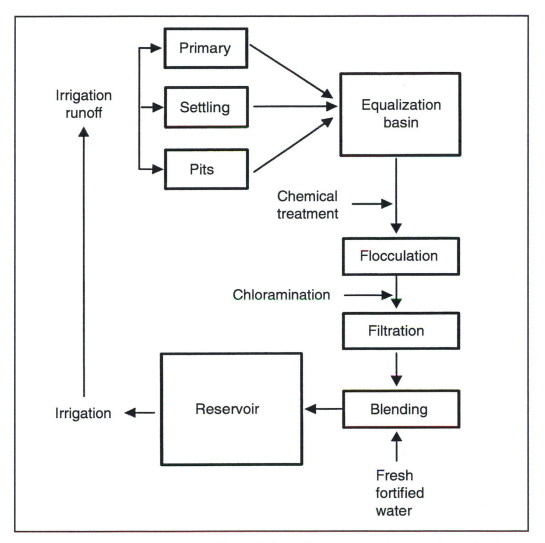

Fig. 11.2 Schematic of a sophisticated system of water clarification. The system uses preliminary settling ponds and pits to remove heavy sediment and floating debris. It also uses a chemical treatment for further flocculation, filtration, and blending to produce water for irrigation.

Sophisticated systems. A sophisticated system uses clay coagulation with an inorganic coagulant such as alum (aluminum sulfate) or ferric sulfate. The aluminum or ferric ion, which is positively charged, neutralizes the negative charges associated with colloidal clay, permitting it to

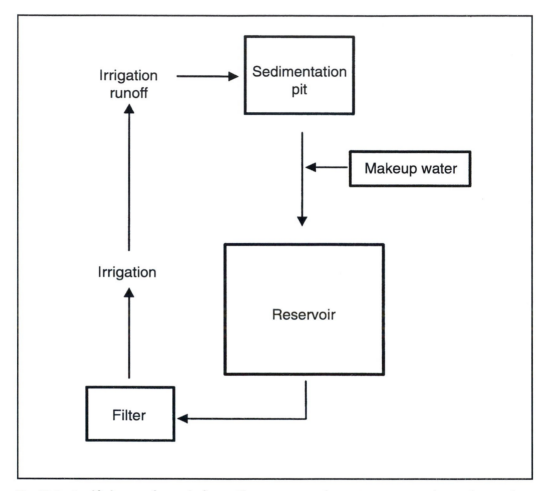

Fig. 11.3 Simplified system of water clarification. The system uses a sedimentation pit to remove heavy sediment and floating debris and minimal filtration to produce water for irrigation.

aggregate into a floc. Then if this floc is treated with an organic polymer such as a polyacrylamide, these flocculated particles will aggregate into larger particles that will settle in minutes rather than days. These polymers can be nonionic, cationic or anionic. Several polymers have to be tested using a jar test after you have determined the best dosage of inorganic coagulant to use.

In the actual process stream, the polymer is injected sufficiently downstream from the coagulant injection to permit the coagulant to mix and react with the colloidal matter before the polymer is added. Static in-line mixers can be used in pipes to provide mixing. You should allow at least one minute for the coagulant to act on the clay colloid before adding the polymer. These flocculated particles will then settle to the bottom of a basin where they can be scraped continuously (like a windshield wiper over a surface). The scraping has to be very slow so that the particles are not re-suspended.

An alternative is to physically clean the pit routinely. The settled sludge must be removed because anaerobic denitrification and biological decomposition of organic matter will cause methane and nitrogen gas bubbles to form in the sludge. When enough bubbles accumulate in the sludge, chunks may break off and float to the top, contaminating the clear water at the surface. One well-designed clarification system allows sludge to be removed through bottom outlets, without being agitated by scraping (Claricone, CBI Walker Co., Aurora, Illinois). I have not tested their unit, but it is the best designed self-cleaning clarifier I have seen. Pilot units are available for testing, which I suggest you do before you make a commitment to buy one (fig. 11.4).

Using alum or ferric sulfate for coagulation results in reduction in the pH of the water. When using alum, the best pH range for precipitation and coagulation is 6.8 to 7.4. A lower or higher pH results in more soluble aluminum in the system. The soluble aluminum concentration should not exceed 1.0 ppm. Higher concentrations may be toxic to some plants. Ammonium hydroxide can be used to adjust pH and neutralize acidity. Use ammonium hydroxide rather than sodium hydroxide because it provides a two-fold benefit: acid neutralization and nitrogen. Ferric sulfate, in contrast, has a wider functional pH range. Ferric iron will precipitate at a pH above 5.5, so if the water requires small amounts, there may be no need for neutralization.

To determine the optimum pH and dosage of coagulant, send water samples to a laboratory for a "jar test" with a gang stirrer. The Aqua-Ben Corp., Orange, California, will do a jar test for prospective customers to determine the optimum coagulant and polymer dosage your particular water requires.

For water treatment, alum is generally sold as a 48.5% liquid solution containing 5.36 pounds hydrated aluminum sulfate/gallon

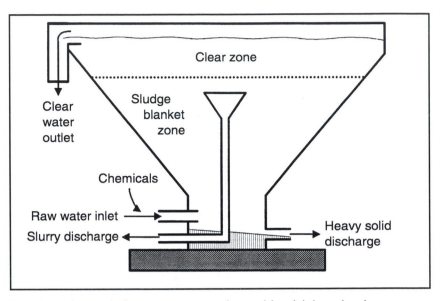

Fig. 11.4 Claricone clarification system removes heavy solids and sludge and produces clarified water.

(0.64 kg/l). Ferric sulfate is generally sold as a salt that must be dissolved to make a liquid concentrate.

The coagulant can be injected with a fertilizer injector that is a proportioning injector which keeps up with the flow rate. If you pump the water from a collection pit, you have a relatively constant flow rate, and you can manually adjust a pump to feed the right dosage on the downstream using a static mixer. Or you can use a rotameter to adjust the flow into the intake side of the pump with a metering type valve. This is a good way to get economical injection and immediate mixing.

Simplified systems. The alternative to a sophisticated system is a simplified clarification system. Simplified systems depend on natural settling of the suspended solids in a large reservoir or pond. If a grower is using soilless or sandless media, the amount of colloidal matter will be minimal, and simple filtration and disinfection will clarify the water sufficiently for reuse. If media contain any soil or sand, simplified settling will mean less clarity.

Direct filtration. For small operations, if the runoff is relatively clean, an alternative that should be investigated is direct filtration. In this case, one can use a pressure sand filter or diatomaceous pool filter. Remember that minute clay particles can pass through the interstices between sand particles, and that pre-flocculation with a coagulant or polymer may be necessary to efficiently remove clay.

Measuring clarity. Clarity is measured with a nephelometer and the units of expression are NTUs (nephelometric turbidity units). A NTU of 0.0 is absolute clarity. Drinking water treatment plants in the United States strive for less than 1.0 NTU, and preferably 0.1 NTU. Monrovia Nursery has achieved a clarity as low as 0.6 NTU from a water originally a 50 NTU. I have found that if you can't see an object 12 inches (30 cm) below the surface of water along the shore of a reservoir, the NTU is approximately 12. I call that the 12/12 rule. As turbid as this may appear "en masse," a sample in a glass jar may appear relatively clear.

For a schematic of sophisticated and simplified water clarification systems see figs. 11.2 and 11.3.

Filtration

After sedimentation, flocculation and/or settling, the water should be filtered. In sophisticated systems, use a dual media gravity filter composed of anthracite coal over sand. In simple systems, a sand filter can be used if clarity is sacrificed for ease of operation. In this case, larger suspended particles rather than colloids would be removed (fig. 11.5).

With dual media systems, the flow through the filter is usually by gravity. Filtration rate should not exceed 5 gpm per square foot (200 l/m/m^2) of filter surface area. For example, for a flow of 50 gpm (2,000 lpm) you would need a filter having 10 square feet (1 m^2) of surface or more. Some provision must be made for backwashing. Reversing the flow through the filter has to be controlled so that the coal is not washed away but is only "suspended." Control the backwash flow to suspend the sand and coal to flush out finer particles that can clog the filter. Then, gradually reduce the backwash flow rate to allow the particles to resettle in the order of their specific gravity, i.e., sand first, and the coal on top of the sand. The filter is then ready for the next cycle of filtration.

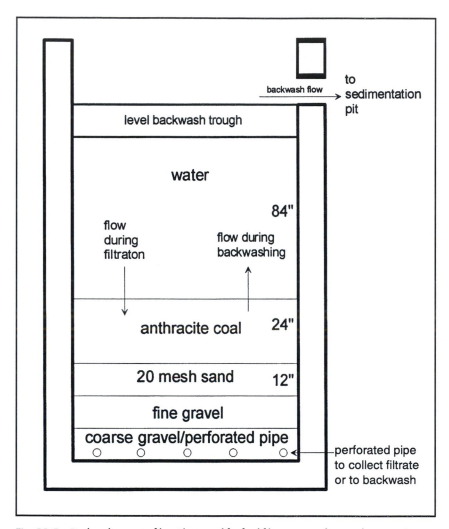

Fig. 11.5 Dual media gravity filter. This is used for final filtration in sophisticated systems. In simple systems requiring less clarity, an all-sand system is used in place of anthracite coal.

Disinfection

Runoff water will invariably be contaminated with various organisms. Ozonization, UV light, chlorination, or bromination can be used. Ozonization requires approximately 20 minutes of retention time. Some air pollution agencies require "off-gas" collection and destruction of residual ozone so that it does not contaminate the air. UV light exposure can be used, but the water has to be clean because suspended particles and/or humic substances will scatter the light. Both UV and ozonization should be done after filtration. UV light or ozonization provides no residual disinfection downstream as does chlorine or bromine.

Chlorine, whether from chlorine gas or from sodium hypochlorite, reacts with the ammonium ion present to form chloramines. Chloramines are also disinfectants, but are slower acting than chlorine. My tests indicate that chloramine is a little more phytotoxic than chlorine. Some plants will tolerate up to 10 ppm, but with the most sensitive crops 2.5 ppm is the limit. If 0.5 ppm residual chloramine can be maintained, adequate disinfection should occur. Remember, the dosage is always higher than the residual since some of the chlorine immediately reacts with contaminants and is decomposed. This is called the demand requirement. The dosage could be many times more than the residual. Disinfection is covered in another chapter in more detail.

Specific problems/adjustments

Correcting pH

In the process of water treatment, it may be necessary to correct pH. Adding alum, ferric sulfate, or chlorine will lower the pH. If alum is used, a pH range of 6.8 to 7.4 is ideal. With ferric sulfate, the pH may be any range desired above 5.6. Ammonium hydroxide can used to raise the pH. The pH usually is adjusted to be close to 7.0. The aqua ammonia used for acid neutralization also serves as a nitrogen fertilizer. My research indicated that the pH drops slightly on a cycle of irrigation due to the conversion of ammonium ion to nitrate ion, but this reduction usually amounts to only a 0.1 unit change in pH. This will vary with soil conditions, temperature, or the culture system used.

Blending

In any agricultural irrigation system, the amount of runoff will be less than the applied water. With outdoor overhead sprinkler systems on the West Coast, the irrigation runoff is approximately 50% of the amount applied. However, this will vary depending on the weather and the percent leaching volume applied. The water lost due to evaporation, transpiration, or soaking into the ground has to be made up with the same amount of fresh or fresh fortified water if a constant feed system is used. This is a good time to adjust your conductivity by varying either the proportion of the fresh water used or the nutrient fortification of the water. In starting up a system, perform frequent chemical analyses to determine the pH, conductivity, and nutrient levels in the system. As you become familiar with changes within the system, testing can be reduced.

One method of blending would be to provide a holding reservoir or tank for the processed runoff and a second reservoir for blended water. The processed water is mixed with makeup water to result in blended water of suitable quality for reirrigation. The rates can be measured by rotameter, conventional meter, or by calculating the flow into a reservoir of known volume. By calculating the flow initially, the subsequent flows should be the same if the head and pump remain the same.

Salinity

Salinity of the captured runoff water will increase with every irrigation cycle. Salinity may increase only slightly, or by as much as 24% on each and every cycle. However, if the processed runoff is blended with makeup water of lower conductivity (fresh water), the salinity generally increases at a reduced rate. Over time, by adding fresh water to makeup water, the system will reach equilibrium. For example, if the makeup water is 50%, the processed water is 50%, and the salinity increases 24% per cycle, then theoretically, equilibrium will be reached at the 7th cycle of irrigation. At this point the salinity should be approximately only 31% greater than the original fresh water. The salinity at equilibrium will be different if: 1) the percent of makeup water is changed, 2) the conductivity of the makeup water changes, 3) the weather changes drastically (excessive rain or evaporation), 4) the growing media changes, or 5) the leaching requirement changes. Remember, conductivity only measures salts that are electrolytes. Urea, for example, is nonpolar and does not conduct electricity. Nevertheless, you can still use electrical conductivity to monitor the salinity trends since the nonpolar substances are only a portion of the total.

Specific salt problems. In examining a water analysis, you can determine the status of each of the elements in the system and see how close they are to a toxic level. Usually, this is not a problem. In systems where trace elements are added to the growing media, some additional trace elements will be added to the water, but they may never reach a toxic level if the original water is of good quality. Boron has to be monitored because the window of tolerance is narrow and generally 0.5 ppm should not be exceeded. More facts on water quality and nutrition are discussed in other chapters. Remember, with a closed system of recycling, you are simply replacing that which has leached from the containers in the first place.

Crop tolerance. The maximum salinity a crop will tolerate varies considerably by species. Some are very sensitive, others actually perform better with higher salinity. There are some ornamentals and greenhouse crops that will tolerate at least seven times higher water salinity than the least tolerant species. The tolerance of the crop grown will need to be determined to provide maximum salinity level for future monitoring. The water conductivity tests should be run in conjunction with soil salinity analyses.

Nitrogen cycling

Since nitrogen compounds are very soluble in water, the nitrogen goes with the water. The concentration of nitrogen usually drops very slightly in a cycle. With a constant feed system, you can generally expect it to be approximately the same concentration in the runoff as the original blended water applied. However the ratio of nitrate:ammonium nitrogen will change due to bacterial conversion of ammonium to nitrate. Therefore, the runoff will be higher in nitrates than the applied water, but the total nitrogen does not change much. One of the great benefits of water recycling is nitrogen conservation and reduced nitrogen use, since the nitrogen is being recycled also.

Pesticide

Very low or undetectable levels of organic insecticides or fungicides are usually present in recycled, processed water from outdoor container crops. These pesticides are usually sprayed on plants, which exposes the pesticide to UV degradation. If a minute amount washes off and gets into the runoff water, the pesticide generally goes through anaerobic biological degradation in the bottom of sedimentation pits and aerobic degradation in the upper levels of the pit. In addition, if chlorination or ozonization is used the pesticide chemically degrades further. Finally, there is adsorption of some pesticides on the colloidal fraction in the water, which is removed either by sedimentation or flocculation. Any residual pesticides are further diluted because the processed runoff is blended with fresh makeup water.

Fungicides applied as drenches result in larger quantities getting into the runoff than from sprays. However, in this case, you might want to recycle it together with the water.

Herbicides must be monitored with caution. Observe the following practices: 1) use herbicides that have a water solubility of less than 5 ppm, 2) use more than one herbicide so that no single herbicide builds up in the system, and 3) do not apply the herbicide on all the property at the same time. Herbicides that have less than 2.5 ppm water solubility are Ronstar, Surflan, Gallery, Barricade, Goal and Prowl or Stomp. Simazine, with a solubility of 5 ppm, has to be used with caution. Spot-spraying with postemergence herbicides, such a cacodylic acid or Roundup, generally does result in dangerous levels of herbicide in the water. These herbicides are strongly adsorbed on the colloidal particles that settle out in the sedimentation pits. My experience indicates that if the above practices are followed, herbicides are usually undetectable in the processed water.

If you're concerned, take a sample from the first irrigation runoff following an application of a herbicide and have a lab run a chromatographic analysis of the sample. The first cycle reveals the worst case scenario.

Pathogens

In any recycling system, one has to be concerned about pathogens in the water. By far the worst are the root rot organisms, such as *Phytophthora* and *Pythium*. Testing the water for *Phytophthora* can be done by using ELISA test kits or by trapping the fungus in floating *Cedrus deodara* needles (Deodor cedar). Fruit traps, such as avocados, apples, pears, or lemons could be used, but I have found that the floating Cedrus needles work very well, and you do not have to excise portions of tissue as you do with fruit.

Float about five to 20 clean, green needles in a device such as a pool chlorinator float. Take the needles out in about two days and place them on a *Phytophthora* selective medium in a petri dish in a separated radial manner. Infected needles will be evident after two days at room temperature. If all of the needles are infected, the water supply is heavily infected. If one or a few needles are infected, a sparse population exists. These tests are easily run using simple techniques and a supply of the medium in petri dishes. Otherwise, give these needles to your Extension Service pathologist to run the test. Remember to store or transport the needles on a moist towel in a way that the individual needles are separated from each other.

Nematodes are by far the most difficult pathogen to kill. They are quite resistant to chlorine and, in general, require about 31 hours exposure at a pH of 6.9 at 0.5 ppm chlorine residual. For one hour of exposure, it takes 10 ppm chlorine to get 100% kill. Also, colder water requires longer exposure times to kill all the nematodes. However, they drown easily, and a sedimentation pit will remove most of them. Better yet, have a clean growing operation so that you don't have pathogenic nematodes in the first place.

Other means of disinfection are ozonization or UV degradation. Ozone is an effective oxidizer and leaves no residual. UV does not work well unless the water has excellent clarity. Even humic acid will absorb UV, making it less effective.

Heating the water is a possibility. Most pathogens do not survive in water held above 132F (55C) for several hours.

In summary, recycling is a viable way to conserve water and nutrients. Sophisticated clarification removes more of the suspended solids and contaminants than a simple system of natural settling. Economics may determine your choice between the systems. Remember these points:

- Monitor the water for pH and salinity. That, with an occasional complete test, will guide you in performing proper treatment for a healthy crop.
- Herbicide use must be restricted to herbicides having very low solubility. Careful use will result in negligible levels in your recycled water.
- Make some provision for adequate disinfection of the water since pathogen dispersal may be a concern.
- Recycling will give your organization a favorable image in your community.

References

Guidance manual. Procedures manual for selection of coagulant, filtration, and sludge conditioning aids in water treatment. 1986. Denver, Colo.: AWWA Research Foundation.

Skimina, C.A. 1986. Recycling irrigation runoff on container ornamentals. *HortScience* 21:32–34.

———. 1987. A 17-year case history of research and implementation of water recycling on container nursery stock. In *Proceedings*, Internat. Plant Prop. Soc. 37:82–87.

———. 1992. Recycling water, nutrients, and waste in the nursery industry. *HortScience* 27:968–971.

Skimina, C.A., and Kabashima, J. 1994. *Recycling and resource conservation.* Harrisburg, Penn.: Pennsylvania Nurserymen's Association, Inc.

U.S. Congress. 1956. Water pollution control act. Public Law 84–660.

U.S. Congress. 1972. Amendments to the water pollution control act. Public Law 92-500.

Water treatment plant operation. 1981. 2 vols. Citrus College, Glendora Calif. ISN 884701-12-4. Ann Arbor, Mich.: Ann Arbor Science Publishers.

Chapter 12

Water, Fertilizer, Pesticides, and the Environment

Don C. Wilkerson

Fertilizers and pesticides are an important part of commercial agriculture and horticulture. In the United States alone, agriculturalists have increased the use of nitrogen fertilizers from 2 million tons (1.8 million metric tons) in 1955 to over 12 million tons (11 million metric tons) in 1990. Pesticide use has more than tripled since 1964, with approximately 1.5 billion pounds (680,000 million kg) per year now being applied. These significant increases are due to the many benefits derived from using fertilizers and pesticides. However, chemicals and fertilizers also pose a potential threat to the environment. Because greenhouse and nursery crop production is so intensive, water and runoff management is increasingly significant.

Runoff from rain and irrigation can concentrate fertilizers and pesticides in smaller collection points where they may enter surface and ground water reserves. Continued, unregulated use of such chemicals could potentially contaminate lakes, streams, ponds, wells, and ground water.

Fish kills, reproductive failure in birds, and acute illnesses in humans and animals have been correlated with contaminated water. However, the exact source(s) of these damaging chemicals is not always apparent. And because we have a poor understanding of the results of long-term exposure to chemicals, the exact identification of the hazards is difficult.

Ground water quality

More than half of the U.S. population relies on underground sources of drinking water. Rural residents are even more dependent on these natural reserves, with more than 90% of rural water from ground water sources.

EPA survey of pesticides in water

Long-term use of agricultural fertilizers and pesticides has created significant concern about the vulnerability of ground water to contamination. In 1990, the Environmental Protection Agency released the results from its five-year National Survey of Pesticides in Drinking Water Wells (NPS). Of the 127 analyses in the survey, nitrate was most frequently detected in NPS wells. Based on the results of the study, EPA estimates that nitrate is present at or above the analytical reporting limit of 0.15 ppm (mg/l) in approximately 45,300 community water systems and 5,990,000 rural domestic wells nationwide (fig. 12.1).

High levels of nitrogen in drinking water have been shown to cause numerous health-related problems. Even "nontoxic" nitrate levels may lower human resistance to environmental stresses and interfere with normal metabolic processes. Ammonia forms of nitrogen in surface water can be directly toxic to fish and other marine life. Nitrogen can also stimulate plant growth, increasing the rate of decomposition, as well as the level of plant toxins. As this process occurs, the supply of oxygen in the water is depleted.

The NPS study also detected pesticides and pesticide degradates much less frequently than nitrate. The EPA estimates that 9,850 community water systems and 446,000 rural domestic wells in the United States contain at least one pesticide or pesticide degradate. DCPA acid metabolites, a degradate of DCPA (dimethyl tetrachloroterephthalate) and the herbicide Atrazine were the two most commonly found chemicals in NPS wells (fig. 12.2).

Greenhouse and nursery crops are among the highest water-consuming plants grown commercially. They also consume relatively high rates of fertilizers and pesticides. As a result, large volumes of runoff are often generated, which could potentially enter surface and ground water sources. Growers in the U.S. and Europe are now working to develop

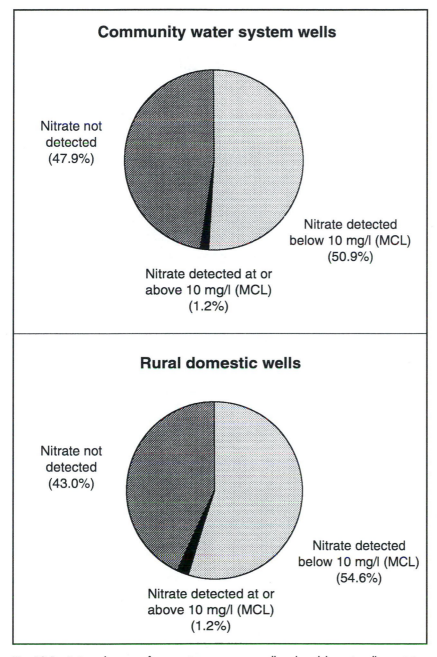

Fig. 12.1   Estimated percent of community water system wells and rural domestic wells containing nitrate (from EPA *National Pesticide Survey*).

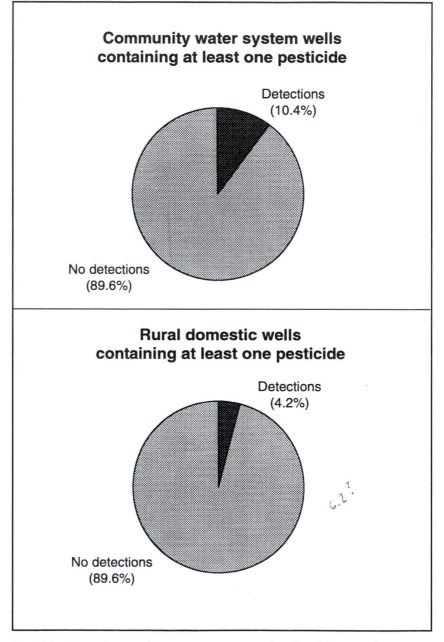

Fig. 12.2 Estimated percent of community water system wells and rural domestic wells containing at least one pesticide (from EPA *National Pesticide Survey*).

water management techniques that will help conserve and protect our natural water resources.

The demand for information on irrigation runoff and how the greenhouse industry impacts ground water has significantly increased as regulations on surface and ground water become stricter. It is critical to the U.S. greenhouse and nursery industry to develop, evaluate, and adapt alternative irrigation and fertilization technologies to reduce water and fertilizer consumption and to reduce pollution of natural water resources. These alternative technologies also require new and improved methods to determine the total fertilizer and water budget for major greenhouse crops.

Regulatory agencies and permits

Federal and state standards for irrigation runoff are not always easy to identify or understand. The EPA has established basic water quality guidelines, and in many areas the EPA is responsible for regulating a state's surface and ground water. In some states, however, water commissions, boards or districts serve as the primary regulatory agencies. To identify what agencies and/or regulations pertain to your situation, contact your county extension office, trade association, or Soil Conservation District.

Submitting samples for analysis. Once you have this information, submit runoff samples for analysis. A simple test for nitrates, as well as other nutrients, is usually inexpensive. A complete analysis, including pesticides, can be costly. If you decide to conduct a thorough pesticide analysis, first inventory the chemicals used in your operation and then determine the chemicals to include. Be aware that the sampling technique, as well as the analytical methodology, can affect results.

After reviewing results from these tests as well as local water quality standards, it should be apparent whether or not you have a problem. Excessive nitrates and phosphates are most common. Check pesticide concentrations carefully to determine if any are above acceptable limits. Monitor runoff water through analysis on a regular basis, and maintain careful records to track water quality.

Water-discharge permits. Many state and federal agencies now require a water-discharge permit to discharge irrigation runoff into surface receiving water. Although permit specifications vary from state to state, the following are common features:

- The permit is usually good for three to five years.
- All irrigation must be retained.
- All or part of storm runoff must be retained (usually at least the first 2 inches [5 cm]).
- No pesticides can be discharged.
- Nitrate- and ammonia-discharge levels must be less than 2 to 10 ppm.
- Discharge pH must be between 6 and 9.
- The discharge must not exceed acceptable levels of suspended solids.

Specific information on regulatory agencies and permits in your area can be obtained through your state Extension Service, Office of Soil Conservation and Stabilization, trade associations, or regional EPA office.

Pesticides and runoff

Pesticide use is receiving its share of attention from regulatory agencies, although most regulations have dealt with worker safety to date. Even so, greenhouse producers must begin to conscientiously look at what they are using and how they are using it from a pesticide standpoint.

Integrated pest management (IPM), today's catch phrase for the new way to control diseases and pests, can help significantly reduce pesticide consumption and at the same time increase pest control effectiveness by using both pesticide and nonpesticide strategies.

Integrated pest management

Integrated pest management for greenhouse crops is complex. Each problem or production objective has a wide range of potentially acceptable solutions. There are also legal implications regarding recommendations and use of any management tactic or pesticide product.

Determine your objective. Design your pest management program to meet a specific production objective. In greenhouse production, this objective is usually to produce pest-free, damage-free plants. However, in some situations, the objective may be to maintain healthy plants, which allows tolerance of minor insect or mite pest damage. Additionally, a preference to use no or low toxicity pesticides may be desirable. This is particularly important in regard to potential surface and ground water contamination. Financial constraints also play a role in determining your IPM objectives.

Sanitation practices. The first steps to take in a program to manage plant pests are preventative, starting with a clean production area. Fumigate or otherwise treat greenhouses prior to establishing a new crop to help eliminate pest problems from previous crops. Where plants at different stages of growth or of different species are grown in the same area, treat pests prior to establishing the next crop. Eliminate weeds and other alternate hosts of plant pests also to help prevent problems on the new crop.

Start with pest-free plants. Selecting uninfected plants, plugs, cuttings, or transplants is critically important. Carefully inspect all plants brought into the production area, and discard or treat those found to be infested. When possible, use pest resistant or tolerant plant species or cultivars to reduce pesticide applications. Become knowledgeable about the susceptibility of a plant species and/or cultivar to pests to help you anticipate problems throughout the production cycle. Use preventative treatments, such as systemic insecticides applied to the growing media at or shortly after planting, to protect young, rapidly growing plants if pest pressure is high at planting time.

Maintain optimum cultural practices. Plants under stress are more attractive to pests and can withstand less injury from them. Use optimum fertilization and irrigation practices to reduce conditions that predispose plants to infestation. Temperature, humidity, and light may also be important factors for pests and the use of certain pesticides.

Early detection is key to good management. Once plants are established, there are several methods you can use to monitor the onset of pest problems. Yellow sticky traps placed around the production area can detect early movement of adult whiteflies, thrips, adult leafminer flies, fungus gnats, and aphids. Plants should be regularly inspected. Pay particular attention to the undersides of leaves, or shake portions of the plants over colored paper to dislodge pests. This method is useful for detecting small, hard-to-see pests such as spider mites and thrips. Regularly inspect plants that are highly attractive to certain insect pests to detect low pest populations. Implement control tactics or programs when a significant number of pests or pest damage is first detected.

Learn to recognize damage produced by major insect pests, and attempt to detect and estimate the pest's population density before selecting a control method. Many of the insect and mite species seen in greenhouses are not harmful. Avoid using pesticides for "ghost" pests or unsolved problems. Become familiar with beneficial insect species (parasites and predators), and consider the use of this free help when making management decisions.

Categorizing pesticides and other greenhouse chemicals

The Soil Conservation Service has developed a data base to estimate the potential risk of various pesticides to water resources (table 12.1). Although the figures given in table 12.1 should not be considered precise, they can be used as a guide to develop a management plan. The following expands on headings and information in table 12.1.

Formulation. The long-term (weeks to months) life of a pesticide is a function of its physical properties and persistence, but its initial life (hours to days) is strictly a function of its formulation. For example, about 30 times more wettable powder than emulsified concentrate is lost if both are applied and immediately subjected to rain or irrigation.

Solubility. The solubility of pesticides in water at room temperature is given in ppm (mg/1). This is the solubility of pure active ingredients and not the formulated product. Solubility is a fundamental property of a chemical and strongly affects the ease of wash-off and leaching through soil. In general, pesticides with solubilities of 1 ppm or less tend to stay at the soil surface and are washed off in the sediment phase of runoff.

Half-life. Half-life, given in days, is the time required for pesticides in soils to be degraded so that their concentration decreases by one-half. Pesticide degradation can be fairly accurately described by assuming that each successive half-life decreases the pesticide concentration by half. For example, a period of two half-lives reduces a soil concentration to one-fourth of the initial amount. "Persistence times," often reported

Table 12.1   Surface loss and leaching potential for commonly used greenhouse pesticides

Common chemical name	Trade name & formulation	Solubility (ppm)	Half-life (days)	Sorption ratio (Koc)	Surface loss potential	Leaching potential
Acephate	Orthene WP	650,000	3	100	small	small
Aldicarb	Temik 10G	6,000	30	30	small	large
Ancymidol	A-Rest	650	20[a]	120	medium	medium
Azinphos-methyl	Guthion 50WP	29	40	1,000	large	small
Benomyl	Benlate WP	2	100	2,100	large	small
Carbaryl	Sevin WP	40	7	229	medium	small
Carbofuran	Furadan 10G	350	30	29	small	large
Chlorothalonil	Daconil WP	0.6	20	1,380	large	small
Cyromazine	Trigard WP	11,000	90	10[b]	small	large
Daminozide	B-Nine SP	100,000	7	10[b]	small	medium
DCNA (Dicloran)	Botran WP	7	10[a]	5,000	large	small
DCPA (Chlorthal dimethyl)	Dacthal WP	0.5	30	5,000	large	small
Demeton-S-Methyl	Metasystox C	33,000	30[b]	51	medium	large
Diazinon	Knox-Out EC	40	30	85	medium	large
Dicofol	Kelthane WP	1[b]	60[a]	8,000,000	large	small
Dimethoate	Cygon C	25,000	7	8	small	medium
Dinocap	Karathane WP	4[a]	20[b]	630[a]	medium	small
Disulfoton	Di-Syston 15G	25	4	2,000	medium	small
Diuron	Karmex WP	42	60	400	large	medium
Endosulfan	Thiodan EC	0.3	43	200,000	large	small
Ethephon	Florel	1,000,000[a]	5[b]	10,000	medium	tot.use
Ethion	Ethion EC	1	350	15,400	large	small
Etridiazole	Terrazole WP	50	20[b]	10,000[a]	large	small
Fenbutatin oxide	Vendex WP	0.005	20[b]	100,000	large	small
Fenvalerate	Pydrin EC	0.1	50	100,000	large	small
Ferbam	Carbamate	120	20[b]	300	medium	medium
Fluvalinate	Mavrik C	0.005	50[a]	1,000,000	large	small
Lindane	Isotox EC	7	90	1,100	large	medium
Malathion	Malathion EC	145	1	1,797	small	small
Mancozeb	Manzate WP	0.5	35	1,000	large	small

Table 12.1 continued

Common chemical name	Trade name & formulation	Solubility (ppm)	Half-life (days)	Sorption ratio (Koc)	Surface loss potential	Leaching potential
Maneb	Maneb	0.5[a]	12	1000[b]	medium	small
Metalaxyl	Subdue EC	7,100	7	16	small	medium
Metaldehyde	Metaldehyde	230	10[b]	240	medium	small
Methomyl	Lannate SP	57,900	8	28[a]	small	medium
Oxamyl	Vydate C	280,000	7	1	small	large
Oxydemeton-methyl	Metasystox EC	1,000,000	20[b]	1[a]	small	large
PCNB	Terraclor WP	0.44	21	10,000	large	small
Permethrin	Pounce EC	0.2	30[a]	10,600	large	small
Phosethyl-Al	Aliette WP	120000	10[b]	10,000[b]	large	small
Piperalin	Pipron EC	10[b]	20[b]	1,000[b]	medium	small
Propargite	Omite EC	0.5	20[b]	8,000[a]	large	small
Trichlorfon	Dylox WP	154,000	27	2	small	large
Triforine	Funginex EC	30	21	500[a]	medium	small

Source: R.L. Becher, D. Herzfeld, K.R. Ostie, and E.J. Stamm-Katovich. 1989. *Pesticides: Surface Runoff, Leaching and Exposure Concern.* Minnesota Extension Service, AG-BU-3911.

[a]Value is estimated.

[b]Value is probably off by a factor of 2-3.

in scientific literature, are the times required for a pesticide to degrade to the point that it is no longer active.

Soil sorption index. Soil sorption index is measured by the Koc value. The Koc measures a pesticide's tendency to be strongly attached, by chemical or physical bonds, to soil particle surfaces. Higher Koc values (1,000) indicate a stronger attachment to soil and a lesser tendency for the pesticide to move, except with sediment movement. Conversely, pesticides with lower Koc values tend to move with water and have a potential for deep percolation below the root zone or to being carried away in runoff water.

Surface loss (runoff) potential. Surface loss potential indicates the tendency of a pesticide to move with sediment in runoff. A "large" rating means the pesticide has a high tendency to move with sediment, while a "small" rating means the pesticide has a low potential to move with sediment.

Leaching potential. The leaching potential indicates a pesticide's tendency to move in solution with water and to leach below the root zone into deep percolation. The ratings of "large," "medium," "small," and "total use" describe the leaching potential. A "large" rating means the chemical has a high potential for leaching. A "total use" rating means the pesticide should not leach with percolating water.

Unfortunately, little is known about the leaching capacity of most pesticides in soil mixtures or soilless growing media. Since a portion of applied pesticides will first move through media, it is important to consider their interaction.

It is safe to assume, however, that producers should try to reduce the application of pesticides with high surface loss and leaching potentials. This is not to say that these chemicals should be eliminated from inventory, but that their use be limited to an "as needed" basis. This information, along with the Soil-Pesticide Interaction Ratings Matrix, is available from the Soil Conservation Service and can be used to determine the overall potential for pesticide loss to surface runoff or leaching.

Handling pesticide wastes

Using information gathered through regular scouting and weighing the economic, worker safety, and environmental implications of various pest control alternatives, you may determine that applying a pesticide is the best way to control a certain pest problem. Before selecting a specific pesticide, compare the mode of action, cost, and application methods for each registered product.

After treatment, leftover spray or drench solution and/or pesticide containers must be disposed of. Improper handling of pesticides poses a real threat to the environment, as well as to the health and safety of workers. Excess application or improper disposal of leftover mixtures, undiluted chemicals, or even pesticide containers can lead to potential contamination of surface and ground water. However, the risk of a serious incident can be reduced if proper management and disposal techniques are used.

Hazardous agricultural wastes, as defined in the 40 Code of Federal Regulations (parts 261.31–261.33), have one of the characteristics of a hazardous waste. Regulated pesticide wastes are those which: 1) contain a hazardous sole active ingredient, 2) are hazardous mixtures, 3) are acutely hazardous waste, or 4) are hazardous waste as identified by an EPA number.

In most areas, pesticides are called hazardous, acutely hazardous, or regulated wastes if they require specific disposal procedures. Disposal of these chemicals usually requires completion of a Uniform Hazardous Waste Manifest before the chemicals can be shipped off-site for treatment, storage, or disposal. This can be costly, so it is important to minimize amounts of hazardous waste.

Management practices

The first step in minimizing chemical waste is to determine the optimum means for pest control. IPM techniques will provide needed protection with reduced use of chemical pesticides. In addition, evaluate biological control alternatives. If a pesticide must be used, minimize waste disposal problems:

- Select the appropriate pesticide.
- Read the label carefully.
- Apply the pesticide properly.
- Clean up thoroughly.
- Store the pesticide securely.
- Dispose of containers safely.

Labels. Once the need for a pesticide product has been determined, carefully review the label. There you'll find mixing and spraying directions, amount to be used over a specific area, equipment requirements, registered crops, spray timing, mixture specifications, as well as other useful information. Review label information before each use. The label also provides guidelines on pesticide storage and container disposal.

Storage. Pesticides should be stored in a locked, dry, cool, well-ventilated area. This will ensure that the chemical will maintain its active ability for the period of time it is stored before use. Safe storage will also prevent nonauthorized personnel from coming into contact with potentially harmful materials. The storage area should be equipped with cleanup supplies, such as clay absorbents, in case a spill occurs. Water, food, or feed should not be stored in the same locked areas as pesticides. Safely storing pesticides will help minimize wastes by preventing spills and loss of chemical activity from degradation by heat, sunlight, or other environmental factors.

Application. Improper pesticide application can create serious waste management problems. Misapplication limits a product's ability to control the target pest(s). As a result, additional pesticide applications are frequently required, and these subsequent applications increase the potential for contamination. Overestimating the volume of pesticide required represents another waste management problem. Preapplication calculations should accurately determine the amount of pesticide needed for a specific area to help avoid excessive, leftover mixture that will have to be disposed later.

Test equipment frequently to determine if it is in proper working order. A trial run with water can be used to determine the spray pressure needed to cover a specific area at the labeled rate. Check all nozzles to make sure they are dispersing properly. Clogged nozzles or an improperly pressurized boom will cause uneven distribution, resulting in over or under application.

Cleanup. Dispose of all remaining mixture according to label instructions. For specific information on the state regulations in your area, contact your local Extension office. Storing excess mixture is not recommended. Many pesticides degrade more quickly when mixed with water or oil. This may weaken or even completely inactivate mixtures saved for later use. Also, these mixtures are more subject to temperature and sunlight factors, which can hasten pesticide degradation. Stored mixtures can also lead to spills and leakage hazards.

Triple rinse all equipment inside and out to minimize pesticide residues. If equipment is rinsed on a loading pad, use a closed storage system to collect the runoff. If a closed system is not available, storage tanks or containers may be used to catch the rinse water. If this material is stored, keep accurate records on the content of each tank. Never store assorted wastes in the same tank.

Rinse water should be applied to an area that would do some good in controlling the target pest(s), but would not create a contamination hazard. Do not apply rinse water to areas previously treated. Reapplying over such an area could increase the potential for contamination or result in longer persistence of the pesticide in that area.

Container disposal. Many areas have specific requirements for disposal of pesticide containers. Check with your county extension office for state regulations. Typically, you should triple rinse all containers with a solvent capable of removing any remaining pesticide and dispose of the runoff according to the disposal instructions on the label. Empty containers should then be punctured, crushed, or otherwise rendered incapable of holding liquid. These containers can then be disposed of at a sanitary landfill or returned to the manufacturer or formulator.

Managing pesticide wastes properly reduces potential hazards to the environment and employees. Although most of these practices are nothing more than common sense, we often tend to cut corners when time is short. However, careful attention to detail in this area is critical if we are to comply with the increasing regulations concerning the environment. Developing an effective waste management program can be relatively painless if you follow these basic guidelines.

Reduce potential contamination through BMPs

Best Management Practices (BMP) reduce those production inputs that contribute to environmental contamination. Both cultural and structural BMPs can greatly limit the amount of contaminants entering the environment, creating a sustainable means of producing quality greenhouse/nursery products. Following are brief descriptions of some of the most commonly used BMPs. The chapters on irrigation system and recycling address several of these factors in greater detail.

Capture and recycle irrigation runoff. This structural BMP can greatly reduce the potential for surface and ground water contamination. However, managing recycled irrigation water can be difficult. Factors such as salinity, alkalinity/pH, specific ion toxicities, pathogens, aquatic weeds and algae, and residual pesticides/herbicides must all be carefully monitored.

High efficiency application systems. Overhead irrigation is inefficient, with an average of only 15% of the water applied reaching the target. Drip and subirrigation systems are much more efficient and can greatly reduce the volume of contaminated runoff entering surface and ground water resources.

Improved irrigation management. Knowing when and how long to run an irrigation system is extremely important. Precise management, based on quantitative soil and plant data, greatly reduces the overall volume of water used and subsequent runoff. Applying irrigation water carefully also helps limit plant stress. Excessive levels of stress often predispose plants to a variety of insect and disease problems, which will then require some form of chemical control (another source of potential contaminants).

Optimum fertility regimes. Selecting the appropriate type and amount of fertilizer to use is an important method of controlling water quality. Slow/control release fertilizers (SRF/CRF) generally reduce the level of nitrates entering irrigation runoff. However, these materials are not immediately available to the plant. Soluble fertilizers provide a more direct way to address plant nutrition, but potential contaminant loads are increased. Generally speaking, floral/ornamental crops receive more fertilizer than they require.

Water treatment. Treating recycled irrigation water can include filtering to eliminate sediment; use of activated charcoal filters to remove selected chemicals; chlorination or other treatments to eliminate pathogens (i.e., ozone, UV light, etc.); back mixing with a fresh water source to reduce salinity; acid injection to correct alkalinity/pH; and/or numerous other treatments. Treating irrigation water can greatly help reduce the accumulation of potential contaminants over long periods of time.

Conducting an environmental audit

Understanding the factors that contribute to environmental contamination can help producers manage this problem. The first step in this process is to carefully audit your operation to identify potential problem areas. This information can then be used to develop short- and long-term management tactics to reduce or even eliminate potential contamination.

The questions posed in this audit cover many of the basic factors to consider when evaluating environmental contamination. Obviously, not all of these questions will pertain to every growing operation, and there may be additional factors to consider that are not covered.

Growers should answer each of these questions as thoroughly and accurately as possible. Compile the information into an organized report and keep it on file. To maintain a current audit, perform periodic updates and revisions.

Site-related considerations

What is the depth of ground water?

What direction does the ground water flow in?

What soil type is your site located on?

Is there a restrictive layer of dense clay between the soil surface and the water table?

What is the depth to bedrock? Is it fractured?

What is the slope of the topography?

If you have a well, is it properly cased? When was it last checked?

What aquifer is the well water drawn from?

Have you ever checked the well water for nutrients, bacteria, or any other contaminants?

Where are the sewer or storm drains or natural drainage points?

Are there sinkholes around your sites?

Where is the nearest down-gradient and up-gradient surface water? How far away is it?

What is the neighboring land use? Rural? Urban? Industrial, commercial, or residential? How is it zoned?

Are there septic tanks in the area?

Are there illegal types of private sewage disposal facilities (e.g., cesspools, disposal wells, etc.) in the vicinity?

Are there other wells nearby, particularly for drinking water?

Are there any abandoned wells onsite or in the immediate vicinity?

What are the conditions of the other wells?

What sampling, if any, is or has been done near your site? By whom?

Who else might have discharges in the area?

Wellhead considerations

Does your pesticide mixing site, if outdoors, have a roof over it?

Do you have an impermeable mixing/loading area?

Who has access to your facilities?

Have you briefed the police and fire departments?

Does your emergency plan have responders identified, current phone numbers, up-to-date product inventories with complete labels and materials safety data sheets (MSDS), and are procedures identified to control, recover, and dispose of products?

Is everyone aware of his or her role(s)?

Is the safety equipment accessible? Is it properly maintained?

Have you ever practiced for an emergency? Have you changed any employees since that time?

Do you have a method to ensure first chemicals in are the first out?

Do you have separate storage areas for pesticides and flammable products?

Do your mixing, growing, and application sites have floor drains? Where do they go? Can you plug them?

Do you have an anti-backup-siphoning device to protect your water supplies?

Do you have a sump pump?

What kind of cleanup facility do you have?

Do you have a plan for legal disposal of unused chemicals including pesticides, acids, concentrates, etc.?

Where are empty containers disposed of? Do you properly rinse them? What do you do with rinse water from your equipment? Do you have a tank for reserving leftover solutions or rinse water?

Do you have secondary containment in case of spills in your storage, mixing, and application areas?

Can you recapture spilled materials?

Do you have absorbent material for spills?

Do you store any material underground, including fuels? If so, how do you check for leaks? How often? Have you reported them to the state as underground storage tanks?

Production considerations

What is the size of your operation?

How many square feet are there under cover, concrete, ground cloth, gravel, soil, other?

Do you have an accurate diagram of your operation?

Where is the principal runoff site(s)?

What is your principal source of irrigation water (percent surface, well, municipal, etc.)?

How are your crops irrigated (percent drip, sub, hand, overhead sprinklers, etc.)?

What is the maximum estimated volume of water used per day?

Do you have a meter on group wells(s) or other water supplies to measure water use?

What is the maximum estimated volume of runoff per day?

Do you have seasonal variations in water use and runoff volume?

What is the average annual rainfall for your location?

What is the maximum volume of rainfall that would occur at your location in a 25-year frequency?

What is the predicted runoff volume from thunderstorms?

What is the average irrigation frequency (i.e., daily, three times per week, etc.) for your crops?

How do you select and manage irrigation frequency and amount?

What size containers do you use? (percent 4-inch [10 cm], 6-inch [15 cm], 10-inch [25 cm], 1-gallon [4 l], 5-gallon [20 l], etc.)

How would you characterize your growing media (porous, high water holding capacity, etc.)?

What types of fertilizers do you use? How is the material applied? How frequently do you apply fertilizer to your crops?

What is your maximum estimated use of fertilizers per year?

Do you monitor the mineral content of irrigation runoff?

What pesticides do you use? What are the primary targets for these materials? How do you select application rates for these chemicals? How frequently are these materials applied? How are these materials applied?

What IPM tactics do you use to reduce pesticide usage?

Are your applicators licensed?

In summary, floriculture and ornamental crop producers need not panic over the environmental issue. Few cases are on record where significant problems have occurred. However, laws, regulations, and policies concerning water and water quality seem to be growing at an exponential rate. It looks like this will be the trend for many years to come. Our industry has a long-standing history of working in concert with the environment, and most growers go out of their way to protect natural resources. A continued understanding of how structural and cultural inputs affect the environment will help in developing long-term, sustainable production practices, while at the same time strengthening our industry.

References

Becker, R.L., D. Herzfeld, K.R. Ostlie, and E.J. Stamm-Katovich. 1989. *Pesticides: surface runoff, leaching and exposure concerns*. Minnesota Extension Service AG-BU-3911, University of Minnesota.

National pesticide survey. 1990. Summary results of EPA's national survey of pesticides in drinking water wells. EPA Office of Pesticide and Toxic Substances. NPS Summary Results Fall 1990.

Wilkerson, D.C., B.M. Drees, D. McWilliams, and J. M. Sweeten. 1991. *Water management guidelines for the greenhouse industry*. Texas Agricultural Experiment Station Publication B-5016. Texas A&M University, College Station.

Glossary

acid fertilizer — a fertilizer that causes a decrease in pH (i.e., increased acidity or decreased basicity) when applied to the soil/growing media. Acidity is primarily due to ammonium, ammonia, and/or urea in the fertilizer.

acidification — the process of making a substance or solution more acid, i.e., lower in pH. In irrigation, it refers to adding acid (sulfuric, phosphoric, or nitric acid) to the irrigation water to create a slightly acid 5.8 to 6.2 pH or reduction to a certain level of alkalinity.

activated alumina — an oxide of aluminum used in water treatment to remove impurities, such as fluoride.

activated carbon — a form of carbon used in water treatment to remove impurities, such as fluoride.

adjusted sodium adsorption ratio (Adj. R_{Na}) — a mathematical term used to estimate the sodium hazard in irrigation water. It is an equation that takes into account the sodium content of water in relation to the salinity, calcium, magnesium, and bicarbonate content. Similar measures of sodium hazard that are reported are: sodium absorption ratio (SAR), adjusted sodium absorption ratio (SAR_{adj}), exchangeable sodium percentage (ESP), sodium percentage, and residual sodium carbonate.

air porosity or air space — the percent volume (volume/volume) of soil/growing media that is filled with air when irrigating media to container capacity. The air in media is primarily in the large macropores.

283

alkaline — indicates a pH above 7.0. Alkaline is also called basic.

alkalinity — a measure of water's capacity to neutralize acids. True alkalinity is the sum of the dissolved bicarbonates, carbonates, hydroxides, ammonia, borates, organic bases, phosphates, and silicates in the water. Most of the time in practice, alkalinity is the sum of the bicarbonates and carbonates (total carbonates) expressed as me/l or ppm.

alum — either aluminum sulfate $[Al_2(SO_4)_3 \bullet (18H_2O]$ or a double salt of potassium aluminum sulfate $[KAl(SO_4)_2 \bullet (12H_2O]]$ used to treat irrigation water and recycled water to flocculate and remove colloidal clay. Aluminum sulfate is more commonly used because of its lower costs and its availability in both liquid and dry forms.

ammonia — a form of inorganic nitrogen (NH_3). It can be toxic at concentrations as low as 2.5 ppm (0.15 mM). Toxicity increases as pH increases. Ammonia is the cause of ammonium toxicity.

ammoniacal — consisting of, containing, or producing ammonia. When referring to a fertilizer, it indicates a fertilizer that contains ammonia or ammonium (such as ammonium sulfate) or a fertilizer that can produce ammonia or ammonium upon breakdown (such as urea).

ammonium — an inorganic nitrogen fertilizer (NH_4^+). Ammonium will always contain a small amount of ammonia in equilibrium.

analysis — see fertilizer analysis.

anion — a negatively charged ion.

anion exchange resin — a positively charged ion exchange resin that removes anions (negatively charged ions) from water.

antagonism — when one nutrient in high concentration suppresses the activity of another nutrient and causes an induced nutrient deficiency.

available water capacity (AWC) — the percent volume (volume/volume) of soil/growing media occupied by water that is available to the plant. It is calculated by determining the container capacity, then subtracting the unavailable water (PWP).

bagasse — an organic growing media component made from sugar cane fiber.

bark — an organic growing media component made from the bark of hardwood or softwood trees. It is usually hammer milled, screened to size, and composted or aged prior to use.

basic — indicates a pH above 7.0. Basic is also called alkaline.

basic fertilizers — a fertilizer that causes an increase in pH (i.e., decreased acidity or increased basicity) when applied to soil/growing media. A fertilizer is basic primarily due to its nitrate content.

best management practices (BMP) — the practice of minimizing production inputs that contribute to environmental contamination.

bicarbonate — partially dissociated carbonic acid in the form HCO_3^-. A water pH between 7.4 and 9.3 will have bicarbonate as the main form of carbonic acid present.

boom system — an overhead irrigation system where the nozzles are mounted on a boom that moves above the plants.

brine water — a water very high in solutes. It may also refer to the byproduct or waste water of water purification systems.

builder's lime — see hydrated lime.

bulk density — the ratio of the mass (weight) of dry soil/growing media to its bulk volume, expressed as grams per cubic centimeter (g/cc) or pounds per cubic foot (lb/cu ft).

calcareous soil — a field soil containing large amounts of free calcium carbonate (i.e., lime), usually with a high pH of 7.6 to 8.3. Common in the southwestern states and areas of low rainfall.

calcined clay — an inorganic growing media component made from clay that is fired (calcined) to harden it, then crushed and screened to size.

calcitic lime — a lime composed of calcium carbonate ($CaCO_3$) derived from calcite. Pure calcitic lime contains 40% Ca. It is also called calcitic limestone.

calcium carbonate ($CaCO_3$) equivalent — on fertilizer labels it is used as the basis for expressing potential acidity (how much calcium carbonate could 1 ton of the fertilizer neutralize?) or potential basicity (how much calcium carbonate would 1 ton of the fertilizer be the equivalent of?).

capillary action — absorption and movement of water through capillary pores due to the forces of capillary attraction. Water from subirrigation systems and some drip systems wet growing media by capillary action.

capillary mat irrigation system — a subirrigation system where container plants are placed on a moistened mat or absorbent material from which water moves into the container by capillary action.

carbonate — completely dissociated carbonic acid in the form $CO_3^=$. At pH 10.3 or above, carbonate is the predominate form present.

carbonic acid — dissolved carbon dioxide in the hydrated form H_2CO_3. At pH of 6.4 or below, carbonic acid is the predominate form present.

cation — a positively charged ion.

cation exchange capacity (CEC) — the milliequivalents (1/1000's of an equivalent) of cation exchange sites present per 100 grams (me/100 g) of dry soil. In soilless organic-based growing media, it is often expressed as milliequivalents per 100 cubic centimeters (me/100 cc) because of the very low weight of dry soilless media. The CEC is a measure of the nutrient holding capacity of cationic nutrients, such as K^+, NH_4^+, Ca^{++}, etc.

cation exchange resin — a negatively charged ion exchange resin that removes cations (positively charged ions) from water.

cellulose acetate-type membranes — a membrane composed of cellulose acetate used in reverse osmosis water purification systems. These membranes are sensitive to pH, but resistant to chlorine.

chelate — derived from the Greek word "chele" meaning claw. A large organic molecule, called a chelating agent, that contains one of the micronutrient heavy metals—iron (Fe), zinc (Zn), manganese (Mn), copper (Cu)—or divalent cations—calcium (Ca), magnesium (Mg)—held in the center by ligand bonds. Used as fertilizers in alkaline soil/media/water to keep Fe, Zn, Mn, and Cu soluble.

chelating agent — a large organic molecule that is able to bond to heavy metal micronutrients—iron (Fe), zinc (Zn), manganese (Mn), copper (Cu)—or divalent cations—calcium (Ca), magnesium (Mg)—by ligand bonds to form a chelate. The most commonly used chelating agents in fertilizers are DTPA, EDDHA, HEDTA, EDTA, citrate, and lignosulfonates.

chlorination — to treat with chlorine as a disinfectant; used in recycled water treatment.

chlorosis — pale green to yellow coloration. The term is usually applied to leaves and is a common symptom of many nutrient deficiencies.

citrate — an organic acid that is sometimes used as a micronutrient chelating agent of iron, zinc, copper, and manganese. Citrate possesses weak chelating ability.

clarified water — partially purified water free of heavy sediments and floating debris.

clarifier — a pit, basin, or tank for removing colloidal material in water treatment systems. Chemicals are added to flocculate the colloidal material, then polymers are added to aggregate the floc and cause it to settle to the bottom. The clear water is then recovered from the top layer.

coagulant — a chemical that causes flocculation, such as alum which acts as a coagulant to flocculate colloidal clay.

coefficient of uniformity (Q) — a measure of how uniformly an irrigation system delivers water, with 1 being perfect and below 0.8 indicating a poorly performing system.

coir fiber — an organic growing media component made from coconut husk fiber.

composting — a process that partially decomposes organic matter.

conductivity — see electrical conductivity.

conductivity meter — an instrument used to measure electrical conductivity of solutions. Also called a solubridge or salts meter.

container capacity — the percent volume (volume/volume) of soil/growing media filled with water after it has been saturated and allowed to drain. It is sometimes called the water holding capacity and is the maximum amount of water that soil/growing media can hold. In field soils, it is called field capacity.

controlled-release fertilizer (CRF) — a fertilizer that is not immediately soluble and available to plants because the nutrients are released over time, from weeks to months. Release is based on either low solubility, biological breakdown, or a semipermeable coating.

critical deficiency limit — the lowest level of tissue nutrient content from which you can expect adequate growth. Below this, deficiencies are likely.

critical toxicity limit — the highest level of tissue nutrient content from which you can expect adequate growth. Above this limit, toxicities are likely.

deciSiemen per meter (dS/m) — the preferred unit to express electrical conductivity. One dS/m = one mS/cm = one mmhos/cm $\cong$ (ppm/700).

deficiency — when the concentration of a nutrient becomes low enough in a plant to cause decreased growth or damage. It is often accompanied by visual symptoms.

deionization — a water purification process for removing ions (cations and anions) from water using ion exchange resins.

distillation — a water purification process where water is heated into vapor form (which leaves impurities behind) and is then condensed to produce purified water.

dolomite — a lime composed of calcium-magnesium carbonate [$CaMg(CO_3)_2$]. Pure dolomite contains 13.1% Mg. Dolomite is often used interchangeably and incorrectly for dolomitic lime.

dolomitic lime — a lime composed primarily of calcium carbonate (calcite, $CaCO_3$), with a lesser content of calcium-magnesium carbonate [dolomite, $CaMg(CO_3)_2$]. Any lime that contains some Mg from dolomite is called dolomitic lime, but the concentration of Mg varies greatly, from 1.3 to 11.7%.

drip irrigation system — an irrigation system where water is delivered to the soil/growing media surface below the plant canopy, usually by small nozzles, emitters, or tubes.

DTPA — diethylenetriaminepentaacetic acid. A chelating agent that is used to chelate ferric (Fe^{+3}) iron. DTPA is used on acid to slightly alkaline soils and in many chelated liquid fertilizer formulations.

ebb-and-flow flooded floor system — an ebb-and-flow subirrigation system that uses molded concrete floors as the flood container.

ebb-and-flow subirrigation system — a subirrigation growing system where containerized plants are placed in watertight trays or molded concrete floors that are flooded when needed with nutrient solution, then drained. Usually the nutrient solution is collected and recirculated. Also called ebb & flow, ebb-and-flood, flood irrigation, and pulsed subirrigation.

ebb-and-flow tray system — an ebb-and-flow subirrigation system that uses watertight trays, usually placed on benches, as the flood container.

EC_e — electrical conductivity of a saturated soil extract.

EC_w — electrical conductivity of water.

EDDHA — ethylenediaminedi-o-hydroxyphenylacetic acid, a chelating agent used to chelate ferric iron (Fe^{+3}); used on highly alkaline soils/media. Very expensive.

EDTA — ethylenediaminetetraacetic acid, a chelating agent used to chelate ferric iron (Fe^{+3}), manganese, copper, and zinc. Used on slightly acid soils/media and in many chelated liquid fertilizer formulations and hydroponic nutrient solutions.

electrical conductivity (EC) — the ability of a solution to conduct electricity due to dissolved or suspended ionic solutes. Used as a measure of soluble salt content of water. Preferred to be expressed as deciSiemen/meter (dS/m), but often expressed as milliSiemen/centimeter (mS/cm), millimhos/centimeter (mmhos/cm), $EC \times 10^{-3}$, or micromhos/centimeter (μmhos/cm). Each dissolved salt has its own unique conductivity, hence, EC is only an approximation of the actual salt content of a solution [ppm $\cong$ (dS/m)(700)].

electrodialysis — a water purification process where water is passed over electrically charged membranes to remove ionic solutes.

electrolytes — any compound or material that forms ions when dissolved in water, thus forming a conductor of electricity, such as all soluble salts.

elemental sulfur — the elemental form of sulfur used to decrease soil pH (increase acidity) in alkaline soil/growing media.

Epsom salt — magnesium sulfate ($MgSO_4 \cdot 7H_2O$); used primarily as a magnesium fertilizer, but it also supplies sulfur. Used to supply Mg without altering soil/growing media pH.

equilibrium reaction (pH$_c$) — a mathematical measure similar to pH, but it also takes into account the alkalinity, calcium, magnesium, carbonate, and bicarbonate content of water.

equivalent — a mole (Avogadro's number) of charges (positive or negative). One mole of a monovalent cation would contain one equivalent of positive charges, whereas one mole of a divalent cation would contain two equivalents of positive charges.

essential element — one of the 17 elements that plants need for normal growth and development and to complete their life cycle. They are: carbon (C), hydrogen (H), oxygen (O), nitrogen (N), phosphorus (P), potassium (K), calcium (Ca), magnesium (Mg), sulfur (S), iron (Fe), zinc (Zn), copper (Cu), manganese (Mn), boron (B), molybdenum (Mo), chlorine (Cl), and nickel(Ni).

evapotranspiration (ET) — the sum of evaporation and transpiration.

expressed sap tissue testing — the use of analytical techniques to determine the nutrient content of plant sap.

ferric — the form of iron in the +3 valency form (Fe^{+3}). Ferric iron is the insoluble form found in most soils and is the form of iron used in most chelates, for example EDTA or DTPA.

ferrous — the form of iron in the +2 valency form (Fe^{+2}). Ferrous iron is the primary form of iron plants absorb. Ferrous iron is only present in the soil in significant quantities under very acid or waterlogged conditions.

fertigation — a term often used to describe the application of soluble fertilizers in the irrigation water. Also called liquid feed.

fertilizer analysis — a sequence of three numbers on all fertilizer labels that gives the percent composition, on a weight basis, of N-P_2O_5-K_2O in the fertilizer.

fertilizer injector — a device attached to the irrigation line to inject a small amount of concentrated fertilizer into the water stream to yield a dilute concentration of fertilizer in the irrigation water. The injector ratio or proportion varies from 1:15 (i.e., dilutes 1 part fertilizer concentrate to every 15 parts of irrigation water) to 1:400. On some injectors the proportion can be varied.

fertilizer ratio — the fertilizer analysis reduced to the least common denominator, which yields the ratio of $N-P_2O_5-K_2O$. For example, a 18-6-12 analysis has a 3-1-2 ratio.

flocculation — the aggregation of particles into larger masses. Flocculation is used in water treatment to aggregate contaminants, which are then precipitated.

flooded floor — see ebb-and-flow flooded floor system.

fog system — a device that dispenses fine droplets of water that stay suspended in the air. Used for temperature and humidity control in greenhouses and propagation.

foliar analysis — nutrient analysis of leaf tissue.

frit — a slow-release fertilizer with the nutrients impregnated into powdered glass. Frit is most commonly used for potassium or iron.

growing media — the substrate in which plant's roots grow. Usually it is a highly amended or totally soilless mixture made from organic and inorganic components. Also called potting soil, soilless media, mix, or substrate.

gypsum — calcium sulfate. Gypsum is used primarily as a calcium fertilizer, and it also supplies sulfur. Most often used as a calcium fertilizer when you do not alter soil/growing media pH.

half-life — the length of time for one-half of a compound to disappear or be used.

hard water — a water high in calcium and/or magnesium.

HEDTA — hydroxyethylethylenediaminetriacetic acid, a chelating agent used to chelate ferric iron (Fe^{+3}). HEDTA is used under moderately alkaline soil conditions. Also abbreviated HEEDTA.

HEEDTA — see HEDTA.

Hoagland's Solution — one of the original hydroponic nutrient solutions. It is still used today with various modification, mainly in research studies.

hollow-fiber membranes — a type of membrane used in water purification systems.

hydrated lime — lime composed of calcium hydroxide [$Ca(OH)_2$]. Hydrated lime is used to raise media pH quickly.

hydroponics — cultivation of plants by placing the roots in liquid nutrient solutions rather than in soil/growing media. The soilless culture or water culture of plants.

immobile — a term used to describe translocation of a nutrient in plants when the nutrient only travels up the stem and into organs via the xylem, but it cannot be loaded into the phloem to travel out of organs or down stems. Deficiencies of immobile nutrients always occur on the young leaves first.

inorganic — a compound or substance that is not carbon based. When used to describe fertilizers, it includes the mineral forms, such as potassium nitrate, superphosphate, etc. When used to describe growing media components, it includes mineral, synthetic, or non-biological forms, such as perlite, vermiculite, sand, etc.

integrated pest management (IPM) — the use of multiple approaches to control pest damage, including variety selection, economic considerations, cultural control, sanitation, timing of planting, biological control, pesticides, etc.

interveinal — between the veins of the leaves.

ion — any atom or molecule that is electrically charged due to the loss of electrons, which results in a positively charged cation; or the gain of electrons, which results in a negatively charged anion.

ion exchange resin — a solid matrix or beads containing fixed positive and/or negative charges that remove ions from water by ion exchange.

leaching — removal of nutrients, salts, pesticides, or other water soluble compounds from growing media with water. Irrigation and rain leaches compounds from soil/growing media, and propagation mist leaches compounds from cuttings.

leaching potential — a measure of a pesticide's tendency to move in solution with water and leach below the root zone into deep percolation in the soil.

leaching requirement (LR) — the fraction of water applied during each irrigation that passes through the root zone and out the bottom of the container or soil profile. An LR of 0.5 means 50% of the irrigation water would pass through the container or soil profile. You can estimate the LR needed to maintain a certain soil salinity level by LR = $EC_w/[5/(EC_e-EC_w)]$; where EC_w is the electrical conductivity of the irrigation water and EC_e is the electrical conductivity of a saturated soil extract.

lignosulfonate — a mixture of sulfonated lignins derived as byproducts of the pulp/paper process. Used as a chelating agent for iron, manganese, copper, and zinc.

lime — technically, calcium oxide (CaO). Practically or agriculturally, it is any material containing the carbonates, oxides, and/or hydroxides of calcium and/or magnesium used to neutralize soil/media acidity. The most common ones used are calcitic lime, dolomitic lime, dolomite, and hydrated lime. Also called limestone.

limestone — see lime.

macronutrient — one of the six essential elements required by plants in larger quantities (0.2 to 7%). They are: nitrogen (N), phosphorus (P), potassium (K), calcium (Ca), magnesium (Mg), and sulfur (S).

major element — see macronutrient.

matric tension — the negative suction pressure or tension developed in soil/growing media due to the attraction of water into capillary pores or adsorbed onto surfaces. It is measured in Pascals (preferred method), bars, or atmospheres of pressure. Also called moisture tension. It can be related to water content by a moisture retention curve.

micronutrient — one of the eight essential elements required by plants in smaller quantities (1 to 600 ppm); iron (Fe), zinc (Zn), copper (Cu), manganese (Mn), boron (B), molybdenum (Mo), chlorine (Cl), and nickel (Ni).

micronutrient mix — a commercial fertilizer that supplies more than one of the micronutrients.

milliequivalent (me) — one-thousandth of an equivalent; see definition of equivalent. Used to express nutrient and salt concentrations in growing media, soil, and plant analyses.

milligram per liter (mg/l) — one thousandth of a gram per liter. The metric equivalent to parts per million (ppm).

millimhos per centimeter (mmhos/cm) — one-thousandth of a mhos per centimeter. The unit most commonly used to express electrical conductivity in the past or on older conductivity meters. The current trend is to use deciSiemen/meter (dS/m), which is numerically equal to mmhos/cm.

mineral nutrient — see nutrient.

minor element — see micronutrient.

mobile — a term used to describe the translocation of a nutrient in plants where the nutrient can travel up the stem and into organs via the xylem and also can be loaded into the phloem to travel out of organs or down stems. Deficiencies of mobile nutrients always occur on the old leaves first.

mobility — term that describes whether a nutrient is mobile or immobile.

model-based irrigation control — an automated irrigation system that is turned on and off based on mathematical models that predict water loss. The model takes into account environmental and plant factors.

moisture content — see matric tension.

moisture tension — the tension, or more precisely the negative pressure, under which water is held in soils/growing media and plants. It is measured in bars, Pascals, or atmospheres of pressure.

necrosis — brown, scorched, or dead areas on plant organs. Necrosis is a common symptom of many nutrient deficiencies.

nephelometer — an instrument using diffused light to determine the turbidity or clarity of water. Sometimes referred to as a turbidimeter.

nephelometric turbidity units (NTU) — a standard unit of measure of the turbidity or clarity of water based on scattering of light by suspended particles of colloids, silica, bacteria, or mineral precipitates. NTU is measured with a nephelometer using formazin as a reference standard.

neutral fertilizers — a fertilizer that does not significantly alter pH when applied to soil/growing media.

nitrate — an inorganic nitrogen fertilizer (NO_3^-). The most stable form of nitrogen found in most soils/growing media.

nitrification — a two-step process of converting ammonium to nitrate by bacteria in soil/growing media. In the first step, ammonium

(NH_4^+) is converted to nitrite (NO_2^-) by the bacterium *Nitrosomonas*, and in the second step nitrite (NO_2^-) is converted to nitrate (NO_3^-) by the bacterium *Nitrobacter*.

Nutricote — Trade name for controlled release fertilizer (usually containing N, P, and K) composed of a pellet of soluble fertilizer surrounded by a semipermeable coating.

nutrient — a term for 14 of the essential elements—nitrogen (N), phosphorus (P), potassium (K), calcium (Ca), magnesium (Mg), sulfur (S), iron (Fe), zinc (Zn), manganese (Mn), copper (Cu), boron (B), molybdenum (Mo), chlorine (Cl), and nickel (Ni)—of the 17 essential elements supplied in the mineral form (exclusive of carbon (C), hydrogen (H), and oxygen (O), which are supplied naturally by carbon dioxide, oxygen, or water). Nutrients are primarily derived from the soil or growing media; also called mineral nutrients. Fertilizers supply nutrients.

nutrient analysis — see tissue analysis.

nutrient film technique (NFT) — a subirrigation growing system. Plants are rooted into porous cubes or containers and placed in sloped troughs where a nutrient solution continuously flows down the troughs in a thin film to supply water and nutrients.This technique is used most in greenhouse vegetable production.

nutritional charting — conducting tissue analysis on a routine basis (for example, weekly) and plotting the results on graph paper to monitor how the level changes over the life of the crop.

organic — a compound composed of a carbon backbone. Usually used to describe something of biological origin. When used to describe fertilizers, it includes those of synthetic origin (for example, urea) or natural plant or animal products (manure, lignosulfonates). When used to describe growing medium components, it applies to components usually of plant origin, such as peat moss, composted bark, etc.

Osmocote — a trade name for controlled release fertilizer (usually containing N, P, and K) composed of a pellet of soluble fertilizer surrounded by a semipermeable plastic polymer coating. The rate of release is several months to over a year, depending on the coating.

overhead irrigation system — an irrigation system that sprays water into the air above plants.

ozonization — to treat with ozone as a disinfectant. Used in recycled water treatment.

parts per million (ppm) — a unit of concentration used to describe substance concentration in a million; may be expressed on a weight, volume, or number basis. The metric equivalent is mg/l.

Pascal — a unit used to express pressure or tension (negative pressure); for example, matric or moisture tension in soil/growing media. In soil, matric or moisture tension is usually expressed as megaPascals (MPa, i.e., 1 million Pa). For conversion, 1 megaPascal = 10 bars = 9.87 atmospheres = 7500 mm Hg = 145 psi of pressure. In soilless growing media, moisture tension is usually expressed as kiloPascals (kPa, i.e., 1 thousand Pa). For conversion, 1 kiloPascal = 0.01 bar = 0.00987 atm = 7.5 mm Hg = 0.145 psi.

peat — an organic growing media component composed of partially decomposed mosses, reeds, and sedges from wet, swampy areas. The most commonly used and highest quality peat is *Sphagnum* peat from northern bogs (Canada, northern Europe), but hypnum and reed-sedge peat is also used.

peat moss — see peat.

peat-lite mix — a common name used to describe soilless growing media mixes containing peat and either perlite or vermiculite. The original peat-lite mixes were developed by Boodley and Sheldrake at Cornell University in the 1970s.

perched water table — a layer of growing media in the bottom of a container that remains saturated with water after irrigation and all drainage from the force of gravity has occurred, i.e., a saturated layer in the bottom of the container at container capacity.

perlite — an inorganic growing media component made from alumino silicate volcanic rock that is mined, crushed, screened to size, then is heated to 1,800F (3215C), which causes it to expand into a lightweight, white aggregate.

pH — negative logarithm of the hydrogen ion concentration. Describes the acidity or basicity of a solution. Below pH 7 is acid, pH 7 is neutral, and above pH 7 is basic or alkaline.

point-source pollution — pollution that is generated from a discrete, relatively small area, such as a greenhouse range or nursery.

polyamide-type membranes — a membrane composed of polyamide polymers used in reverse osmosis water purification systems. They are resistant to pH but sensitive to chlorine.

polyphosphate — a polymer of orthophosphates that is used as a phosphorus fertilizer or as a weak chelating agent of the heavy metal micronutrients (Fe, Zn, Cu, Mn).

polystyrene — an organic polymer that is used to make styrofoam.

porometer — an instrument developed by the North Carolina State University Horticultural Substrates Laboratory to determine the physical properties of soil/growing media.

postplant fertilizer — a fertilizer application made to the plant/growing media after sowing seed or transplanting.

potential acidity — the pounds of calcium carbonate ($CaCO_3$) estimated to be required to neutralize the acidity caused by adding 1 ton of an acid-forming fertilizer to soil/growing media. The higher the potential acidity of a fertilizer, the more likely it will cause the soil/growing media pH to decrease over time (i.e., become more acid).

potential basicity — the pounds of calcium carbonate ($CaCO_3$) estimated to be equal to the addition of 1 ton of a base-forming fertilizer to the soil/growing media. The higher the potential basicity of a fertilizer, the more likely it will cause the soil/growing media pH to increase over time (i.e., become more basic or alkaline).

preplant fertilizer — a fertilizer application incorporated into growing media prior to sowing seed, transplanting, or potting.

primary nutrients — the macronutrients nitrogen (N), phosphorus (P), and potassium (K).

pulsed subirrigation — see ebb-and-flow system.

quick lime — see hydrated lime.

ratio — see fertilizer ratio.

recirculating system — a term often used to describe a closed irrigation system where the plants or containers are placed in trays or troughs, and the irrigation solution is recirculated between the trays/troughs and storage tanks; usually applied to a zone in a production facility.

recycling system — a term often used to describe a system where the irrigation runoff from the entire production facility (greenhouse or nursery) is collected, treated, stored, then reused for irrigation.

reverse osmosis system — a water purification system where the water is forced under high pressure through a very fine membrane that filters out dissolved solutes.

rock wool — inorganic growing media component made from basalt rock, steel mill slag, or other minerals that are liquefied at high temperatures and then spun into fibers. Rock wool in its pure form may also be used as cubes (stock plant production) or slabs/cubes (cut flower production).

rock wool culture — a subirrigation growing system where plants are rooted into bags or containers of rock wool and irrigated with drip tubes or in troughs that are periodically flooded.

runoff potential — a measure of a pesticide's tendency to move with sediment in runoff water.

salinity — a term used to describe the salt content of soil, growing media, or water.

salt — a compound that dissolves in water and dissociates into cations (positively charged ions) and anions (negatively charged ions). All soluble inorganic fertilizers dissolve to form salts.

sand filter — a filter composed of layers of different sized sand and gravel that is used to filter particulate material out of water.

saturated media extract (SME) — a method of soil/growing media extraction where the soil/growing medium is mixed with just enough water to make a paste, and then some of the water is vacuumed out or squeezed out for testing.

scaling — the buildup of deposits of calcium and/or magnesium carbonates, hydroxides, or hemihydrates. Occurs in water lines, tanks, and other plumbing.

secondary nutrients — the macronutrients calcium (Ca), magnesium (Mg), and sulfur (S).

sedimentation pit — a reservoir, pit, or tank used to produce clarified water by removing sediment and floating debris from waste or recycled water.

sensor-based irrigation control — an automated irrigation system that is turned on and off by moisture sensors, called tensiometers, placed in the soil/growing media.

Siemen — the currently accepted unit for expressing electrical conductivity. Replaces the formerly and most commonly used term: mhos. Reported as deciSiemen/meter, which is abbreviated dS/m.

silt density index (SDI) — a measure of the clarity or turbidity of water due to suspended colloids, silica, bacteria, or mineral precipitates.

single superphosphate — see superphosphate.

slow-release fertilizer (SRF) — see controlled-release fertilizer.

sodium adsorption ratio (SAR) — Similar to adjusted sodium absorption ratio, except it does not take the water's bicarbonate content or salinity into account.

soil permeability — the property of a soil to allow water to percolate through.

soil sorption index — a measure of a pesticide's tendency to attach to soil particles as measured in Koc value. Higher Koc indicates stronger attachment, and lower Koc indicates a greater tendency for leaching.

solenoid valve — an electrically activated valve used to control water flow in irrigation systems.

soluble salts — a salt that is soluble in water. Salts include most inorganic fertilizers (such as ammonium, nitrate, potassium, sulfate, phosphate) and mineral salts dissolved in irrigation water (such as sodium, bicarbonate).

spaghetti irrigation system — a type of drip irrigation where the water is delivered in small diameter (spaghetti) tubes that are often weighted at the end to keep them in place when irrigating pots or hanging baskets.

sphagnum peat moss — a type of peat derived from bogs composed of mosses from the genus *Sphagnum*. To be classified as sphagnum moss peat, the peat must contain at least 75% *Sphagnum* moss fiber and 90% organic matter. It is generally considered the highest quality peat.

styrofoam — an inorganic growing media component made from expanded and solidified polystyrene foam that is formed into small flakes or beads.

subirrigation system — an irrigation system that delivers water onto a surface where containerized plants are placed. Water enters the container through drain holes by capillary action from below. The surface may be an absorbent mat (capillary mat), trough, tray, or molded concrete floor (ebb-and-flow).

substrate — see growing media.

subsurface irrigation system — see subirrigation system.

sufficiency range — the recommended range of nutrients in plant tissue that yields acceptable growth. Also called normal, acceptable, or optimum range by various analytical labs.

sulfur-coated fertilizer — a slow-release fertilizer composed of a pellet of soluble fertilizer coated with a layer of sulfur that causes slow release. The most common is sulfur-coated urea (SCU), but other nutrients are available. Some sulfur-coated urea products may also include a light polymer coating to further control release.

superphosphate — a granular phosphorus fertilizer derived by dissolving raw rock phosphate with acid. Use of sulfuric acid produces single superphosphate (0-20-0, plus Ca and S), and use of phosphoric acid produces treble (or triple) superphosphate (0-45-0).

tensiometer — a sensor with a porous ceramic tip that when placed in the soil/growing media measures moisture tension (matric tension) of the water in the soil/growing media. This can be related to moisture content with a moisture tension curve.

thin-film composite membrane — a very thin, layered membrane containing a polyamide layer used in reverse osmosis water purification systems. They are resistant to pH but sensitive to chlorine.

tissue analysis — the use of analytical techniques to determine the nutrient content in plant tissue.

total carbonates (TC) — the sum of bicarbonates and carbonates. Often used to express alkalinity.

total dissolved solids (TDS) — the total of nonvolatile solutes dissolved in water. Often called total dissolved salts. For most water it reflects the soluble salt content. Usually expressed as ppm or mg/l.

total porosity — the percent volume (volume/volume) of soil/growing media comprised of pores. The pores are filled with air and/or water.

toxicity — when the concentration of a nutrient or chemical becomes high enough in a plant to cause damage.

trace element — see micronutrient.

treble superphosphate — see superphosphate.

triple superphosphate — see superphosphate.

trough culture — a subirrigation growing system where containerized plants are placed in sloped troughs, down which nutrient solution flows as needed. Usually the nutrient solution is collected and recirculated.

UC mix — a group of growing media mixes containing various ratios of sand to peat. Developed by Baker at the University of California in the 1950s.

unavailable water (PWP) — the percent volume (volume/volume) of soil/growing media occupied by water that is unavailable to the plant. It is also called the permanent wilting percentage (PWP) and is the water content at which the plant permanently wilts and will not recover unless additional water is added to the soil/growing media. It is determined by measuring the percent of water present at a moisture tension of 1.5 megaPascals (approximately 15 bars or atm).

urea — an organic nitrogen fertilizer [$CO(NH_2)_2$] that is soluble and can be taken up directly by the plant, thus acting like an inorganic fertilizer. In the soil/growing media, the urease enzyme of bacteria readily converts it to ammonium and carbon dioxide, so it behaves like an ammonium fertilizer.

urea formaldehyde — a slow-release nitrogen fertilizer composed of a polymer of urea and formaldehyde. Availability is based on low solubility and biological breakdown. Also called ureaform.

vermiculite — an inorganic growing media component made from a micalike ore of aluminum-iron-magnesium silicate that is fired (heated) to cause the layers to expand into an accordion-like structure.

Water Pollution Control Acts — the laws set by Congress (Public Law 84-660 and 92-500) that set the standards for clean water.

water softener — a water treatment system where a cation exchange resin is used to remove the hard water salts calcium and magnesium and replace them with the soft water salt sodium, and in some applications potassium.

zero-leach — a term used to indicate no or very minimal drainage (i.e., leaching) from a container after irrigation, i.e., a leaching fraction of zero or near zero.

Index